T0342554

For a New West

For a New West

Essays, 1919–1958

Karl Polanyi

Edited by Giorgio Resta and
Mariavittoria Catanzariti

Preface by Kari Polanyi Levitt

polity

First published in Italian as *Per un nuovo Occidente* © il Saggiatore S.p.A, Milan 2013

This English edition © Polity Press, 2014

Polity Press
65 Bridge Street
Cambridge CB2 1UR, UK

Polity Press
350 Main Street
Malden, MA 02148, USA

ISBN-13: 978-0-7456-8443-7
ISBN-13: 978-0-7456-8444-4(pb)

A catalogue record for this book is available from the British Library.

Typeset in 10.5 on 12 pt Sabon
by Toppan Best-set Premedia Limited
Printed and bound in Great Britain by Clays Ltd, St Ives PLC

The publisher has used its best endeavours to ensure that the URLs for external websites referred to in this book are correct and active at the time of going to press. However, the publisher has no responsibility for the websites and can make no guarantee that a site will remain live or that the content is or will remain appropriate.

For further information on Polity, visit our website: politybooks.com

Contents

Editors' Note and Acknowledgments

The texts collected in this volume are archived at the Karl Polanyi Institute of Political Economy at Concordia University (Montreal). Many of them are difficult to decipher, either because of the handwritten comments and corrections by the author, or as a result of the bad state of conservation of the paper. We strived to provide a transcription as faithful as possible to the text and to the intentions of the author, pointing out in the footnotes the most serious doubts about the interpretation of the documents. Typing mistakes and awkward sentences have been corrected to make the reading easier. The original emphasis has been rendered, as usual, through italics. The sources to the originals in the Polanyi Archive have been listed in each chapter and the dates of the documents have been given wherever possible.

The editors would like to express their deepest gratitude to Kari Polanyi Levitt, for her continuous encouragement and support and for giving permission to publish her father's works, and to Marguerite Mendell and Ana Gomez, for their kind assistance in accessing the Polanyi Archive and for their guidance in deciphering the manuscripts. Our heartfelt thanks go to Michele Cangiani and David Lametti, for their thoughtful comments and suggestions, and to Manuela Tecusan at Polity, for her invaluable advice and support in completing the English edition of the book. The usual disclaimer applies.

Preface

Kari Polanyi Levitt

Recent years have witnessed a remarkable resurgence of interest in the work of Karl Polanyi and *The Great Transformation* has been translated into more than fifteen languages, including Chinese, Korean, and Arabic. Special issues of reviews and journals have been devoted to the intellectual legacy of Polanyi, and his analysis of the development of capitalism is increasingly referred to in influential political forums – most recently the one at Davos in 2012, where it is reported that the ghost of Karl Polanyi was haunting the deliberations of the assembled global elite. The unfolding world economic crisis has once again posed the fundamental question of the place of economy in society – the central theme of my father's entire oeuvre. To understand the profound challenge faced by our democracies in the most serious crisis since the 1930s, we need to revisit history. To this end, Giorgio Resta and Mariavittoria Catanzariti have provided us with an Italian translation of as yet unpublished lectures and manuscripts of Karl Polanyi from the early 1920s to his death in 1964. This fascinating collection of essays revisits the collapse of the liberal economic order and the demise of democracies in the interwar years. Both the present danger to democracy, which results from the unleashing of capital from regulatory control, and the prevailing neoliberal ideologies of market fundamentalism suggest a careful rereading of this volume.

To gain a better understanding of this collection of essays, let me share a brief account of the life and social philosophy of Karl Polanyi and my reflections on the contemporary relevance of *The Great Transformation*.

My father was a passionate man. He strongly believed that intellectuals have a social responsibility. In early articles and speeches in Hungary, he assumed, for himself and his generation ("Our Generation," as he called it), the moral responsibility of the disaster of 1914 and the ravages of the Great War. For him, freedom was inseparable from responsibility. I believe his critique of market society was grounded in an aversion to the commercialization of daily life and, more generally, to the impersonalization of social relations. In his view, any form of socialism would have to ensure the responsibility of people for their communities, their societies, and their democracies. For these reasons he distrusted the idea of a centrally planned economy, with its inherent concentration of political power. In 1920s Vienna he engaged the principal advocate of economic liberalism, Ludwig Von Mises, in a debate on the feasibility of a socialist economy carried in the pages of the most important social science journal of the German-speaking world. Polanyi outlined a functionalist associational model of a socialist economy, where the interests of individuals as workers, consumers, and citizens could be reconciled through organized negotiation between constituent representatives. There are evident similarities with the guild socialism of G. D. H. Cole and the Austro-Marxism of Otto Bauer.

At that time he was earning what he called an honest living as a journalist. I cannot get too much into family anecdotes but his mother, my grandmother, had definite ideas as to the profession of each of her children. My father was to be a lawyer, my uncle Michael was to be a doctor, and the oldest brother, Adolph, was to follow in the footsteps of his father, as an engineer and entrepreneur. However, Adolph would have none of it and at a very early age traveled about as far as anybody could at that time – all the way to Japan. He later moved to Italy, where eventually he fell afoul of Mussolini and emigrated to Sao Paulo, where he lived for many years and died. To resume, my father, who articled in the chambers of his prosperous uncle, decided to become what another family member described as a "drop-out" from the bourgeois world he was meant to inhabit. I think he was a superb journalist and political analyst. I have read all of the articles he wrote for *Der Oesterreichische Volkswirt*, the leading financial and economic weekly of German-speaking Europe at the time, which was modeled on the London-based *Economist*. He was senior editor of international affairs. With the accession of Hitler to office in 1933, the shadow of fascism crept over Austria. The owner and publisher of the journal regretfully decided he could no longer keep a prominent socialist like Polanyi on his editorial board. My father was advised to find a job in England. Within a few years, he found employment as a lecturer for the Workers' Educational Association, an adult education extension of the Oxford and London universities. The subjects he was required to treat were contemporary international relations, with which he was of course familiar, and English social and economic history, which was entirely new to him. The lectures he prepared for evening classes held in the public libraries of provincial towns in Kent and Sussex became the skeleton of *The Great Transformation*. At this time he also produced a course entitled "Philosophies in Conflict in Modern Society," which is translated and published for the first time in the present book.

Like Marx before him, he located the origins of industrial capitalism in England – specifically, in the 30 years from 1815 to 1845 when the legislative and supportive infrastructures for markets in labor and land were instituted. The free market for money was of course older, dating to the abolition of the laws that prohibited usury – considered as sinful by Christian doctrine. Together, the markets for labor, land, and money had the effect of disembedding the economy from society. The economy assumed a life of its own, and society was reconfigured to serve the requirements of the economy. This was a very strange and historically unprecedented state of affairs, which, however, released an enormous energy of economic growth.

My father's intellectual ancestry, I suggest, runs from Karl Marx to Max Weber, Ferdinand Tönnies, and two students of primitive economies (now called economic anthropology): Thurnwald of Germany and Malinowski of Vienna. I mention this in connection with the contemporary debate on social rights and economic crisis, because in no era of in human history, recorded or unrecorded, do we find that individuals or individual families were permitted to fall into destitution or suffer starvation, unless the community as a whole fell on hard times. In primitive societies, failing harvests could bring severe shortage of food, but individual families could never be without the basic necessities of life while the rest of the community was provided for. The idea that fear of hunger and love of gain could become the motivating drivers of economic life is historically very recent – as recent as the early nineteenth century. For these reasons alone, without taking the story any further, I can say that a share in the social product as a citizen right would have won Karl Polanyi's support, both as a means of decommodifying access to economic livelihood and on grounds of moral justice.

Taking into account the contemporary debate on social rights and global public goods, I suggest that there are three distinct reasons why my father would have supported a universal basic income: the first is economic, the second is social, and the third (and not least important) is political. The economic arguments are well known and have many times been repeated. You do not need to be a Keynesian to understand that people in need who receive a basic income will spend it on consumption goods, thus creating market opportunities for producers. Furthermore, the accelerating rate of technological innovation requires ever less labor input into industrial activity, from mining and manufacturing to transportation and commerce. And this is true on a global scale. In these conditions, it is no longer reasonable to consider earnings from wage employment to be the only – or even the principal – entitlement to the social product. In light of the increasingly precarious nature of the labor market, a basic income provides a platform from which people can organize economic activities with some relief from the debilitating stress of making ends meet.

The social argument is one of justice. Where there is a perception of social injustice, there will be problems of social cohesion. In these conditions, the state will be ineffective in negotiating conflicting claims to the social product. Such a society lacks the capacity to advance in terms of economic development. It is now recognized that societies that are more egalitarian and less riddled by inequities and injustices have been more successful at achieving economic growth and development. Speaking as an economist, I believe that mobilization for effective economic development ultimately rests on the degree of social cohesion and on the perception of social justice, releasing the energies generated by the hope and belief of the people that their sacrifices and efforts will result in a fair and equitable share of the social product.

The third reason why my father would support a basic income relates to his concern about freedom in a technologically advanced society, as expressed in the last chapter of *The Great Transformation*. In the 1950s, while teaching at Columbia and commuting between New York and Canada, he became increasingly preoccupied with the trend toward uniformity, conformity, and what he called "averagism," which was manifested in a reluctance to dissent from prevailing opinions. This was the United States in the 1950s; and he suggested that a highly advanced technological society had within it the seeds of totalitarianism. I remind you that he wrote this before the role of the media had become so evident, before the total corporate control of the media had become so powerful, and certainly before what we witnessed in the United States after September 11, 2001, when the cost of dissent from official views became virtually prohibitive.

My father believed that the protection of liberty required the institutionalization of nonconformity. He saw this as a virtue of English classical liberalism. But these liberties were available only to the privileged upper classes that benefitted from the rentier incomes of the late nineteenth and early twentieth centuries. Incidentally, most of this came from colonial possessions and extensive overseas investments of Britain and France. This was the *belle époque* period in England and France, in Vienna, and more generally in Western Europe. It produced great cultural achievements, but it was confined to limited sectors of the population. My father was familiar with classical Greek literature and particularly admired Aristotle, whom he credited with the discovery of economy as a distinct sphere of social life. But Greek democracy was dependent on the work of slaves. In bourgeois society, of which my father's family was a beneficiary, cultural expression was effectively limited to a privileged elite.

Polanyi believed that creativity was a basic human attribute and need and that the capacity to exercise it should be granted to the whole of humankind. In his view a popular culture was the collective wisdom, knowledge, tradition, and common sense of ordinary people. This had nothing to do with what is known as pop culture; rather it meant that different societies would have created different democracies, rooted in the collective pool of their unique popular culture. This is developed in an essay entitled "Jean-Jacques Rousseau: Is Freedom Possible?," written in 1953 and translated into Italian a few years ago.[1] This fascinating piece treats the classical issues of liberty and equality in the era of the Enlightenment. He finds in the writings of Rousseau support for his contention that the ultimate foundation of government must rest on that reservoir of wisdom, knowledge, tradition, and common sense of the people that is the popular culture. In a note penned a few days before his death, he wrote: "The heart of the feudal nation is privilege; the heart of the bourgeois nation is property; the heart of the socialist nation is the people, where collective existence is the enjoyment of a community of culture. I myself never lived in such a society."

As suggested earlier, I offer a few comments on the relevance of *The Great Transformation* to our times. It should be understood that, in Polanyi's writings, the great transformation referred to the transformation from the nineteenth-century liberal order, which collapsed in 1914, to measures taken by nations to protect economic livelihood, whether through national fascisms, Soviet social planning, or the New Deal in the United States.

In continental Europe conflicts between industrialists and parliaments dominated by socialist majorities brought the democratic political process to a virtual standstill. In a paper entitled "Economy and Democracy,"[2] written in 1932, he noted the conflicting interests of the economy, represented by industrial capitalists, and democracy, represented by parliamentary majorities. Where the interests of industrialists predominated over socialist majorities in parliaments, the result was the suspension of democracy and the advent of fascism. Where the conflict was resolved in favor of political and also economic democracy, the result would be socialism. The suspension of democracy in South America and the installation of military dictatorships in the 1960s and 1970s were justified on the grounds of securing economic stability. The restoration of democracy was the result of 20 years of popular political mobilization against entrenched economic interests.

It is well known that the two penultimate chapters of *The Great Transformation* were written in haste and left for colleagues to edit from notes. My father was impatient to return from America to England in 1943, when it was clear that Nazism had been defeated at Stalingrad, the turning point of the war. He wished to participate in the discussion of the postwar world. His optimism was reflected in the penultimate chapter, where he wrote that labor, land, and money would no longer be commodities, countries would be free to adopt suitable domestic economic regimes, and the price of necessities and staple foods would be fixed and protected from market forces. In an 1945 essay entitled "Universal Capitalism or Regional Economic Planning"[3] he expressed the opinion that only the United States believed in universal capitalism and that the laissez-faire market capitalism of the nineteenth century was now history. We now know that this is not quite what happened, although the introduction of the welfare state, an increased role for government in economic and social advancement, and the achievement of full employment represented a significant and successful compromise of the conflicting interests of capital and labor.

The Great Transformation has enjoyed a steady readership since its publication in 1944, but it was not until the end of the twentieth century that it emerged as a truly transformative critique of a predatory capitalism that is destroying the natural and social environment that sustains life on earth. The conflict between capitalism and democracy, noted by Polanyi in the interwar period, has now assumed new and global dimensions. In the past 30 years capital has succeeded in rolling back many of the gains of the welfare state in North America – and now also in Europe – and has shifted the burden of taxation from the rich to the rest. The increases in productivity have gone to the profit of upper-income earners while the lower quintiles in the United States and Canada, where real median wages and salaries have hardly increased in 30 years, have been reduced to poverty. Since capital was freed from all regulation and control, the concentration of financial wealth cannot meaningfully be described in numbers anymore and has significantly increased in the fallout of the financial crisis of 2008. Even the most powerful governments are now hostage to the dictates of financial capital.

In 1933 my father wrote a remarkable essay called "The Mechanism of the World Economic Crisis."[4] He maintained that the ultimate source of the breakdown of the world economic order was not the stock exchange mania or the crash of Wall Street in 1929, or even the end of pound sterling gold convertibility in 1931, but the attempt by Britain, France, and the United States to restore the pre-1914 liberal economic order in conditions where empires of kaisers, kings, tsars, and sultans had come crashing down in a political earthquake. The human and social costs of the war were irreconcilable with the punishing reparations demanded from Germany and the structural adjustments required of weaker impoverished countries of continental Europe by the victorious western creditors.

This invites us to view the financial crisis of 2008 from the larger perspective of globalization and shifting power relations. In the western heartlands of capitalism a malaise of stagflation and declining returns on domestic investment triggered a neoliberal regime change in the 1970s, while East Asian economies initiated high-growth policies of industrialization. The shift of the growing points of the world economy from North and West to South and East, first discernible in the early 1990s, is now an inescapable fact of changing global power relations. While the European Union and the United States are still the largest markets, real production in the Global South has now surpassed that of the Global North in purchasing power terms. There is an unwinding of the traditional dependence of the rest of the world on export markets in Europe and North America, which has characterized the world economy since the middle of the nineteenth century.

It is the countries that were more closely integrated into the financial structure and trade relations of the capitalist centers that have been hit the hardest by the recent crisis – principally in the eastern and Mediterranean peripheries of Europe and in the southern peripheries of the United States. The crisis is far from resolved: the Eurozone is in question. The ability of the United States to reflate an economy of indebted households and businesses in the context of income inequalities that surpass the record levels of the 1920s and in a dysfunctional political system is also in question. By contrast, emerging economies that resisted excessive liberalization, maintained control over banks and the external capital accounts, and channeled their investment into their domestic economies recovered rapidly from the financial crisis and resumed strong economic growth.

Notes to Preface

1. Available in Italian translation as "Jean-Jacques Rousseau, o è possibile una società libera?" in Karl Polanyi, *La libertà in una società complessa* (Turin: Bollati-Boringhieri, 1987), 161–9.
2. "Wirtschaft und Demokratie," *Chronik der großen Transformation: Artikel und Aufsätze, 1920–1945*, vol. 1 (Metropolis-Verlag: Marburg, 2002 [1932]), 149–54.
3. Originally published in *The London Quarterly of World Affairs*, 10 (3), 86–91.
4. "Der Mechanismus der Weltwirtschaftskrise," *Der Oesterreichische Volkswirt*, 25 (suppl.), 2–9.

Introduction

Giorgio Resta

Karl Polanyi has been described as an "outdated" thinker, and not for purely chronological reasons.[1] Born in Vienna in 1886 to a Hungarian father and brought up amid the intellectual fervor of Budapest,[2] Polanyi was one of the most acute investigators of the disappearance of the "world of yesterday." After serving in the Great War as an officer in the Austro-Hungarian army and witnessing the Hungarian Revolution, Polanyi took part in the extraordinary cultural and political laboratory of socialist Vienna before migrating to London after the rise of national socialism. He eventually settled permanently in North America, whence he observed the tensions of the Cold War.[3] It is the ideas of Karl Polanyi rather than the man himself that seem outdated, mostly because of their distance from the ones that dominate the present age. They are, according to Michele Cangiani, ideas "of another time" and "of another place," born of a now distant historical context and a singular life experience.[4] Polanyi never interpreted his role as an intellectual to be that of a detached and impassive "historical notary"; he was instead animated by an intense civic passion and an anti-deterministic faith in the possibility of "shaping our social destiny"[5] and making it respond to the needs of the human personality. The construction of a *new West* – centered on the values of freedom, pluralism, and social justice (the true heritage of the "cultural West," wasted by the errors of the "political West"),[6] and hence open to dialogue with other cultures rather than turned in on itself and on its economic monologue – represented, even in his final years, the central objective of Polanyi's intellectual and political efforts.[7] As an adolescent, Polanyi already developed a firm belief in the possibility of making democracy real, thereby securing the effective liberation of the human being through socialism.[8] This faith was the constant guiding force throughout his *Lebensweg* and served as a never-ending intellectual inspiration that guided and focused his research. Thanks to his passion and goals, that research often evinced a pioneering spirit.

> Break with the peace within you
> Break with the values of the world
> You (cannot be) better than the times
> But to be of the best . . .

These verses, taken from Hegel's poem "Entschluss" [literally "Unclosing"], were much loved and often quoted by Polanyi (if in abbreviated form).[9] They reflect not only his ideals but also that tension between the value of human freedom and the "reality of society" that represents one of the dominant themes of his work.[10] He was a scholar who swam against the current; hence he can seem even more out of synch with the spirit of the times today. And yet, over the past thirty years or so, his decidedly unorthodox ideas have attracted ever-growing interest and attention in the social sciences. *The Great Transformation* has become a classic and has been translated into over fifteen languages.[11] Even his later works, most notably *Trade and Markets in the Early Empires*, have exerted a considerable influence in various fields – for example economic anthropology, historical sociology, or economic history.[12]

The rebirth of the intellectual legacy of Karl Polanyi should not come as a surprise. Few other analyses of modern society prove to be as original and profound as those of this Hungarian author; Polanyi has always demonstrated a marked ability to see beyond the confines of a particular field and to "read" reality from a variety of complex – and never reductionist – perspectives. Polanyi succeeded in maintaining an admirable balance between his different approaches, combining the sensibilities of the legal scholar (he studied jurisprudence at the Universities of Budapest and Kolozsvár),[13] the economist (this discipline captured his attention already in Vienna, where he was co-director of the political and economic weekly *Der Österreichische Volkswirt*),[14] the historian (a skill he refined most of all during his time in London)[15] and the anthropologist (his interest in anthropology, already evident in *The Great Transformation*, became especially marked after his migration to North America).[16] This methodological richness on the one hand exposed his work to some inevitable criticisms,[17] on the other hand allowed

him to develop a wider perspective on social phenomena, as well as
certain instruments of analysis that are of indubitable significance
even to contemporary thought, from the distinction between formal
and substantive meaning in economics to the notion of embeddedness
and the category of "double movement." Yet, beyond these tools of
analysis, it is the subjects he studied and the problems he raised that
are still of central importance today, albeit within a greatly changed
frame of reference (one need only think of the current importance of
financial economics).[18] Suffice it to list a few: the problem of the
relationship between economy and democracy;[19] the trend to universal commodification;[20] the question of control over technology;[21] the
regulation of transnational trade.[22] It comes as no surprise, then, that
Joseph Stiglitz, in the foreword to the latest American edition of *The
Great Transformation*, observes: "it often seems as if Polanyi is
speaking directly to present-day issues";[23] or that Polanyi's warning
about the destructive tendencies of a self-regulated economy resounds
especially today, in the midst of a new and dramatic crisis of the
capitalist economy – and that it does so with such intensity, from city
squares to university classrooms, that it has inspired talk of a true
"Polanyi's revenge."[24] The questions posed by Polanyi some seventy
years ago have not lost their relevance – on the contrary, they reassert
themselves with even greater intensity in the context of contemporary
"supercapitalism"; the latter has indeed provided further evidence
that the general loosening of market constraints represents a serious
threat not only to the environment but to the fundamental feasibility
of democracy.[25]

Whereas the persistence of the problems criticized by Polanyi adds
to the evidence for his critique of "market society," it could, conversely, represent a trap: there is a risk of trivializing the content of
these problems by dissociating the author's arguments from their
original context, thus losing sight of their original presuppositions
and implications. As has been rightly observed, and as Polanyi himself
taught in his lessons on historicism, both history and ideas from the
past can "serve to better understand the present only so long as the
differences are not smoothed over."[26] For this reason, when we
approach the work of Polanyi today, it is important not to limit
ourselves to his major works but to consider the entirety of his
output: this consists of numerous essays, conference papers, and
incidental writings that, while less known, contain much material of
interest and contribute to a better understanding of his intellectual
evolution. Italian readers find themselves in a particularly privileged
position in this regard due to the wealth of collections of the minor
writings of the author that have been published in recent years,

mostly thanks to the efforts of Alfredo Salsano and Michele Cangiani.[27]

The writings presented in this volume constitute a new contribution to the ever growing collection of Polanyi's published works, making available a series of unpublished pieces taken from the archive of the Polanyi Institute for Political Economy in Montreal.[28] They span the entire breadth of his career: from "The Crucial Issue Today," written in German and dating back to 1919 and his time in Vienna, to the eponymous work of this volume, "For a New West," composed a few years before his death in 1958 and intended as the opening chapter in a book of the same name, which Polanyi never completed.[29]

For a New West is a collection of heterogeneous works. With the exception of pieces originally intended for publication in books or periodicals, most of the works are lecture notes and addresses for conferences, together with lessons and university courses delivered in England, before the completion of *The Great Transformation*, and in the United States, following the last of Polanyi's many migrations. As the reader will quickly gather, the interest of these works extends well beyond simple intellectual curiosity. In them Polanyi not only anticipates and synthesizes ideas developed in his major works – like the short circuit between self-regulating markets and parliamentary democracy, or the distinction between formal and substantive concepts of "the economic" – but also pauses to dwell on questions elsewhere addressed only in passing. These include the relationship between class structure and the nature of English culture,[30] or between public opinion and the art of governing;[31] the relevance of the education system for the nature of American society;[32] the problems of pacifism and war as "institutions";[33] and the idea of a sociology of knowledge.[34] These pieces can serve to improve our understanding of Polanyi's thought, offering examples of the breadth of his interests, of his extraordinary ability to deconstruct the many sides of society, and at the same time of the internal coherence of his intellectual journey.[35]

In chronological order, the first work is "The Crucial Issue Today: A Response," completed, according to the archives, in 1919. It was probably written in Vienna, as Polanyi refers to the Hungarian Soviet Republic as a concluded episode; and his migration to Austria coincided chronologically with the rise to power of the reactionary government of Miklós Horthy.[36] That piece, though tightly bound up with the political events of the era, still merits rereading, as it prefigures certain ideas and questions he would develop more thoroughly in the 1920s; also, certain key elements of his philosophy of politics emerge here.[37] In particular, Polanyi tracks the genealogy of liberal socialism – a movement to which he had been drawn since his Hungarian period[38] – outlining how it differs from Marxism and identifying the unifying principle behind the assumption that "freedom is the foundation of all true harmony."[39] This presupposition constitutes the crux of Polanyi's own social philosophy: in this essay he already distances himself clearly from both "the anarchic market of the capitalist profit economy" and the communist centrally planned economies.[40] His rejection of unregulated capitalism is based primarily on its dependence on the exploitation of labor, which, recalling the thesis of Eugen Dühring,[41] he traces to "the *political* law of coercive property in land in land that actually prevails and nullifies free competition,"[42] and hence to the absence of free access to arable land. Here the theme of enclosure crops up: this concept will be thoroughly investigated in Chapter 3 of *The Great Transformation* and will assume a crucial role in Polanyi's analysis of the rise of the market economy.[43] Second, Polanyi finds unregulated capitalism unacceptable because its intrinsic dynamic leads it to "bring production into conflict with social need,"[44] so that it would provide no protection for collective interests. The idea that self-regulated markets are structurally unsuited to create an economic environment that serves a social function – a concept encountered here in its embryonic state – would find fuller expression in his writings from the 1920s on the subject of socialist calculation. In that later work he develops the argument that "private economy, by its very nature, cannot recognize the adverse effects of production on the life of the community."[45] In the 1930s, moreover, he put forward the thesis that, barring some form of regulation (*Übersicht*) of the economic players regarding the consequences of their choices, the market economy will ignore personal responsibility, will fracture social cohesion, and will create disincentives to individual moral action.[46] Yet he asserts with equal force his position on the second prospect – that of the nationalization of the means of production and of a centrally planned economy. This prospect conflicts, above all, with the ideal of freedom of choice, which Polanyi applies not only to individuals, but also to medium-sized groups. According to Polanyi,

> Liberal socialism is fundamentally *hostile to force*. For liberal socialism, not only the state as an organism exercising domination over persons, but also the state as an administrator of things is, practically speaking, a necessary evil and, theoretically speaking, a superfluous and harmful construct. Any attempt to use state power to replace what

can only arise through the life and activity of the individual inevitably has devastating consequences.[47]

Moreover, this solution was technically impractical for one fundamental reason: eliminating the system of free trade would make it impossible for economic processes to function. No method of statistical verification would be capable of creating an effect analogous to the free flow of supply and demand. In an observation that reveals Polanyi's affinity with the "Austrian" view of the market,[48] he writes: "The economy is a living process that can by no means be replaced by a mechanical apparatus, however subtly and ingeniously conceived." This particular kind of market is characterized as "a peculiar sense organ in the literal sense, and without it the circulatory system of the economy would collapse."[49] The economy envisioned by liberal socialism – and by Polanyi himself[50] – is not, then, a centralized economy without free trade, but a cooperative economy in which labor, consumption, and production are all represented and problems are solved in concert:

> This is why cooperative socialism is synonymous with market economy; not the anarchic market of the capitalist profit economy as a field in which the plunder of the surplus value concealed in the prices is realized, but the organically structured market of equivalent products of free labor.[51]

This text contains, then, two ideas that would be central in Polanyi's work: his critical view of self-regulating markets; and his insistence on the value of freedom as a suitable criterion for evaluating any political and economic system.

While the exploration of cooperative socialism would find a fuller exposition only a few years later, in Polanyi's rebuttal of von Mises' thesis regarding the unfeasibility of a socialist economy,[52] the theme of freedom would remain central to Polanyi's thought.[53] It was by means of this concept that the valorization of the uniqueness of the individual, in contrast to any type of social collectivism, married so well with a radical criticism of that form of liberalism that, as Giacomo Marramao has written,

> presupposes the individual, that is, assumes the individual is already formed and is not instead the product of some outside process, and so renders the individual meaningless; by reducing him or her to an *a-tomon* – an *in-dividuum* – we sever those connections to the critical constitutive processes that alone can make him an individual.[54]

The unavoidable tension between the freedom of the individual and the "reality" of social boundaries constitutes one of the key problems faced by Polanyi and comes up often in his work. He says as much in "The Meaning of Peace":

> The recognition of the inescapable nature of society sets a limit to the imaginary freedom of an abstract personality. Power, economic value, coercion are inevitable in a complex society; there is no means for the individual to escape the responsibilities of choosing between alternatives. He or she cannot contract out of society. But the freedom we appear to lose through this knowledge is illusory, while the freedom we gain through it is valid. Man reaches maturity in the recognition of his loss and in the certainty of ultimate attainment of freedom in and through society.[55]

However, it is only in Polanyi's post-World War II writings that the problem of "freedom in a complex society" – the title of the last chapter of *The Great Transformation* – becomes absolutely central.[56] Some of these writings are collected in this volume ("For a New West," "Economics and the Freedom to Shape Our Social Destiny," "Economic History and the Problem of Freedom," "New Frontiers of Economic Thinking"). Among the myriad questions raised by Polanyi in these writings, two in particular merit closer consideration.

The first question regards controlling the forces of technology, economic organization, and science in an increasingly artificial social context, characterized by very real threats to the survival of the human race (we are now, after all, in an era of Cold War, with the impending risk of nuclear arms race). Polanyi's main concern is "restoring meaning and unity to life in a machine civilization"[57] – a concern reinforced by his awareness of the historical responsibility of the West for the paths of industry, science, and economy, which have influenced worldwide development since the Industrial Revolution. That event, as he writes in "For a New West," constitutes a watershed moment in the history of mankind:

> Three forces – technology, economic organization, and science, in this sequence – each from separate and undistinguished parentage, linked up, inconspicuously at first, to form, hardly a hundred years ago, into a social maelstrom that is still engulfing new and new millions of people, in an irresistible rush.[58]

The sequence outlined by Polanyi (who here synthesizes in a few brush strokes the central analysis of *The Great Transformation*) is very precise: first came the introduction of new industrial machines; then followed the process of market organization – which, contrary to liberal doctrines, was not at all "natural," but rather the result of deliberate institutional choices;[59] finally, about a century later, science was added to the mix. "All three then gathered speed: technology and science formed a partnership, economic organization made use of its chance, forcing the efficiency principle in production (both by market and planning) to vertiginous heights."[60] Subordination of those forces (science, technology, and economic organization) "to the will for a progress that is human and to the fulfillment of a personality that is free has become a necessity of survival." It falls to the West, then, the genitor of industrialized society, "to discipline its children."[61] And this not only because of its historical responsibility, but also because it is only in this way that the West can re-establish dialogue with the other cultures of the world and demonstrate a genuine concern for the problems of the entire human race. The alternative is to repeat the mistakes of the past, and in particular the mistaken assumptions that colonialism represents progress and capitalism represents democracy. Polanyi's fierce criticism of the "political West" (that is, of the collective choices made by capitalist states) does not spare the intellectuals; for he believes that, through their conformity and willingness to acquiesce in the impositions of government propaganda, they have betrayed the true patrimony of western civilization, namely personal universalism.[62]

It is on this point that Polanyi raises his second major question, namely the "dogmatic belief in economic determinism" as an ideological barrier to capitalist reforms that promise economic freedom and equality. Knowing full well that such a reform would necessitate "fulfilling the requirements of social justice, as a consciously pursued human aim,"[63] Polanyi seeks, in "Economics and the Freedom to Shape Our Social Destiny," to refute the thesis according to which any restriction of economic freedoms would automatically have a negative effect on civil liberties. This argument, as is well known, is central to *The Road to Serfdom*,[64] where von Hayek maintains that the introduction of any economic planning will lead to the inevitable disappearance not only of the unregulated market, but also of freedom itself. But Polanyi equates this with the equivalent and opposite argument (adopted in Marxist trends) according to which a change in economic organization would bring with it the disappearance of free institutions – insofar as these are a "bourgeois fraud."[65] Both positions, the liberal and the Marxist, suffer from the same problematic assumption: dogmatic faith in economic determinism, or rather the belief that economic relations do not only limit but rather *determine* the cultural aspects of societies – the "institutions of freedom" among them.[66]

In order to illustrate the falsity of this assumption, Polanyi turns to history, demonstrating that, even if the determinist model may appear feasible in the context of nineteenth-century market society, where humans (labor) and their natural habitat (land) are reduced to commodities and bound by the powers of a self-regulating market, this is not the case in most situations. Even admitting that economic and technological factors play a large part in determining the cultural attitudes of a society, these attitudes are not *determined* by the means of production.

> But the pattern of culture, the major cultural emphasis in society, is *not* determined by either technological or geographical factors. Whether a people develops a cooperative or a competitive attitude in everyday life, whether it prefers to work its technique of production collectively or individualistically, is in many cases strikingly independent of the utilitarian logic of the means of production, and even of the actual basic economic institutions of the community.[67]

The same can be said for the propensity of a community to guarantee civil liberties by means of specific institutions:

> Emphasis on liberty, on personality, on independence of mind, on tolerance and freedom of conscience is precisely in the same category as cooperative and harmonious attitudes on the one hand, antagonistic and competitive attitudes on the other – it is a pervasive pattern of the mind expressed in innumerable ways, protected by custom and law, institutionalized in varied forms, but essentially independent of technique and even of economic organization.[68]

Here Polanyi emphasizes the intrinsic weakness of the thesis according to which the disappearance of civil liberties follows from the restriction of freedoms of the market. Citing various examples, Polanyi ably shows that "under private enterprise public opinion may lose all sense of tolerance and freedom,"[69] while, in contrast, a satisfactory level of civil liberty can be guaranteed even in a heavily regulated economy. He concludes the analysis in "General Economic History" in no uncertain terms, by returning to the question of determinism:

> In truth, we will have just as much freedom in the future as we desire to create and to safeguard. Institutional guarantees of personal freedom are in principle compatible with any economic system. In market

society alone will the [‡]. . .[‡] economic mechanism lay down the law for us. Such a state of affairs is not characteristic of human society in general, but only of an unregulated market economy.[70]

At the heart of Polanyi's argument lies the recognition of the specificity of nineteenth-century market economy.[71] In that particular case, the economic factor arguably played a determining role in relation to social institutions. Once the normative and cultural obstacles preventing inclusion of land and labor in competitive markets had been lifted, the basis was established for a completely autonomous economy and a radical overturning of the relationship between that economy and the other social spheres. This came about thanks to an institutional shift: the fear of hunger and the desire for wealth drove individuals to engage with the processes of production. This is the well-known thesis of the disembedded economy as a distinctive feature of the "market society" – a society where economic activity is no longer a constituent part of social, cultural, and religious institutions but society itself is instead absorbed in the network of economic activity. That thesis is developed in *The Great Transformation* and in two chapters in Part IV of this volume.[72] For Polanyi, ignoring the historical or cultural specificity of that period and elevating the deterministic approach to a general rule leads to two fundamental errors. Applied to the future, the proposed model generates mere prejudice, as we have seen. But, applied to the past, it creates an unsustainable anachronism.[73]

This last position lies at the core of the research in economic history that Polanyi conducted after his move to the United States. It found expression in a series of books (*Trade and Markets in the Early Empires*; *Dahomey and the Slave Trade*; *The Livelihood of Man*) and articles that had notable influence in the fields of anthropology and sociology. The characteristic features of Polanyi's approach are outlined clearly in Parts II and III, especially in Chapters 5 ("The Contribution of Institutional Analysis to the Social Sciences"), 14 ("General Economic History"), and 15 ("Market Elements and Economic Planning in Antiquity"). Chapter 14 is of particular interest, insofar as it reproduces the introductory lessons of a course of the same name that Polanyi taught at Columbia University in the early 1950s; it contains a clear exposition of his methodological approach.[74] Polanyi proposes that the fundamental objective of "economic history" is to study *"the place occupied by the economy in society as a whole*, in other words the changing relation of the economic to the noneconomic institutions in society" [p. 133]. If one is to pursue these goals, which Polanyi also identifies in the work of Max Weber, the analytical tools developed by neoclassical economics are of little help – indeed they risk falsifying irreparably our perception of observed phenomena. Instead, Polanyi intends to address the problem of theoretically analyzing "primitive" or archaic, pre-industrial economies through the adoption of an institutional method of investigation focused on uncovering the essential rather than the merely formal meaning of "economics."[75]

As Polanyi explains in the 1950 essay "The Contribution of Institutional Analysis to the Social Sciences" (reproduced here as Chapter 5 in Part II), this means that economics has to be thought of as the interaction between humans and their environment, which takes place for the sake of satisfying the material needs of the former; economics is not only a set of choices linked to "the relationship between ends and scarce means that have alternative uses" – as it is according to the neoclassical paradigm.[76] This insight, which is further elaborated upon in later works[77] and constitutes one of the most enduring and notable elements of Polanyi's thought, is the most fitting antidote to the "economistic fallacy" – the logical error of "equating the human economy in general with its market form."[78] In this way Polanyi establishes the conditions for an authentically operational and dogma-free study of essentially every type of economy that has ever existed or currently exists (in doing so, he proves to be, along with Marcel Mauss, one of the finest interpreters of the comparative method in the social sciences).[79] Empirical economies can then be described on the basis of the "manner in which the economic process is instituted at different times and places," and hence also on the basis of the relationship that exists in every society between economic and noneconomic institutions.[80] If a similar approach allows Polanyi to produce significant results in the fields of history and economic anthropology – beginning with the crucial distinction between the three forms of trade integration, reciprocity, and redistribution discussed here in Part III[81] – it is also worth noting that his earlier studies, some of which are reproduced in Part II, demonstrate a marked sensibility for institutional perspectives.

Polanyi's insistence on the role of public or governmental power in relation to the emersion of the system of self-regulated markets, and hence in relation to the demystification of the liberal model of market economics as a "natural" process, is consistent with the postulates of the German historical school, in particular those of Schmoller and Bücher.[82] In "Culture in a Democratic England of the Future," instead, Polanyi repeatedly references the works of Thorstein Veblen and investigates, in a particularly acute and brilliant manner, the stratification into classes of English society and the relationship of that process with the establishment of a cultural "elite."[83] The broad scope of political and social history is outlined (with a particular focus on the rise of fascism) in a series five of lectures (gathered here under one chapter); in them Polanyi focuses on the intersection between models of democracy and forms of economic organization.[84] On the other hand, the penetrating analysis of American society pays special attention to the relationship between the education system and economic processes in the United States.[85]

Polanyi, then, returns to proposing, in various ways, the fundamental theme of economy as a "cultural reality." That concept is at once a main focus of Polanyi's thought and a litmus test for his own ideological distance from the central themes of American economic neo-institutionalism[86] – a school of thought that originates with Douglass North and Oliver Williamson. These themes are only superficially convergent with his own.[87] Neo-institutional analyses privilege the logic of an economic calculation made by competing individuals in conditions of scarcity; following Mauss' typical unidimensional view of the human being as an "economic animal,"[88] they seek to explain the persistence and mutability of institutions, and also their impact on economic development.[89] In contrast, Polanyi does not address institutions from the point of view of "economic functionalism,"[90] according to which the sole purpose of institutions is the lowering of costs and the amassing of wealth. He considers institutions to be not so much factors that are important in terms of payoff and behavioral ties (of both individuals and organizations), but rather integral parts of a culture, and hence transmitters of meanings capable of orienting the values and desires of a community and its constituent parts.[91] On the one hand, this line of thinking emphasizes – as the German historical school had already done – the interdependence between the economy and institutions, both economic and noneconomic: "For religion or government may be as important for the structure and functioning of the economy as monetary institutions or the availability of tools and machines themselves that lighten the toil of labor."[92] On the other hand, the idea of an economy as a cultural and institutional reality leads Polanyi – in contrast to the neo-institutionalists – to emphasize the specificity of the market economy and its ideological corollaries, which, far from presenting intrinsic truths about human nature and the order of things,[93] seem to be exclusively the products of a *contingent historical form* and hence do not lend themselves to universalization.[94]

If it is true that "nothing obscures our social vision as effectively as the economistic prejudice,"[95] then Polanyi's writings contain a sophisticated critique of that ideology and a demystification of each of the axioms of orthodox economics – in particular, utilitarian rationality, the paradigm of scarcity, and the distinction between economic and noneconomic matters. In fact his analysis sets out to establish, with the help of empirical material drawn from anthropological studies – the authors referenced include Thurnwald, Malinowski, and Boas – that the model of *Homo economicus* and its corollaries are cultural constructs that emerged in parallel with the nineteenth-century affirmation of a specific institutional arrangement, characterized by free and interdependent markets of land and labor.[96] Institutions, then, create the underlying incentives for individual action and the attendant model of rationality, and not vice versa. Therefore, while it is possible to maintain that a market society gives rise to economic calculation,[97] it is not possible to explain the institutional changes and the emersion of the system of the self-regulating market simply through the logic of maximizing utility.

The points raised by Polanyi are of particular relevance not only for sociologists and economic anthropologists, but also for legal scholars who have experienced firsthand what is usually referred to as economic imperialism:[98] the tendency to present economic analysis as a general theory of human behavior or, in the words of Foucault, a "grid of intelligibility" encompassing all social interactions and individual behaviors, including those of a noneconomic nature.[99] The encroachment of economics upon areas traditionally under the purview of other disciplines – such as individuality, familial interactions, and criminal behavior (consider the studies of Gary Becker) – has increased the contact and intersection between economics and law well beyond their traditional areas of overlap such as anti-trust legislation. Modern "law and economics" has demonstrated its analytic power first in a purely descriptive way, but then in a progressively normative fashion, by testing not simply the justice of laws and judicial institutions, but their efficiency as well[100] – to the point of legitimizing the contemporary appeal to pseudo-scientific techniques for the quantitative measurement of judicial systems according to the criterion of efficiency.[101] In this last case – and especially in the version proposed by the theory of legal origins, advanced by the World Bank in its celebrated *Doing Business* reports[102] – the law has been reduced to a mere vector of economic development and is investigated from a purely functionalist standpoint: a questionable approach with regard to both its premises and its effects.[103] If the plurality of the methods of investigation of social phenomena is something to appreciate and to welcome, we should exercise caution regarding the recent phenomenon of uncritically accepting that analytical models developed in other fields of study should solve different sorts of problems from the ones they were designed for: their careless use can give rise to reductionist and counterproductive results.

The works of Polanyi, particularly "How to Make Use of the Social Sciences" (most likely written in the 1930s),[104] offer insight into this question as well. That piece is interesting above all for a reconstruction of the author's intellectual evolution, since it develops arguments about the relationship between nominalism and essentialism in the methodologies of the natural and social sciences. Karl Popper (known as "Karli" in Polanyi's family, who would often receive him at their apartment on the Vorgartenstrasse in Vienna)[105] makes exact references to Polanyi's ideas in *The Open Society and Its Enemies*, but only mentions private conversations with him rather than any specific writings.[106] More specifically, Polanyi emphasizes that the possibility of aggregating the various sciences is limited on account of the particularities of their different methods and of the relative "innate interest."[107] He also insists that there is a fundamental difference between the natural and social sciences, which has less to do with their different methods and more with the difference in the impact that their respective fields have on the shaping of tastes and the framework of human values: "man's attitude toward his material environment is directed by definite ends, which are but little influenced by the rise of [the natural] sciences,"[108] while the social sciences instead "have a massive influence on man's wishes and purposes" – so much so that they impact his very existence "radically and immediately."[109] It follows, then, that the function of the social sciences is twofold and their usefulness must be judged by considering both aspects: "it is not enough to inquire how far they assist us in attaining our ends; we must also ask how far they help or *hinder us* in clarifying them."[110] Here the *normative* dimension of the social sciences becomes clear, and with it Polanyi's distance from more naive approaches, which focus on the *Wertfreiheit* [ethical neutrality] of those sciences. Polanyi's thesis is that, while the pursuit of methodological purity and the gradual elimination of "metaphysical remnants" from the field of inquiry of the social sciences "may have enhanced man's ability to attain his ends, they certainly diminished his faculty of knowing what they are."[111] There is, then, an intrinsic tension between the drive toward progress in the social sciences and that of preserving "the dignity of metaphysics in its insistence on the comprehensive character of common human awareness as the matrix of art, religion, morality, personal life, and science."[112] But is it possible to protect the matrix of science without interfering with its progress? "Is a creative compromise possible, which would leave scope for progress, while protecting us from the danger of losing our way in our search for it?"[113] The conditions established by Polanyi for answering these questions are clear: the pitfalls attendant upon the scientific handling of human affairs can only be avoided by understanding the necessity of a "directed existence"[114] – in other words, only by establishing a fairly stable consensus regarding certain guiding principles, which are "deliberately protected from corrosive influence as the Roentgen manipulator's hands are from the effects of X rays."[115] Use of the social sciences "is not a technical problem of science. It is a matter of providing such a definition of the meaning of human society as will maintain the sovereignty of man over all instruments of life, including science."[116]

The points raised in these writings are demanding ones, which have not lost any relevance over the years. On the one hand, the development of the life sciences has greatly amplified the destabilizing tendencies of the natural sciences and has led to the rise of juridical rules and principles, for instance of dignity and precaution, which are intended to re-establish a strong foundation and to actualize a series of measures aimed at preserving human sovereignty over the manipulation of life.[117] On the other hand, the universalization of economic reasoning as a sort of new secular religion renders ever more important a critical reflection on the impact that normative assumptions taken from the social sciences (in this case, from economic science) have on any system of human values and desires. All the shortcomings of the alleged *Wertfreiheit* of the social sciences come once again to the surface, and the importance of the critical, historical, and institutional perspectives presented by Polanyi is reconfirmed. Rereading these works today provides an excellent antidote not only against a naively "scientistic" attitude, but against reductionism of any kind; reductionism that – to cite Polanyi once more – has produced the "barrenness of the cultural West in its encounter with the world at large."[118]

Translated by Carl Ipsen and Michael Ipsen

Notes to the Introduction

1. Michele Cangiani, "L'inattualità di Polanyi," *Contemporanea*, 5.4 (2002), 751–7. Regarding the question of the outdated character versus contemporary relevance of Polanyi's thought, see also Alain Caillé and Jean-Louis Laville, "Actualité de Karl Polanyi," in Michele Cangiani and Jérôme Maucourant, eds., *Essais de Karl Polanyi* (Paris: Seuil, 2008), 565–85.

2. Gareth Dale, "Karl Polanyi in Budapest: On His Political and Intellectual Formation," *Archives européennes de sociologie*, 50.1 (2009), 97–130, which explores among other things Polanyi's relationships with György Lukács, Oszkár Jászi, and Karl Mannheim; see also Karl Polanyi's autobiographical notes "L'eredità del Circolo Galilei," in Karl Polanyi, *La libertà in una società complessa*, edited by Alfredo Salsano (Turin: Bollati Boringhieri, 1987), 199–214.

3. For detailed biographical notes, see Kari Polanyi-Levitt and Marguerite Mendell, "Karl Polanyi: His Life and Times," *Studies in Political Economy*, 22 (1987), 7–39.

4. Cangiani, "L'inattualità di Polanyi," p. 751.

5. See Chapter 2 in this volume, "Economics and the Freedom to Shape Our Social Destiny."

6. See Chapter 1 in this volume, "For a New West."

7. It is worth mentioning that Polanyi's final project involved the creation of a new journal entitled *Co-Existence*, which intended to look at international politics and economics from a pluralist perspective that ran counter to the logic of the universal market. The first issue was published a few days after Polanyi's death; see Kari Polanyi-Levitt, "Karl Polanyi and *Co-Existence*," in Kari Polanyi-Levitt, ed., *The Life and Work of Karl Polanyi: A Celebration* (Montreal, Canada: Black Rose Books, 1990), 253–63, especially pp. 259–62 (the article was originally published in *Co-Existence*, 2 (1964), 113–21).

8. See Kari Polanyi-Levitt, "Karl Polanyi as Socialist," in Kenneth McRobbie, ed., *Humanity, Society, and Commitment: On Karl Polanyi* (Montreal, Canada: Black Rose Books, 1994), 115–34.

9. Polanyi-Levitt, "Karl Polanyi and *Co-Existence*," p. 253.

10. On this aspect of Polanyi's philosophy, see Gareth Dale, *Karl Polanyi: The Limits of the Market* (Cambridge: Polity, 2010), esp. pp. 31–44; Abraham Rotstein, "The Reality of Society: Karl Polanyi's Philosophical Perspective," in Polanyi-Levitt, *Life and Work*, 98–110.

11. See Kari Polanyi-Levitt, "The Origins and Significance of *The Great Transformation*," in Polanyi-Levitt, *Life and Work*, 111–26.

12. Carl Levy, "La riscoperta di Karl Polanyi," *Contemporanea*, 5.4 (2002), 767–70; Caillé and Laville, "Actualité de Karl Polanyi."

13. As noted in Sally C. Humphreys, "History, Economics, and Anthropology: The Work of Karl Polanyi," *History and Theory*, 8 (1979), 165–212, at pp. 165, 168. Political economy and constitutional history, moreover, made up a part of legal studies.

14. According to Kari Polanyi-Levitt, it was in this phase that Polanyi expanded on the thoughts of the Vienna School and of many American and British economists (Polanyi-Levitt, "Karl Polanyi as Socialist," p. 125).

15. On this subject, see Margaret R. Somers, "Karl Polanyi's Intellectual Legacy," in Polanyi-Levitt, *Life and Work*, 152–60.

16. In this regard, see Mihály Sárkány, "Karl Polanyi's Contribution to Economic Anthropology," in Polanyi-Levitt, *Life and Work*, 183–7.

17. For a discussion of the main criticism of Polanyi's economic history, see Caillé and Laville, "Actualité de Karl Polanyi," at pp. 569–71; Dale, *Karl Polanyi*, pp. 137–87. On Fernand Braudel's criticism of Polanyi, see Alfredo Salsano, "Polanyi, Braudel e il re del Dahomey," *Rivista di storia contemporanea*, 15 (1986), 608–26.

18. For a basic overview, see the 2007 volume in the series Cahiers lillois d'économie et de sociologie, entitled *Penser la marchandisation du monde avec Karl Polanyi* and edited by Richard Sobel – particularly the chapters by Franck Van de Velde, Geneviève Azam, and Richard Sobel himself.

19. See Michele Cangiani, *Economia e democrazia: Saggio su Karl Polanyi* (Padua: Il Poligrafo, 1998).

20. See the essays collected in Ayşe Buğra and Kaan Ağartan, eds., *Reading Karl Polanyi for the Twenty-First Century: Market Economy as a Political Project* (New York: Palgrave Macmillan, 2007).

21. On this subject, consult Alfredo Salsano's "Presentazione" in his edition of Polanyi, *La libertà in una società complessa*.

22. See Christian Joerges and Josef Falke, eds., *Karl Polanyi: Globalisation and the Potential of Law in Transnational Markets* (Oxford: Hart, 2011).

23. Joseph E. Stiglitz, "Foreword," in Karl Polanyi, *The Great Transformation: The Political and Economic Origins of Our Time* (Boston, MA: Beacon Press, 2011), vii–xvii, at p. vii.

24. Lisa Martin, "Polanyi's Revenge," *Perspectives on Politics*, 11.1 (2013), 165–74.

25. See Robert B. Reich, *Supercapitalism: The Transformation of Business, Democracy, and Everyday Life* (New York: Alfred A. Knopf, 2007) – and also the preface to the Italian edition by Guido Rossi (*Supercapitalismo. Come cambia l'economia globale e i rischi per la democrazia*, Rome: Fazi, 2008).

26. Cangiani, "L'inattualità di Polanyi," p. 751.

27. Some of the most important volumes are the following: Polanyi, *La libertà in una società complessa*; Karl Polanyi, *Cronache della grande trasformazione*, edited by Michele Cangiani (Turin: Einaudi, 1993); Karl Polanyi, *Europa 1937: Guerre esterne e guerre civili*, edited by Michele Cangiani (Rome: Donzelli, 1995).

28. For information regarding the formation and work of the Polanyi Institute, see Ana Gomez, "The Karl Polanyi Institute of Political Economy: A Narrative of Contributions to Social Change," *Interventions économiques*, 38 (2008), 1–18, at p. 2.

29. On the basis of the notes of P[aul] M[eadow] from March 25, 1962 (File 24–2, Karl Polanyi Archive), we can ascertain that such a volume would have covered the following arguments: (1) "The West as a Civilization and the Political West"; (2) "The Idols of the Old West: Science, Technology, and Economic Organization"; (3) "The Dual Character of the Consequences: (a) The Internal and External Achievements of the Old West; (b) The Idols Revealed as a Threat to Physical

Survival"; (4) "The Core Values of the New Non-Western Nations
and the Industrial Process"; (5) "The Failure of Western Leadership
after the Second World War"; (6) "The Limited Basis for a New
West"; (7) "Some Specific Issue for the New West: Modus Vivendi;
Grotius Extended; Foreign Trade Monopolies; the Use of Priorities in
Settling International Disputes; Protection of the Intellectuals from
Contractual Pressure"; (8) "On the Rejuvenation of the West and
Personal Freedom."
30. See Chapter 9 in this book, "Culture in a Democratic England of the
Future."
31. See Chapter 13 in this book, "Public Opinion and Statesmanship."
32. See Chapter 10 in this book, "Experiences in Vienna and America:
America."
33. See Chapter 8 in this book, "The Roots of Pacifism."
34. See Chapter 11 in this book, "How to Make Use of the Social
Sciences."
35. For a discussion of the unpublished works from the 1930s, see Giandomenica Becchio, "Gli inediti di Karl Polanyi negli anni Trenta," *Rivista
di filosofia*, 88.3 (1997), 475–82, and also Gareth Dale's richly docu-
mented monograph.
36. Polanyi-Levitt and Mendell, "Karl Polanyi," pp. 13, 21.
37. On this phase in Polanyi's life and intellectual development, see Lee
Congdon, "The Sovereignty of Society: Polanyi in Vienna," in Polanyi-
Levitt, *Life and Work*, 78–86; Dale, *Karl Polanyi*, esp. the chapter "The
Economics and Ethics of Socialism" (pp. 19–45).
38. Dale, "Karl Polanyi in Budapest," pp. 113, 115–16.
39. See Chapter 16 in this book, "The Crucial Issue Today: A Response,"
p. 167.
40. On this subject, see Polanyi-Levitt, "Karl Polanyi as Socialist," p. 126.
41. For a more in-depth analysis, see Alberto Chilosi, "Dühring's 'Sociali-
tarian' Model of Economic Communes and Its Influence on the Development of Socialist Thought and Practice," *Journal of Economic
Studies*, 29.4/5 (2002), 293–305.
42. See Chapter 16 in this book, "The Crucial Issue Today: A Response,"
p. 168.
43. Karl Polanyi, *The Great Transformation* (Boston, MA: Beacon Press,
1957), pp. 33–42.
44. See Chapter 16 in this book, "The Crucial Issue Today: A Response,"
p. 169.
45. On the market economy, Polanyi also wrote:

it lacks any mechanism to understand the need for health, repose and
spiritual and moral fulfillment among the producers and those who
inhabit the world of production; for by means of long-term retroactive
effects the common good is either furthered or harmed by the different
ways in which production and the means of production are organized.
That economic model is even less capable of advancing the positive

goals of the common good – the spiritual, cultural, and moral goals of the community – insofar as their realization depends upon material factors. Finally, that model is entirely incapable of responding when economic objectives touch upon the general goals of humanity, for example the need for international aid or maintaining peace between peoples. (Karl Polanyi, "La contabilità socialista," in his *La libertà in una società complessa*, p. 19).

46. Dale, *Karl Polanyi*, p. 10, which includes reference to a passage taken from the unpublished 1937 essay "Community and Society: The Christian Criticism of our Social Order" (File 21-22, Karl Polanyi Archive). It is worth reproducing that passage here:

The market acts like an invisible boundary isolating all individuals in their day-to-day activities, as producers and consumers. They produce for the market, they are supplied from the market. Beyond it they cannot reach, however eagerly they may wish to serve their fellows. Any attempt to be helpful on their part is instantly frustrated by the market mechanism. Giving your goods away at less than the market price will benefit somebody for a short time, but it would also drive your neighbor out of business, and finally ruin your own, with consequent losses of employment for those dependent on your own factory or enterprise. Doing more than your due as a working man will make the conditions of work for your comrades worse. By refusing to spend on luxuries you will be throwing some people out of work, by refusing to save you will be doing the same to others. As long as you follow the rules of the market, buying at the lowest and selling at the highest price whatever you happen to be dealing in, you are comparatively safe. The damage you are doing to your fellows in order to serve your own interest is, then, unavoidable. The more completely, therefore, one discards the idea of serving one's fellows, the more successfully one can reduce one's responsibility for harm done to others. Under such a system, human beings are not allowed to be good, even though they wish to be so.

47. See Chapter 16 in this book, "The Crucial Issue Today: A Response," p. 172.
48. See Giandomenica Becchio, "The Early Debate of Economic Calculation in Vienna (1919–1925). The Heterodox Point of View: Neurath, Mises and Polanyi," *Storia del pensiero economico*, 2007, at pp. 133–4.
49. See Chapter 16 in this book, "The Crucial Issue Today: A Response," p. 170.
50. See the essay "Il 'guild socialism' (uomini e idee)," in Polanyi, *Libertà in una società complessa*, 3–6. For a more in-depth look at Polanyi's idea of guild socialism, see Cangiani, *Economia e democrazia*, pp. 127–8; Polanyi-Levitt, "Karl Polanyi as Socialist," pp. 115–16.

51. See Chapter 16 in this book, "The Crucial Issue Today: A Response," pp. 170–7.
52. For Ludwig von Mises position, see Lawrence H. White, *The Clash of Economic Ideas: The Great Policy Debates and Experiments of the Last Hundred Years* (Cambridge: Cambridge University Press, 2012), pp. 35–7.
53. A fundamental starting point for piecing together the evolution of Polanyi's philosophy of freedom is his essay "Über die Freiheit," written toward the end of the 1920s, which can be found in Karl Polanyi, *Chronik der großen Transformation: Artikel und Aufsätze (1920–1940)*, edited by Michele Cangiani and Claus Thomasberger, vol. 1 (Marburg: Metropolis, 2002), 137–64. Gregory Baum discusses it broadly in his *Karl Polanyi on Ethics and Economics* (Montreal and Kingston, Canada: McGill–Queen's University Press, 1996), at pp. 24–7 and 35–7.
54. Giacomo Marramao, "Dono, scambio, obbligazione: Il contributo di Karl Polanyi alla filosofia sociale," *Inchiesta*, 27.117/18 (1997), 35–44.
55. See Chapter 7 in this book, "The Meaning of Peace," p. 84.
56. See in particular the writings collected in Polanyi's Italian volume *La libertà in una società complessa*, especially in the third section: "Jean-Jacques Rousseau, o è possibile una società libera?" "Libertà e tecnologia," "La macchina e la scoperta della società," "La libertà in una società complessa."
57. See Chapter 2 in this book, "Economics and the Freedom to Shape Our Social Destiny," p. 33.
58. See Chapter 1 in this book, "For a New West," p. 31.
59. As observed by Polanyi in *The Great Transformation*, p. 141: "While laissez-faire economy was the product of deliberate state action, subsequent restrictions on laissez-faire started in a spontaneous way. Laissez-faire was planned; planning was not." Analysis of the political–juridical aspect of the institution of markets in land and labor is developed in the second part of *The Great Transformation*, especially in chs. 6 and 7.
60. Chapter 1 in this book, "For a New West," p. 31.
61. Ibid.
62. For Polanyi's ideas about "a new West" that date from that era, see Paul Meadow's notes entitled "Karl Polanyi's Theses Concerning the 'New West'" in the Karl Polanyi Archive, file 24–2 (on which see also n. 29).
63. See Chapter 2 in this book, "Economics and the Freedom to Shape Our Social Destiny," p. 33.
64. Friedrich A. von Hayek, *The Road to Serfdom* (Chicago: University of Chicago Press, 1994 [1944]). For an interesting reconstruction of the intellectual and biographical genesis of the work, see Kari Polanyi-Levitt and Marguerite Mendell, "The Origins of Market Fetishism (Critique of Friedrich Hayek's Economic Theory)," *Monthly Review*,

41 (1989), 11–32; also the important volume edited by Philip Mirowski and Dieter Plehwe, *The Road from Mont Pèlerin: The Making of the Neoliberal Thought Collective* (Cambridge, MA: Harvard University Press, 2009), and particularly the essay by Robert van Horn and Philip Mirowski, which is based on archival documents yet unpublished: "The Rise of the Chicago School of Economics and the Birth of Neoliberalism," 139–80.

65. See Chapter 3 in this book, "Economic History and the Problem of Freedom," p. 40.
66. See Chapter 14 in this book, "General Economic History," p. 137.
67. See Chapter 3 in this book, "Economic History and the Problem of Freedom," pp. 41–42.
68. Ibid., p. 42.
69. Ibid.
70. See Chapter 14 in this book, "General Economic History," p. 145.
71. Somers, "Karl Polanyi's Intellectual Legacy," pp. 152–3.
72. See Chapters 18 and 20 in this book, "The Eclipse of Panic and the Outlook of Socialism," pp. 205–8, and "Five Lectures on the Present Age of Transformation: The Trend toward an Integrated Society."
73. See Chapter 3 in this book, "Economic History and the Problem of Freedom," p. 39.
74. For a useful account, see Daniel J. Fusfeld, "Karl Polanyi's Lectures on General Economic History: A Student Remembers," in McRobbie, ed., *Humanity, Society and Commitment.* For an evaluation of Polanyi's thoughts on the postwar trends in economic anthropology, see Sárkány, "Karl Polanyi's Contribution to Economic Anthropology."
75. See Michele Cangiani, "From Menger to Polanyi: The Institutional Way," in Harald Hagemann, Tamotsu Nishizawa, and Yukihiro Ikeda, eds., *Austrian Economics in Transition: From Carl Menger to Friedrich Hayek* (New York: Palgrave Macmillan, 2010), 138–53; Riccardo Motta and Franco Lombari, "Traffici e mercati: L'istituzionalismo di Karl Polanyi," *Materiali per una storia della cultura giuridica*, 1 (1980), 231–52, especially pp. 248–52; J. Ron Stanfield, "Karl Polanyi and Contemporary Economic Thought," in Polanyi-Levitt, ed., *Life and Work*, 195–6; Walter C. Neale, "Institutions," *Journal of Economic Issues*, 21.3 (1987), 1177–205.
76. In *An Essay on the Nature and Significance of Economic Science* (London: Macmillan, 1945), Lionel Robbins defines economics as "a science which studies human behaviour as a relationship between ends and scarce means which have alternative uses" (p. 16).
77. See in particular Karl Polanyi, "The Economy as Instituted Process," in Karl Polanyi, Conrad M. Arensberg, and Harry W. Pearson, eds., *Trade and Market in the Early Empires* (Glencoe, IL: Free Press, 1957), 243–69; and Karl Polanyi, "Carl Menger's Two Meanings of 'Economic,'" in George Dalton, ed., *Studies in Economic Anthropology* (Washington, DC: American Anthropological Association, 1971), 16–24.

78. Karl Polanyi, *The Livelihood of Man* (New York: Academic Press, 1977), p. 6.
79. In this regard, see Gérald Berthoud, "Toward a Comparative Approach: The Contribution of Karl Polanyi," in Polanyi-Levitt, *Life and Work*, 171–82.
80. See Polanyi, "The Economy as Instituted Process."
81. See Chapters 14 and 15 in this book, "General Economic History" and "Market Elements and Economic Planning in Antiquity."
82. Somers, "Karl Polanyi's Intellectual Legacy," p. 155. On this point, see also Sabine Frerichs, "Re-Embedding Neo-Liberal Constitutionalism: A Polanyian Case for the Economic Sociology of Law," in Joerges and Falke, eds., *Karl Polanyi*, 65–84, at p. 81. Frerich contrasts the reconstructions of von Hayek and Polanyi regarding the relationship between law, society and the market, stating:

Hayekian economic liberalism confirms and approves the liberal nature of market society: markets are conceived as spontaneous orders that arise from the interaction of economically "free" individuals (bottom-up aspect), while any form of social interventionism is criticized as a coercive form of order (top-down aspect). Polanyi's liberal socialism gives a reversed image: while "self-regulating" markets are seen as artificial institutions imposed on "commodified" individuals (top-down aspect), social policies draw on the self-protective impulses of social movements (bottom-up aspect).

83. See Chapter 9 in this book, "Culture in a Democratic England of the Future."
84. See Chapter 17 in this book, "Conflicting Philosophies in Modern Society."
85. See Chapter 10 in this book, "Experiences in Vienna and America: America."
86. See Douglass C. North, "Markets and Other Allocation Systems in History: The Challenge of Karl Polanyi," *Journal of European Economic History*, 6 (1977), 703–16. It is worth noting, however, that North's ideas have evolved significantly since the writing of this piece, signaling a major detachment from the precepts of neoclassical economics. In that regard, see Claude Menard and Mary M. Shirley, "The Contribution of Douglass North to New Institutional Economics," in Sebastian Galiani and Itai Sened, eds., *Institutions, Property Rights, and Economic Growth: The Legacy of Douglass North* (Cambridge: Cambridge University Press, in press), at http://hal.inria.fr/docs/00/62/42/97/PDF/2011–Menard_Shirley_North_and_NIE–CUP.pdf (accessed April 2, 2014).
87. On the differences between Polanyi's institutionalism and the "new" economic institutionalism, see Michele Cangiani, "Karl Polanyi's Institutional Theory: Market Society and Its "Disembedded" Economy,"

Journal of Economic Issues, 45 (2011), 177–98; Michele Cangiani, "The Forgotten Institutions," in Mark Harvey, Ronnie Ramlogan and Sally Randles, eds., *Karl Polanyi: New Perspectives on the Place of the Economy in Society* (Manchester: Manchester University Press, 2008), 25–42; Cangiani, "From Menger to Polanyi"; Jérôme Maucourant and Sébastien Plociniczak, "Penser l'institution et le marché avec Karl Polanyi," *Revue de la régulation*, 10 (2011), at http://regulation.revues. org/9439 (accessed February 21, 2013); on the relationship between Polanyi and "old" economic institutionalism, see Walter C. Neale, "Karl Polanyi and American Institutionalism: A Strange Case of Convergence," in Polanyi-Levitt, *Life and Work*, 145–51.

88. See Marcel Mauss, *Essai sur le don: Forme et raison de l'échange dans les sociétés archaïques* (Paris: Presses Universitaires de France, 2007), p. 238.

89. For a precise summary of his views on the relationship between institutions and economic processes, see Douglas C. North, "Institutions and the Performance of Economies over Time," in Claude Ménard and Mary M. Shirley, eds., *Handbook of New Institutional Economics* (Berlin-Heidelberg: Springer, 2005), 21–30, where the author clarifies the general premise that "the continuous interaction between institutions and organizations in the economic setting of scarcity and hence competition is the key to institutional change"; and see also Douglas C. North, *Institutions, Institutional Change and Economic Performance* (Cambridge: Cambridge University Press, 1990) and Oliver E. Williamson, "Transaction Cost Economics," in Richard Schmalensee and Robert Willig, eds., *Handbook of Industrial Organization*, vol. 1 (New York: North Holland, 1989), 136–84.

90. Michele Cangiani and Jérôme Maucourant, "Introduction," in Cangiani and Maucourant, eds., *Essais de Karl Polanyi*, 9–46, at pp. 9–10, 28–9.

91. In this regards it seems pertinent to recall the principal differences between "old" and "new" institutionalism and their relation to the work of Polanyi. For further discussion, see Helge Peukert, "Bridging Old and New Institutional Economics: Gustav Schmoller and Douglass C. North, Seen with Old Institutionalists' Eyes," *European Journal of Law and Economics*, 11 (2001), 91–130; see also Malcolm Rutherford, "Institutionalism between the Wars," *Journal of Economic Issues*, 34.2 (2000), 291–304; James R. Stansfield, "The Scope, Method, and Significance of Original Institutional Economics," *Journal of Economic Issues*, 33 (1999), 230–55.

92. Polanyi, "The Economy as Instituted Process."

93. As is so often presented by the prophets of the creed of liberalism, which ultimately brings to mind Donato Carusi, *L'ordine naturale delle cose* (Turin: Giappichelli, 2011), pp. 122–4.

94. On this point, compare the considerations of Caillé and Laville, "Actualité de Karl Polanyi," p. 567.

95. See Polanyi, *The Great Transformation*, p. 159.

96. See Polanyi, *The Livelihood of Man*, pp. 5–7.
97. Obviously there are certain limits: the empirical results of field studies in cognitive and behavioral economics would seem to reshape models of utilitarian rationality assumed by orthodox theory. See the studies collected in Matteo Motterlini and Massimo Piattelli Palmarini, eds., *Critica della ragione economica: Tre saggi: Kahneman, McFadden, Smith* (Milan: Il Saggiatore, 2005); see also Dan Ariely, *Predictably Irrational: The Hidden Forces that Shape our Decisions* (New York: Harper, 2010), especially from p. 75 on.
98. Steven G. Medema, "The Trial of Homo Economicus: What Law and Economics Tells Us about the Development of Economic Imperialism," in John B. Davis, ed., *New Economics and Its History* (Durham, NC: Duke University Press, 1997), 122–42.
99. See Michel Foucault, *The Birth of Biopolitics: Lectures at the Collège de France, 1978–1979* (Basingstoke: Palgrave Macmillan, 2008), at pp. 243–4.
100. For a historical reconstruction of the development of the economic analysis of law, see Ejan Mackaay, "History of Law and Economics," in *Encyclopedia of Law and Economics*, accessible online at http://encyclo.findlaw.com/tablebib.html; for the internal affairs of the Chicago School, see especially the important reconstruction of Robert van Horn, "Reinventing Monopoly and the Role of Corporation: The Roots of Chicago Law and Economics," in Mirowksi, and Plehwe, *The Road from Mont Pèlerin*, 204–37.
101. For an introduction to this debate, see the studies of Antonio Gambaro, "Misurare il diritto?" *Annuario di diritto comparato e di studi legislativi* (2012), 17–47; and Ralf Michaels, "Comparative Law by Numbers? Legal Origins Thesis, Doing Business Reports, and the Silence of Traditional Comparative Law," *American Journal of Comparative Law*, 57 (2009), 765–95.
102. A synthesis of the assumptions and of the fundamental thesis shared by the exponents of the theory of *legal origins* (who are all economists) can be found in Rafael La Porta, Florencio Lopez-de-Silanes, and Andrei Shleifer, "The Economic Consequences of Legal Origins," in *Journal of Economic Literature*, 46.2 (2008), 285–332. For a description of the contents and idea behind the project Doing Business, see the documents of the World Bank at http://www.doingbusiness.org/ (they are publicly available).
103. Certain critiques (which, in truth, are not all to be agreed with, insofar as they are affected by issues of national pride) are expressed in the volume edited by the Association Henri Capitant des amis de la culture juridique française: *Les Droits de tradition civiliste en question: À propos des rapports* Doing Business *de la Banque Mondiale* (Paris: Société de Législation Comparée, 2006). See also Catherine Valcke, "The French Response to the World Bank's Doing Business Reports," in *University of Toronto Law Journal*, 60.2 (2010), 197–217; Louisa Antoniolli, "La letteratura in materia di misurazione del diritto: Breve

itinerario ragionato," *Annuario di diritto comparato e di studi legislativi*, 2012, 453–485.

104. See Chapter 11 in this book, "How to Make Use of the Social Sciences."

105. This information is drawn from an interview with Kari Polanyi-Levitt. For the early relationship between Karl Popper and Karl Polanyi, see Malachi Haim Hacohen, *Karl Popper: The Formative Years, 1902–1945: Politics and Philosophy in Interwar Vienna* (Cambridge: Cambridge University Press, 2002), pp. 117–20.

106. Karl R. Popper, *The Open Society and Its Enemies*, vol. 1: *The Spell of Plato* (London: Routledge, 1947), p. 190, n. 30. On this point, see the notations in Humphreys, "History, Economics, and Anthropology," p. 170.

107. See Chapter 11 in this volume, "How to Make Use of the Social Sciences," pp. 109–10. Regarding interest in elements of a particular type, and hence the existence of a "problem" that plays a crucial role in the development of science, see Chapter 12 in this volume, "On Political Theory"; see also Karl R. Popper, *The Poverty of Historicism* (Boston: Beacon Press, 1957).

108. See Chapter 11 in this volume, "How to Make Use of the Social Sciences," pp. 113–14.

109. Ibid., pp. 114, 117.

110. Ibid., p. 114.

111. Ibid.

112. Ibid., p. 116.

113. Ibid.

114. Ibid., p. 117.

115. Ibid., p. 115.

116. Ibid., p. 118.

117. In general, see the considerations of Jürgen Habermas, *The Future of Human Nature* (Cambridge: Polity, 2003). For a particular reference to the rise of the paradigm of dignity, see Stefano Rodotà, *Il diritto di avere diritti* (Rome: Laterza, 2012), especially from p. 179 on.

118. Ch. 1 in the present volume ("For a New West"), p. 29.

Part I

Economy, Technology, and the Problem of Freedom

1

For a New West*

Some of us still recall World War I, which awakened our generation to the fact that history was not a matter of the past, as a thoughtless philosophy of the hundred years' peace would have us believe. And once started, it did not cease to happen.

I will seek to evoke the scenes we have witnessed and take the measure of our frustrations. Great triumphs and grave disappointments have been met with. However, it is not a balance of our experiences, achievements and omissions that stands to question; nor am I scanning the horizon for a mere break. The time has come to take note of a much bigger change.

There are signs of a barrenness of the cultural West in its encounter with the world at large. What matters here is not the level of its achievements in science or the arts, which flourish as only rarely before, but the weight of its mind and life values as measured by the rest of mankind. The material and scientific products of the West are avidly consumed by the nascent nations, but with an unconcealed contempt for the interpretations set upon them by ourselves. That cultural entity, the West, of which the thinkers and writers were the traditional vehicles, is no longer listened to; not on account of a hostile public, as we persuade ourselves to believe, but because it has nothing relevant to say. We must face this fact squarely, even if it

*File 37–12, Karl Polanyi Archive: typescript dated October 16, 1958, with corrections in the author's hand. There are two older versions of this same text, namely from September 21, 1958 and from July 28, 1958: "For a New West," 37–12 and "The New West," 37–12, respectively.

means laying bare the essential nature of our civilization, as it is now revealing itself, together with the unexpectedly changed circumstances in which our ultimate convictions will have to prove themselves from now onward.

Since this is not a theoretical disquisition, I will simply imagine myself addressing a public that is fairly sure to remember the opening scenes.

The Russian Revolution of 1917 was patently a continuation of the French Revolution of 1789 in its eastern advance. It smashed autocracy, gave land to the peasants, liberated oppressed nationalities, and in addition promised to rid the industrial system of the blemishes of exploitation. In its heroic age, Soviet socialism was given selfless support by the writers and artists of the West. They steeled their muscles in an epic defence of freedom, democracy, and socialism against the pagan upsurge of Teutonic fascism. Hitler's persecution of Bolsheviks and Jews was in the last resort directed against Christian universalism and its derivatives in the industrial present. His onslaught on traditional values, root and branch, created the modern West. Hence its ascendancy over the civilized world and beyond, to the tribal communities of inner Asia and tropical Africa – a moral triumph crowned by the victory of the political West and its ally, the Soviet people, those beggars of yesterday, over Germanic might. But the raising of the level of economic life in Russia from the ethical indifference of a capitalist market system to the conscious responsibility of a socialist basis did not by itself prevent human degradation. The defeat of fascism was almost reversed by Stalin's crimes. The disillusioned West lost status, stature, and self-confidence. A shift in the continental balance of power then evoked the specter of a third world war. A power vacuum had resulted from the disappearance of German and Japanese hemispheric structures, creating enmity between America and Russia – islands of world power in an empty ocean – which inevitably was a permanent menace to peace. The blast of Hiroshima multiplied a thousandfold the threat of that vacuum. By sheer weight of numbers Russia's army overshadowed Eurasia and was a nightmare to Washington. The replacement of Chiang by Mao on the Chinese continent hit America as if it had been defrauded of its heritage. The British felt threatened in the Near East and the Balkans. The West now emerged as a designation for a political power grouping. An atomic attack on Soviet Russia became a possibility. Even a Bertrand Russell advocated preventive war. Thinkers, writers, and artists, deprived of a substance of their own, shut their eyes to reality. The national uprisings in Asia – a link in the chain reaction started by the American, French, and Russian Revolutions

– were misread for a communist ramp. Propaganda for policies set by government officials, themselves mere cogs in the wheels of history, appeared as the only function to which western intellectuals now felt confident to aspire. Yet at the root of this lack of creativity there lay a real change in the life conditions of the world as a whole.

As the dust settled, the awe-inspiring feature of the moral landscape emerged. Not the Cold War, nor the civil wars in Asia stood out. The mushroom was the symbol of unspeakable perils, born from forces responsible for our own origins. And mankind began to grasp the true nature of the development that held it in its grip.

The Industrial Revolution was a watershed in the history of mankind. Three forces – technology, economic organization, and science, in this sequence – each from separate and undistinguished parentage, linked up, inconspicuously at first, to form, hardly a hundred years ago, into a social maelstrom that is still engulfing new and new millions of people, in an irresistible rush. The contraptions were the beginning; a movement toward a deliberate organizing of markets followed; science – almost a century later, but with an explosive effect – joined up last. All three then gathered speed: technology and science formed a partnership, economic organization made use of its chance, forcing the efficiency principle in production (both by market and planning) to vertiginous heights. Western culture is what science, technology, and economic organization, mutually reinforcing one another, unbridled and unrestrained, are making of man's life. Their subordination (science and technology, as well as economic organization) to our will to a progress that is human and to the fulfillment of a personality that is free has become a necessity of survival. It falls to the West to discipline its children. For the sociologist, nuclear fission, the atom bomb, and the Asian revolutions may well seem to fall into unrelated fields: science, technology, and politics. Actually they are proximate steps in the growth of an industrial civilization. Progress may be geographical, theoretical, practical. The directions vary, the tendency to advance is the same. For the West, they represent *one* problem: How to find creative answers to responsibilities to which it is committed by its past.

The tasks of the cultural West are interlaced with the rebirth of a continent. Industrialization is, for Asia, not an absolute; it is accomplished under reservations. What these imply, only time will unfold. The West is held responsible for the industrial, scientific, and economistic road on which our world has embarked. We are in the dock. Also, the leaders of western thought, entangled in power politics, were the moral victims of the Cold War and its violent perversion of minds. They lost caste, when democracy was made synonymous with capitalism – in the USA – and national status was identified with colonial possessions – in Britain and France. Western spiritual ascendancy, gained in the long battle against Hitlerism, was frittered away in the hopeless support of a decaying past.

But the perspectives in which we grew up have dissolved. Universalism postulated our identification with the wide world, the *oikoumenē*. Its conquest by a technological civilization is unexpectedly producing separate and distinct cultures, all of them industrial, yet not only different on the capitalism–socialism axis but different, moreover, on other scales, some which are based on incommensurable core values. To penetrate and internalize the position in which the West is placed is the task. A circumscribed, reduced West is both a concentrated and radical West and an adjusted, tolerant West. It is the parent of the industrial society as well as of its derivatives, and an equal member of a family of such societies. It is the offshoot of a universalism of a preindustrial type and the first representative of a universalism of a postindustrial type. It is a result of early illusions and of late recognitions of a unique sort. It has passed through the liberal utopia of unrestricted freedom and the illiberal utopia of general regulationism. It has probed authoritarianism and libertinism; traditionalism and anti-traditionalism; class elite and mob rule. It has passed through the methodological discoveries of general law and historical specificity; of empiricism and phenomenology; of logical positivism and symbolism; of Thomism and existentialism. So have other cultures. But none in the same way. Western universalism – this is the Jewish–Christian inheritance – was the claim to a way of life of universal validity. This received a massive topical content when the West became the bearer of an industrial civilization which, whether capitalist or socialist, soon comprised almost half of the planet. We were somehow thinking about and for the rest. It was not a conversation, rather a spirited monologue. Since no answer came, we carried on in our train of thought – unsustained, but also uncontradicted. No one was overruled, bossed around, or made to listen. It was just that we were without a partner.

2

Economics and the Freedom to Shape Our Social Destiny*

Dogmatic belief in economic determinism in its different forms has become a chief obstacle to the progress of mankind. The total view from which pessimism results is this:

All thinking persons recognize the precariousness of the human condition today. Man is not a simple being, and he can die in more than one way. War or no war – man, in the material and moral cast for the sake of which we cherish our humanity, may be unable to maintain himself in the future in the technological environment which he has created. The Moscow Trials, Oswiecim, Hiroshima are portents.

Since the venture of a progressively artificial surrounding cannot – and indeed should not – be voluntarily discarded, we must adapt life in such a surrounding to the requirements of human existence. The problem of restoring meaning and unity to life in a machine civilization must be faced. But, on whatever level we approach the question – whether that of cultural unity or emotional balance, or even only that of bare national survival – adjustment implies fulfilling the requirements of social justice, as a consciously pursued human aim. It is here that grave doubts set in. For, among the requisites of meaningful purpose, the safeguarding of the freedom of conscience stands out for us – a demand that cannot be compromised without

* File 37–4, Karl Polanyi Archive: undated conference paper. Some portions of this piece have also been printed in "Our Obsolete Market Mentality: Civilization Must Find a New Thought Pattern," published in *Commentary*, 3 (1947), 109–17.

voiding all our other aims as well. Yet justice appears unattainable except at the cost of freedom, and this is so for reasons that seem to be rooted in economics. Laissez-faire appears therefore as the price we pay for[a] freedom. For the freedoms we cherish – and this cannot be gainsaid – grew up in the interstices of our economy and must (it is argued) necessarily disappear with it. Behind this and rigid ominous economic determinism, which we meet more and more often, there stand strong convictions, both as to the preeminent role of the economic agent in our present world and as to its decisiveness in human history in general.

This appreciation of our total situation contains, I submit, both an essential truth and a radical fallacy. Justly, we deem our institutions to be determined by the economic aspect of life; but, quite mistakenly, we ascribe this fact to some immanent and timeless quality of the economic as such.

The society we live in: In contrast to tribal, ancestral, or feudal societies, ours is a market society. The institution of the market is here the basic organization of the community. Blood tie, ancestor worship, or feudal allegiance is replaced by market relations. Such a state of affairs is new; for an institutionalized supply–demand–price mechanism – a market – was never more than a subordinate feature of social life. On the contrary, the elements of the economic system were found, as a rule, imbedded in other than economic relations, such as kin, religion, or charisma. The motives for which individuals participated in economic institutions were not usually themselves "economic," that is, they did not arise from fear of otherwise going without the necessities of life. It is precisely such a fear of individual starvation as an inducement to hunt, catch, till, or harvest that was unknown in the majority of societies – in effect, in all except the society of classical laissez-faire, or such as were modeled upon it.

For never before the nineteenth century was the production and distribution of material goods and services in society organized through a market system. This stupendous innovation was achieved by drawing the factors of production, labor, and land into that system. Labor and land were themselves made into commodities; that is, they were treated as if they were produced for sale. Of course they were not actually commodities, since they were either not produced at all (as land), or, if they were, this was not for sale (as labor).

---

[a] Editors' note: The original here reads *of* ("the price we pay of freedom"). We interpret this to mean "the price of freedom that we pay," i.e. "the price we pay for (the sake of) freedom" rather than "the price we pay in/from/out of our freedom," i.e. by giving it away.

The true scope of such a step can be gauged if we remember that labor is only another name for man, and land for nature. The commodity fiction handed over the fate of man and nature to the play of an automaton running in its own grooves and governed by its own laws.

Market economy thus created a new type of society. The economic or productive system was entrusted to a self-acting device. An institutional mechanism controlled the resources of nature as well as the human beings in their everyday activities.

In this way an "economic sphere" came into existence that was sharply delimited from other institutions in society. Since no human aggregation can survive without a functioning productive apparatus, this had the effect of making the "rest" of society a mere appendage to that sphere. This autonomous sphere, again, was regulated by a mechanism that controlled its functioning. As a result, that controlling mechanism became determinative of the life of the whole body social. No wonder that the emergent human aggregation was "economic" to a degree previously never even approximated. "Economic motives" now reigned supreme in a world of their own, and the individual was made to act on them under penalty of extinction.

In actual fact, man was never as selfish as the theory demanded. Though the market mechanism brought his dependence upon material goods to the fore "economic" motives never formed with him the sole incentive to work. In vain was he exhorted, by economists and utilitarian moralists alike, to discount, in business, all other motives but material ones. On closer investigation he was still found to be acting on remarkably "mixed" motives, not excluding those of duty towards himself and others – and maybe secretly even enjoying his work for its own sake.

However, we are not here concerned with actual, but only with assumed motives. For views on man's nature are built not on the psychology, but on the ideology of everyday life.[b] Accordingly, hunger and gain were singled out as "economic motives" and man was supposed to be acting on them in practice, while his other motives appeared more ethereal and remote from the humdrum existence. Honor and pride, civic obligation and moral duty, even self-respect and common decency were not deemed irrelevant to production and were significantly summed up in the word "ideal." Hence man was believed to consist of two components, one more akin to hunger and

[b]Editors' note: The original word order here betrays strong influence of German syntax: "For not on the psychology, but on the ideology of everyday life are views on man's nature built."

gain, the other to honor and power. The one was "material," the other "ideal"; the one "economic," the other "non-economic"; the one "rational," the other "non-rational." Utilitarian philosophers went so far as to identify the two sets of terms, thus endowing the "economic" with the aura of rationality. He who would have refused to imagine that he was acting for gain alone was thus considered not only immoral, but also insane.

The picture of man and society that was induced by this condition of affairs was this:

As regards man, we were made to accept the notion that his motives can be described as "material" and "ideal," and that the incentives on which everyday life is organized spring from the "material" motives.

As regards society, the kindred doctrine was propounded that its institutions were "determined" by the economic system.

Under a market economy both assertions were, of course, true. *But only under such an economy*. In regard to the past, such a view was no more than an anachronism. In regard to the future, it was a mere prejudice. For this new world of "economic motives" was based on a fallacy. Intrinsically, hunger and gain are not more "economic" than love or hate, pride or prejudice. No human motive is, per se, economic. There is no such a thing as a *sui generis* experience – in the sense in which one may have a religious, aesthetic, or sexual experience. These latter give rise to motives that broadly aim at evoking similar experiences. In regard to material production, these terms lack self-evident meaning.

The economic factor, which underlines all social life, no more gives rise to definite incentives than the equally universal law of gravitation.

Assuredly, if we do not eat, we must perish, as much as if we were crushed under the weight of a falling rock. But the pangs of hunger are not an individual, but a collective affair. If an individual is hungry, there is nothing definite for him to do. Made desperate, he might rob or steal, but such an action can hardly be called productive. With man – the political animal – everything is given not by natural, but by social circumstances. What made the nineteenth century think of hunger and gain as "economic" was simply the highly artificial and deliberate organization of production under a market economy.

But the market mechanism also created a delusion of economic determinism as a general law.

Under a market economy, again, such determinism holds good. Indeed the working of the economic system here not only "influences" the rest of society, but determines it – just as, in a triangle, the sides not merely influence but determine the angles.

Take the stratification of classes in society. Supply and demand in the labor market were identical with the classes of workers and employers which personified them. The social classes of capitalists, landowners, tenants, merchants, brokers, professionals, and so on were delimited by the corresponding markets for land, money, capital; for their uses; or for various services. For the income of these classes was fixed by the market, their rank and position by their income.

While social classes were directly, other institutions were indirectly determined by the market mechanism. The forms of state and government, marriage and the rearing of children, the organization of science and education, religion and the arts, the choice of profession, habitation, settlements, the very aesthetics of private life had to comply with the utilitarian pattern or at least not interfere with the working of the market mechanism, on which the livelihood of all depended. It was almost impossible to avoid the erroneous conclusion that, as "economic" man was the "real" man, so the economic system was "really" society.

The stringency with which the market mechanism works was falsely imputed to the strength of economic motivation. As a matter of fact there was no connection between the two. The market mechanism knows nothing but rigid alternatives, whatever the motives of the individuals who participate in the market. The supply–demand–price system works the same way whether the motives of individuals are weak or strong, rational or irrational, utilitarian, political, or religious. The discovery of economic determinism by nineteenth-century thinkers was nothing but the discovery of the market and of the formal necessity by which it moves between inevitable alternatives, whether these are geared to the economic system or not[c] – in other words, whatever the real or fictitious commodities transacted in the market. Economic determinism as a sociological phenomenon is coterminous with the market, outside of which it can exist only in a shadowy form.

So spurious are the foundations of economic determinism. Economic factors affect the social process in innumerable ways (and vice versa), but nowhere except under a market system are the effects more than limiting. Neither sociology nor history contradicts this thesis. And anthropologists rightly deny that the emphasis embodied

---

[c]Editors' note: The original here has a lacuna, completed by us. It reads: ". . . the formal necessity by which it moves between inevitable alternatives are geared to the economic system or not . . ."

in a culture is dependent upon technological – or even economic – organization. Attitudes as opposite as cooperation and competition have been found to be prevalent in different societies endowed with almost identical tools and a very similar economic environment. What could be more vital to the whole cultural and moral atmosphere of a community than the predominance of cooperative or competitive attitudes? What could prove to go deeper into the substance of humanity's ideal heritage than the distinction between the principles of solidarity and self-assertion? And yet even such extreme ideological divergences are unaffected by economic factors.

Now free institutions, I submit, are nothing but expressions of persuasive principles such as cooperation and competition, which, until proof to the contrary, should be deemed independent of the technological and organizational aspects of the economy. Freedom finds its institutional expression in the prize set on personality, integrity, character, and nonconformity. Free institutions depend upon the valuation set on civic liberties. And, as John Stuart Mill wrote, the organization of trade, whether public or private, is not a question of individual freedom as he meant it. The freedoms involved in the organization of trade and business have but little to do with the valuation of the freedom of conscience and its institutional safeguarding. The latter is a matter of the total culture of a society, and where emphasis lies in such a culture is not determined by economic factors.

It is not for the economist, but for the moralist and the philosopher to decide what kind of society we should deem desirable. An industrial society has one thing in abundance, and that is material welfare more than is good for it. If, to uphold justice and the freedom to restore meaning and unity in life, we should ever be called upon to sacrifice some efficiency in production, economy in consumption, or rationality of administration, an industrial civilization can afford it. The economic historians' message to philosophers today should be: we can afford to be both just and free.

3

Economic History and
the Problem of Freedom*

The problem that I have been asked to discuss appears clear and simple. *The problem of freedom* consists in our ability to maintain the inheritance of freedom in a changing world. But say as much as "changing world," and you are in for alarums and excursions from right and left – especially from the right and the left, the children of Light and the children of Darkness being equally unhelpful (and unclarifying, I am afraid); in effect, sometimes one would wish to be quite sure which was which.

I mean by freedom concrete institutions, civic liberties – *freedoms* (in the plural) – the capacity to follow one's personal conviction in the light of one's conscience: the freedom to differ, to hold views of one's own, to be in a minority of one, and yet to be an honored member of the community in which one plays the vital part of the deviant. It is freedom to follow what the Anabaptists – and the Quakers after them – called the "inner light" – or, in terms of political theory, to be in safe possession of the priceless achievement of John Stuart Mill's century.

I admit that there may arise a dilemma of national security versus civic liberties. To ignore it is to bury one's head in the sand. However, it need not prove fatal to liberty, if tackled in a spirit that is open both to the realities of the situation and to the transcendent principle of political freedom.

* File 35–10, Karl Polanyi Archive: lecture held in 1949 for the Graduate Public Law and Government Club.

Also, I readily admit that I do not mean by freedom the right to sweat one's fellows, to make inordinate gains without commensurate service to the community, or to keep technological inventions from being used for the public benefit, or the liberty to profit from public calamities engineered from private advantage. If such freedoms disappear, it is all to the good. John Stuart Mill, though at that time a convinced upholder of laissez-faire economy, rejected the defense of private trading or private enterprise as a matter of individual freedom, as unrelated to the fundamental values of freedom of thought, mind, and conscience.

Let me repeat my first statement. The problem of freedom consists in our ability to maintain our inheritance of freedom in a changing world. For it is held that *change must destroy free institutions*. This is argued in two very different keys: in Milton's language, that of Satan and that of the angelic host.

Satan argues: "Don't worry, go ahead; free institutions are a bourgeois fraud, and change will *inevitably* do away with these ideologies of capitalism."

The other side echoes the premise that change will do away with freedom, but draws the opposite conclusion: "Stop! Do not try to reform capitalism, for if you interfere with free enterprise you will *inevitably lose* your freedom."

Between the Marxist determinism of the powers of darkness and the laissez-faire determinism of the seraphic host, we find ourselves the victims of two kinds of inevitabilities: *Marxist inevitability*, which sometimes almost exultantly proclaims the inevitability of the loss of our freedoms, unless we resign ourselves to the status quo, changelessness and certain destruction; and *laissez-faire inevitability*, which proclaims precisely that fatal changelessness in a changing world, compliance with laissez-faire preconceptions, under the threat of an (allegedly) otherwise inevitable serfdom. In my conviction, these are merely two different forms of the same creed of *economic determinism* – a materialistic legacy of the nineteenth century – *which economic history does not bear out*.

Marxist determinism is based on some kind of railway timetable of social development: Upon slave society follows feudalism, upon feudalism capitalism, upon capitalism socialism. Ideologies move in parallel – after a kind of Auguste Comte timetable of theology, metaphysics, positive science. Everything is ultimately predetermined – including ideologies, institutionalized or not. In the long run the *economic basis of society*, that is, technology, pulls into line the conditions of production, in other words the property system, and both together pull into line the superstructure of institutionalized ideas and valuations. Irrigational technique not only produces a slaveholders' society, but such a society must also ultimately produce fetish idolatry; the hand mill not only produces a feudal society, but such a society must also ultimately produce a church religion; the steam engine not only produces a bourgeois society, but such a society must also eventually produce the ideologies of liberty, equality, and fraternity; electricity, and a fortiori the atomic age, must produce socialism, under which liberty, equality, and fraternity disappear again as ruling ideologies and are replaced by dialectical materialism.

Now, there is an element of essential truth in all this. Technology and ecology decisively limit the basic structure of human society and may deeply influence its ideology. But only under market economy do economic factors not only limit, but *determine* culture. Only here does the economy *determine* the shape and form of society. Economic determinism is here a massive fact. *But only here.* As a description of earlier periods, it is a mere anachronism, while as a forecast of the future it is no more than a prejudice.

"Marxism," as well as laissez-faire, mirror nineteenth-century conditions. A market economy is an economy organized through markets, that is, through a supply–demand–price mechanism. No one can, in principle, exist under such conditions unless he buys goods on markets with the help of income derived from selling other goods on other markets. But what makes a market economy is its self-regulating character. This springs from the inclusion of the factors of production, labor, and land into the system. No society before our own ever permitted the fate of labor and land to be decided by the supply–demand–price mechanism. Once this is the case, society is economically determined. Why? Because labor is only another name for man, and land for nature. Market economy amounts to the handing over of man and his natural habitat to the working of a blind mechanism running in its own grooves and following its own laws. No wonder that the picture of economic determinism arose for a society governed by the action of an economic mechanism. This was a picture of actuality.

But, as the economic historian is bound to add: of a unique actuality. Normally the economic factor is merely a limiting factor in human history. – Sure, no powerful navies are ever developed in countries that have no coast; nor are polar bears hunted in tropical waters. But the pattern of culture, the major cultural emphasis in society, is *not* determined by either technological or geographical factors. Whether a people develops a cooperative or a competitive attitude in everyday life, whether it prefers to work its technique of production collectively or individualistically, is in many cases strikingly independent of the utilitarian logic of the means of production, and even of the actual basic economic institutions of the community. The very same occupations and techniques of production are worked in the spirit of antagonistic competition by one group of people, while another prefers to work them in a harmonious spirit of mutuality and noncompetition. The work of modern cultural anthropologists like Margaret Mead, Forde, or Thurnwald has made this abundantly clear. Yet it was such a mistaken belief in economic determinism as a general law that made many Marxists – not, to my knowledge, Marx himself – prophesy that our personal freedom must disappear together with the free enterprise system. Actually, there is no necessity for this whatever. Emphasis on liberty, on personality, on independence of mind, on tolerance and freedom of conscience is precisely in the same category as cooperative and harmonious attitudes on the one hand, antagonistic and competitive attitudes on the other – it is a pervasive pattern of the mind expressed in innumerable ways, protected by custom and law, institutionalized in varied forms, but essentially independent of technique and even of economic organization. Under private enterprise public opinion may lose all sense of tolerance and freedom, while under the strictest regulation of a war economy the power of a free public opinion was greater in Britain and in the USA than ever.

German and Russian planned economies certainly were accompanied by an almost total absence of civic liberties. But where's the proof that institutionalized freedoms were ever intended in Germany, or in Russia since the setting aside of the new constitution? And whether intended or not: the laissez-faire argument hinges on the alleged effects of the absence of freedom of choice in employment. Yet reliable investigation has shown that, in practice, *no* individual direction of labor even took place either in Germany or in Russia. Political intolerance and political regimentation were entirely a matter of propaganda, supplemented by political and administrative methods. Yet police methods would be applicable in any police state, laissez-faire economy or not: That crucial *link* was missing. Or take more recent developments: Is there any evidence that, during the

---

[a]Editors' note: This paragraph was deleted in pencil by the author: "But this self-same determinism reappears today with another emphasis. Ironically enough, it is often voiced by those who imagine themselves to be the protagonists of anti-Marxism. We are warned by people of good will that, unless we uphold the market system in its nineteenth-century form, which is in principle identical with that of a market economy, we inevitably lose our freedoms."

relatively free economy period of 1946–8 in the USA, civic liberty standards improved, as against 1932–45? As everyone knows, the opposite was the case; but – *again* – for reasons independent of economic policies and directly related to more general factors. Or, finally, England: According to laissez-faire standards, England has long passed the line that separates freedom from serfdom. The government has, formally, absolute powers with regard to the direction of labor, and on very rare occasions has even used them. But has Britain ceased to be the country whose standards of civic liberties are a model for the world?

But this self-same determinism reappears today *with another emphasis*. Ironically enough, it is often voiced by those who imagine themselves to be the protagonists of anti-Marxism. We are warned that, unless we uphold the market system in its nineteenth-century form, which is in principle identical with that of a market economy, we inevitably lose our freedoms.

But is there more truth in the new adage than there was in the old? True, appreciation for freedom of conscience, freedom of speech, of religion, of association, and so on was institutionalized together with the spread of the market system. True, the rights of radical, religious, national minorities were increasingly safeguarded as the century became older. The basic argument is that these freedoms would necessarily and *inevitably* disappear again, together with the economic institutions of the period. Such views are being strongly held by well-meaning persons of integrity, among them Professor Hayek.

The origins of these gloomy prophecies lie in the beginnings of market economy. They are no truer today than they were then. It was prophesied that under our economic system of private ownership we can have liberties only as long as we do not have *democracy*, for under democracy capitalism would either be destroyed by the mob or survive only at the cost of liberty, in other words under a dictatorship. Nothing could be more deterministic, and at the same time more untrue. This view was strongly held by Lord Macaulay, the typical representative of Whig opinions – the views of the enlightened but uniquely class-conscious aristocracy of Britain.

I beg your leave to read to you parts of a letter that he wrote in 1857 to an American friend living in New York: the Honorable H. E. Randall. Judge for yourselves how much truth there was in the forebodings of economistic prejudice.

You are surprised to learn that I have not a high opinion of Mr. Jefferson, and I am surprised at your surprise. I am certain I never wrote a line and I never in Parliament, in convention, or even on the hustings, a place where it is the fashion to court the populace, uttered a word indicating the opinion that the supreme authority in a state ought to be entrusted to the majority of citizens told by the head; in other words, to the poorest and most ignorant part of society. I have long been convinced that institutions purely democratic must, sooner or later, destroy liberty or civilization, or both.

In Europe, where the population is dense, the effect of such institutions would be almost instantaneous. What happened lately in France is an example. In 1848 a pure democracy was established there. During a short time there was a strong reason to expect a general spoliation, a national bankruptcy, a new partition of the soil, a maximum of prices, a ruinous load of taxation laid on the rich for the purpose of supporting the poor in idleness. Such a system would, in 20 years, have made France as poor and as barbarous as the France of the Carlovingians. Happily, the danger was averted and now there is a despotism, a silent tribune, an enslaved press; liberty is gone, but civilization has been saved. I have not the smallest doubt that if we had a purely democratic government here the effect would be the same. Either the poor would plunder the rich and civilization would perish or order and property would be saved by a strongly military government, and liberty would perish.

You may think that your country enjoys an exemption from these evils. I will frankly own to you that I am of a very different opinion. Your fate I believe to be certain, though it is deferred by a physical cause. As long as you have a boundless extent of fertile and unoccupied land, your labouring population will be far more at ease than the labouring population of the Old World; and while it is the case, the Jeffersonian policy may continue to exist without causing any fatal calamity. But the time will come when New England will be as thickly peopled as Old England. Wages will be low and will fluctuate as much with you as with us. You will have your Manchesters and Birminghams. Hundreds of thousands of artisans will assuredly be sometimes out of work. Then your institutions will be fairly brought to the test. Distress everywhere makes the labourer mutinous and discontented and inclines him to listen with eagerness to agitators who tell him that it is a monstrous iniquity that one man should have a million while another cannot get a full meal. In bad years there is plenty of grumbling here and sometimes a little rioting. But it matters little, for here the sufferers are not the rulers. The supreme power is in the hands of a class, numerous indeed, but select, of an educated class, of a class which is and knows itself to be deeply interested in the security of property and the maintenance of order. Accordingly, the malcontents are finally yet gently restrained. The bad time is got over without robbing the wealthy to relieve the indigent. The springs of national prosperity soon begin to flow again: work is plentiful, wages rise and all is tranquillity and cheerfulness.

I have seen England three or four times pass through such critical seasons as I have described. Through such seasons the United States will have to pass in the course of the next century, if not of this. How will you pass through them? I heartily wish you a good deliverance, but my reasons and my wishes are at war and I cannot help foreboding the worst. It is quite plain that your government will never be able to restrain a distressed and discontented majority. For with you the majority is the government and has the rich, who are always a minority, absolutely at its mercy. The day will come when, in the state of New York, a multitude of people, none of whom has had more than half a breakfast or expects to have more than half a dinner, will chose the legislature. Is it possible to doubt what sort of legislature will be chosen? On one side is a statesman preaching patience, respect for vested rights, a strict observance for public faith. On the other is a demagogue ranting about tyranny of capitalists and usurers and asking why anybody should be permitted to drink champagne and to ride in a carriage while thousands of honest people are in want of necessities. Which of the two candidates is likely to be preferred by a workingman who hears his children cry for bread?

I seriously apprehend that you will, in some such season of adversity as I have described, do things which will prevent prosperity from returning; that you will act like people in a year of scarcity, devour all the seed corn and thus make the next year not of scarcity but of absolute distress. The distress will produce fresh spoliation. There is nothing to stay you. Your constitution is all sail and no anchor. As I said before, when society has entered on this downward progress, either civilization or liberty must perish. Either some Caesar or Napoleon will seize the reins of government with a strong hand or your republic will be as fearfully plundered and laid waste by barbarians in the twentieth century as the Roman Empire was in the fifth, with this difference: that the Huns and Vandals who ravaged the Roman Empire came from without, and that your Huns and Vandals will have been engendered within your country, by your own institution.

Thinking this, of course, I cannot reckon Jefferson among the benefactors of mankind.[b]

---

[b] Editors' note: Polanyi does not give his source for this long extract – or any other source, for that matter – since these were notes not intended or revised by him for publication. All the references to sources have been supplied by us. In this case, the letter can be found at http://books.google.it/books?id=uI5DAAAAYAAJ&pg=PA86& dq=You+are+surprised+to+learn+that+I+have+not+a+high+opinion+of+Mr.+Jefferso n&hl=it&sa=X&ei=TEc3U6uYNOr8ygOd24GIBA&ved=0CDQQ6AEwAA#v=one page&q=You%20are%20surprised%20to%20learn%20that%20I%20have% 20not%20a%20high%20opinion%20of%20Mr.%20Jefferson&f=false (accessed in April 2014).

May I conclude by saying: America is still there. She is a democracy and has lost neither her freedom nor her prosperity. And it is my firm belief that, another century hence, a reformed American economy, stable, just, and prosperous will be the answer to the Macaulays of today: the answer of a people stronger than ever in its liberties and freedom.

4

New Frontiers of Economic Thinking*

Some of our most urgent problems spring from the need of adjusting the forms of our social life to the technology we have adopted. ‡. . .‡a

The sphere of life in which such adjustment would have to be made is of course the economic. What, broadly, is implied in this? And what new light does economic science throw upon our problems? That is the question.

Let us repeat the pragmatic definition of the economic sphere of life: "the way we make sure that we do not go without the necessities of life." And, if some of us sometimes do, is it for most of us most of the time even approximately true? And then there are the leaders of American industry who earn several hundred thousand dollars a year, and yet surely the level of our production owes much to their exertion. Do these exertions actually spring from fear of otherwise starving? And, if not, is this fear of theirs even an appreciable factor in that achievement of superabundant plenty?

Not at all. The Trobriand Islanders of the South Sea grow normally twice as much yam fruit as they need and allow it to rot. They phrase their economic life in terms of plenty, while according to our standards we are surrounded by scarcity. We, according to their standards, are surrounded by plenty but freeze our economic life in terms of scarcity. That is why we are able to accept the fiction that the millionaires are actuated by fear of starvation.

* File 20–7, Karl Polanyi Archive: undated typescript, probably from the late 1950s (according to the archival inventory).
a Editors' note: Unreadable handwritten comments.

But the truth behind the fiction is that, in principle, a man must either earn his wages or make a profit. Otherwise he goes without income, and how can he then be sure of providing himself even with the necessities of life?

It is to ensure that everybody tries to sell whatever he may possess in order to make an income that our society is organized as it is. And everything else has been subordinated to the requirements of the system. The property owner sells the use of his capital or land, the worker sells the use of his labor power – and their incomes are actually prices that they attain on the market: price of the use of capital, called interest; price of the use of land, called rent; price of the use of labor power, called wages. The entrepreneur sells his services and is recompensed by profit – a difference between the price of cost of the goods and the selling price of the product.[b] His income also depends on the market.

As you see, the market system determines their incomes, which are prices determined by different markets: markets for the use of labor power, capital, land, or whatever they possess. Only the entrepreneur has no direct market for his services: he must take the risks. That's maybe why he tends to disappear in large-scale industry, being replaced by the manager, who gets his safe salary.

I am not going to go much further into the nature of our economy here. My point was to show that we rightly assume that our market economy appeals to what we call "economic motives," that is, fear of hunger and hope of gain.

But, by calling hunger and gain "economic motives," do we not prejudge the very possibilities of adjustment of the economic sphere of life? Let us consider the point.

In one sense, the answer must be yes. Since market economy takes care of the production and distribution of material goods, and hunger and gain (as we define them) are ensuring the working of that system, it is justifiable to call them economic motives, since they happen to be the motive on which the economic system rests.

But are they economic in any other sense? Are they intrinsically economic? In the sense in which aesthetic motives or religious motives are aesthetic or religious, that is, as the outcome and expression of an experience the quality of which is self-evident? Not at all. There is nothing economic about hunger: if a man is hungry, there is nothing specific he can do. Being hungry is certainly no indication of how to go about production. It may induce him to commit robbery, but that

[b]Editors' note: This is what the original seems to say, though in a very compressed form: "a difference of the price of cost goods and product."

is not economic activity. Neither is the cerebral drive of gain specifically economic. Its idea, and maybe its urge, if such a thing exists, have no connection with the production and distribution of material goods, unless such a connection be provided by some elaborate economic mechanism – which would be begging the question.

The point is of very real importance. Unless we see this clearly, we must assume that an economic system is necessarily run on economic motives – meaning motives that are intrinsically economic, as we uncritically assume hunger and gain to be.

No worse and more unscientific narrowing down of our freedom of action is conceivable. The task of adjusting our economic system to technology and justice would have become insoluble.

It would be truer to say that at no time before the setting up of market economy has the economic system made the individuals' fear of hunger a motive for their participation in production. The community as a whole may be – and usually is – continuously concerned about food, but this concern is not passed on to the individual in the form of a concern about individual share as depending upon his participation in hunt or catch, tillage or harvest. In primitive society institutional safeguards are provided against fear of hunger as an individual's motive for action in the economic sphere. The same is true of medieval society, and indeed even of the mercantile system. The tendency is throughout to avoid what we call the economic incentive. This does not mean that the connection between social dividend and the amount of the share in it can be severed – this would be obviously impossible. No more than is available can be distributed, and under many economic institutions one's share may depend upon one's own exertions. But that is not the point. An individual's fear of hunger is entirely different from the apprehension of being better or less better off, and it is precisely the whip of hunger that is absent in poorer societies than our own.

This is even truer of the motive of gain made on exchange. It is either entirely absent or, insofar as it is present, it is ostracized and put under a negative premium. Surely many exceptions will come to your mind. But their importance should not be exaggerated. We tend to look at the past with the eyes of the present and recognize the familiar trends more easily than the unfamiliar ones. What counts is the character of the dominant institutions of an age, since these set the limit to the growth and scope of the secondary ones. The presence of merchants need not imply the dominance of commercial attitudes, just as the presence of monasteries today does not make society intermonastic. The presence of markets is a harmless fact, and the use of money is, as a rule, a subordinate trait. It does not imply a monetarized society; and the presence of markets in an economy does not in any way involve the existence of a market economy.

Now, what is this market economy of ours, which is run on economic motives and the adjustment of which looms so large today? It is the dominance of the market pattern. Primitive society is based on kinship systems. Feudal society, on the personal tie. Our society is embedded in the market pattern.

The criterion is simple. The mere presence of markets need not involve the existence of markets for labor and land. These two pillars of social existence are everywhere sheltered from the action of the market. For what we, in our jargon, call labor and land is merely the economist's name for man and his natural *environment*. As soon as these are organized in markets, that is, the fate of man and his habitat are left to the action of the market – then and then only has the market grown into the dominant institution of society – like kinship, monastery, feudal tie, and other types of social patterns.[c]

Formally[d] this is expressed in this. The market system becomes autonomous and automatic; for, once the factors of production, labor, and land have markets of their own, then capital, which is a combination of labor and land, can move from one market to another oriented on the single aim of equalizing profits. This is what we mean by a self-regulating market system – that is, by a system of markets comprising free markets for labor and land.

Now clearly such a system could not exist for a day without destroying the human society delivered up to it. People would perish, nature would return to dust in the grips of this blind mill – a tower of Babel whirling itself to destruction.

Naturally, such a state of affairs has never actually existed (although some economic theorists still postulate it as the foundation of practical policies). The rise of the market pattern to dominance was accompanied by a movement in the opposite direction, protecting the substance of human society – man and nature – against the working

---

[c]Editors' note: "Social patterns" is supplied by us (and see previous paragraph) in place of "society" (picked up from the line above) – which is either a slip of pen or (more likely?) shorthand of the kind uses in notes. The context makes it clear that Polanyi does not intend to say that the items listed here are "societies," but he may have found it difficult to find a common classificatory name for all of them.

[d]Editors' note: Corrected from "formerly" in the original. This slip of pen is interesting and representative enough for the errors one finds in Polanyi's English typescripts not revised for publication. There are numerous such errors – trivial ones; we are not, on the whole, recording them here, since this is not a textual–critical edition, but anyone with philological–linguistic interests in Polanyi's text can consult the originals in the archive.

of the Satanic mill. Especially labor and land were never completely abandoned to its mercy, while unfortunately our mind and thoughts were – and indeed had to be – exposed to the desiccating samum ["poison wind"] of economistic prejudice. The institutions, however extreme, were at least met by institutional counterforces, protecting society to some extent; but in the field of philosophical and religious thought the commercialist influence reigned supreme. Thus our picture of man was deeply influenced by economic assumptions; and so was our view of man's freedom to shape his world according to his ideals.

As regards man . . .^e

---

^eEditors' note: The text breaks off here.

Part II

Institutions Matter

5

The Contribution of Institutional
Analysis to the Social Sciences*

We of the economic department sometimes fail to realize that human economy is not altogether a concern restricted to our own department – not even from the academic angle. No society can exist without some kind of economy, and all social sciences must include the word "economic" in their vocabulary. The sociologist, the anthropologist, the historian, the political scientist, the social psychologist – they all have to deal, each in his own way, with economic factors, economic motives, economic interests, economic classes, economic conditions and developments that involve every element of the human economy. Thus it comes to pass that all social scientists find themselves time and again in the unenviable position of having to make up their minds about the meaning of economic terms. And, in all fairness, who can blame them for their belief that the economist "knows"? And so they turn to the economist. But then the fact is in the fire. Since economics, as we know, embodies an unending but on the whole not unsuccessful attempt to disagree on all essentials, social scientists are bound to be disillusioned if they really expected to learn from us what terms such as money, capital, capitalism, saving, investment, equilibrium, and the like mean – not to mention the term "economic" itself. (Incidentally, they should not be *too* much amused at our expense, for they find themselves in a very similar predicament as regards their own terms.) But even this is not all. Recently they have been warned by one of our colleagues that they had better give

* File 30–18, Karl Polanyi Archive: lecture delivered in 1950 at the Graduate Economics Society of Columbia University, New York.

up all hope, since, whatever definition economists decided upon, this could not and would not benefit them. Briefly, they were given to understand, openly, that the economist's definitions of economic terms were useless to them by definition. Professor Ellis at least has left no doubt on this point. "Economics," he said in his chairman's address to the American Economic Association, "is concerned only with the processes and results of individual choice on the *market*." With regard to economic analysis (though *not* to economic theory in the wider sense), Professor Ellis is emphatically right, and social scientists who disregard the limitation under which strictly *formal* or scarcity economics stands do so at their own peril. It is an application of that branch of the logic of rational action that deals with scarce means; the application is to market-organized economies.

The point deserves amplification. Neither economic history, with which I am personally connected, nor the other social sciences can avoid dealing with the economic sphere. With the *anthropologist*, the danger is that of an unconscious dependence on economistic prejudice: this is doubly dangerous on account of the conscious rejection of such dependence, in all its forms. Such self-delusion is perilous. Professor Melville Herskovits gave an instance of it in his controversy with Professor Knight: Herskovits, a pioneer of the anthropologists' emancipation from economic influence, nevertheless unwittingly threw the door wide open to the reception of economic analysis. Except for the business cycle, he wrote – I am quoting from memory – trade, money, markets, capital, investment, saving, and all the other phenomena of modern economic life equally occur in savage society . . .

Mrs. Quiggin, the Cambridge University ethnologist, author of a very useful study on "primitive money," offers another example of the self-delusion that accompanies the anthropologist's *imperfect emancipation* from the economist. Wittily and aptly, her book opens on a note of defiance: "Everyone except an economist knows what money means, and even an economist can describe it in a chapter or so . . ."[a] A veritable declaration of independence, one would think. However, that did not prevent her from swallowing hook, line, and sinker a definition of money that she borrowed from the work of the anthropologist Thilenius – who in turn had lifted the definition bodily from the models of the monetary theorist Bendixen. You can imagine the consequences. What advantage can a classifier of primitive money objects derive from definitions such as Bendixen's theory of token

[a] Editors' note: A. H. Quiggin, *A Survey of Primitive Money* (London: Methuen, 1963), p. 1.

money? "Classic" or perfect money, according to Bendixen, is "money based on *bills and notes* resulting from commercial transactions."[b] No wonder that, under such 100 percent nominalist influence, Mrs. Quiggin decided that *only* token money was "true" money, and that all primitive money objects were, properly speaking, *only money substitutes . . .*

It's the same old ironical story: What starts as a declaration of independence ends up as a manifestation of dependence, all the more complete for its unconscious nature.

The *sociologist* is familiar with economic theory, maybe with the one exception of Herbert Spencer, whose relations with economics are especially ironical. Somehow or other Spencer managed *not* to write a "Principles of Economics" – nobody knows how. That didn't prevent him from enunciating the crudest views on economics and economic policy ever uttered by a scholar. Compared to him, Bastiat was a meticulous empiricist. To crown it all, he erected a truly impressive edifice of *organicistic* sociology, which was, however, in utter contradiction to his *atomistic* economic individualism – and he made no pretence of bridging or harmonizing the two. With Durkheim, Pareto, and Max Weber the position is different. These critical thinkers incorporated economic theory consciously and attempted to attune their system to its requirements. Durkheim's identification of the moral problem of *society* with that of the division of labor explicitly assumed that specialization was basic to human economy. Now this thesis, as Adam Smith established it, referred to the economic specialization of individuals. But, as Thurnwald has shown, conditions in early society in no way correspond to this. On the contrary, often whole villages are found to be specialized in one and the same industry, mostly producing for collective export without any internal trade being in evidence. Pareto's circulation of elites was merely an application of the law of competition to a set of power positions; not to speak of his concept of the rational, which merely reflected utilitarian market appraisal. And even Max Weber's oeuvre suffered from his attempt to fuse the Mengerian concept of rationality, as well as Mises's concept of money, with the entirely different concepts derived from Karl Marx and Carl Buecher. All this may account largely for the scant contribution made by anthropology and sociology to the problem of *economic organization*, a fact for which the inadequate tools put at their disposal by the economists are primarily responsible.

[b]Editors' note: This quotation is almost certainly from F. Bendixen, *Das Wesen des Geldes* (3rd ed., Munich: Duncker & Humblot, 1922) – arguably from Ch. 2.

Last, not least, it is the *historian* who is forced to borrow his economic concepts from wherever he can find them. These giants of economic historiography – Boeckh on ancient Greece, Cunningham on England, and Schmoller on Germany – produced their work before the authority of economics had made itself fully felt. Fortunate men. With them economy history was still following in the footsteps of Montesquieu and Adam Smith. In effect both Cunningham and Schmoller rejected Ricardian economism – an act of insubordination for which they were rigorously ignored by economists. But with the turn of the century the intellectual climate changed. Economism swept the board; it became axiomatic. Economic history was the victim. Though the release of Babylonian and Egyptian sources, the triumphs of archeology and numismatics, enlarged our historical knowledge enormously, not even an Eduard Meyer was able to glean *economic* history from the rich new fields. More than a hundred years after the excavation of Niniveh and of the places of Senacherib and Sargon, almost fifty years after the discovery of Hammurabi's Code in Susa, with several hundred thousand private documents to boot, *no economic history of the cuneiform civilization has been as yet attempted.* In 1910ᶜ Weber wrote that the time for it had not yet come. And Rostovtzeff, in his latest masterpiece, still restricted himself to the brief comment that Mesopotamia offered a very mixed spectacle . . . Instead of contributing to the strength of historiography, the *economic* aspect of history worked out as its weakness. The more business documents of ancient Mesopotamia were revealed, and the more assiduously contemporary thought was infused into the material, the more confused, admittedly, the picture of her economic file became. Economic history, maybe more than any social science, was dependent for its terms on the professional economist, and perhaps nowhere has formal economics as conspicuously failed to enlighten as in this case.

It may be now time for me to elucidate somewhat the title of my talk, which I elliptically called "The Contribution of Institutional Analysis to the Social Sciences." Institutional analysis stands here as an abbreviation for a more definite approach to the *economic* aspects of *human society in general* than formal or scarcity economics could provide. Essentially, it is that variant of institutional economics that represents a shift back from the formal to the more popular substantive meaning of "economic." It insists that the substantive meaning should be consistently adhered to throughout the social sciences, with

---

ᶜEditors' note: Corrected in the original typescript from "1919" by the author's hand.

the single exception of market phenomena, where the formal or scarcity definition alone can lead to an effective theory.

My main purpose tonight is to outline the characteristics of such an approach, especially as *applied to economic history*. It will then be easy to see what kind of contribution it[d] may be expected to make to *other* social sciences, *notably anthropology and sociology*.

Its main characteristic is, as I have just said, its sole reference to the substantive meaning of economic. With this goes its second characteristic: that it is free of the economistic or modernizing associations that accompany the formal meaning. Let me briefly define my terms.

"Economic" in the substantive sense means here "with reference to material want satisfaction," the adjective "material" adhering primarily to the *means* employed, and only in a subsidiary fashion to aims and ends – that is, to a definite group of physical wants.

The *economy* is defined as an aggregate of economic elements embodied in institutions, these elements being listed as needs and wants, material resources, services, the activity of production, transportation and consumption of goods, and so on. The list can, if necessary, be lengthened or shortened. But scarcity is *not* among these elements.

Economic institutions are institutions comprising a *concentration* of economic elements. Economic institutions do not consist of economic elements only, nor are economic elements found only in economic institutions.

Economic motive is a phrase the definition of which is mainly pragmatic, since it is doubtful whether such a motive really exists. The term "economic" in "economic motive" is therefore made to follow common usage and to designate three kinds of motives:

(a) to *labor for pay alone* – that is, irrespective of the sociological relationship involved in the situation;
(b) to *make gain on barter or exchange* – the term "barter" or "exchange" being defined as a reverse movement of goods, where the behavior of the partners reflects the resulting terms of exchange;
(c) to *act primarily for fear of otherwise going without the necessities of life* (fear of individual starvation).

It should be noted that an "economic institution," in so far as its economic character is concerned, is a matter *of degree*, and it should

---

[d]Editors' note: "It" here refers to the approach proposed (institutional analysis).

not therefore be assumed that the mere presence of economic elements is sufficient to transform an institution into an economic one. This is important, since the substantive definition of "economic" includes almost everything and economic elements are present almost everywhere. However, the *economy* is an aggregate of elements embodied in *economic institutions*, and institutions are not economic unless they comprise a concentration of such elements.[e] It is in this sense that we may describe a factory or a granary as an economic institution, while Christmas or Congress are not economic institutions, in spite of their economic importance in the substantive sense.

At this point it may be called to the attention of the sociologist, the anthropologist, the political scientist, that these definitions of economic institutions and motives allow questions of the following form to be put: What is the relation of economic to noneconomic institutions in a definite society? And to what *extent* are economic institutions in a definite case run on economic motives?

These may be only alternative ways of approaching the problem of the place occupied by the economy in human societies. All social sciences may be thus in a position to contribute to the clarification of this central problem of general economic history.

Now, having briefly dealt with the definitional system that is based on the substantive meaning of "economic," let us see in what manner this definition can rid us of the incubus of an economistic or modernizing misinterpretation of the past.

What is the *modernizing or economistic* attitude?

Superficially, it may seem as if it consisted merely in hypostatizing a gainful, profit-seeking, selfish, competitive, and combative nature of man in economic matters. If this were so, the rectifying of the position would be outside the competence of the economist, for such motivations or behavior patterns are a matter for cultural anthropology, and it is for the cultural anthropologist to decide about their presence or absence. Whether someone misreads a savage society as a modern chrematistic one or, as Veblen ironically preferred to do, misreads modern capitalism as a prestige-haunted savage society, it makes no difference on this point: in either case the statement turns on merely motivational and valuational facts, that is, it remains within the purview of cultural anthropology.

Fortunately the matter does not stop here. The gainful, chrematistic, and so on attitudes that we feel to be "modern" wherever and in

---

[e] Editors' note: From "and it should not therefore be assumed . . ." until here, this sequence was probably deleted by the author. We choose to keep it in the Italian translation, and we retain here as well.

whatever surroundings we meet them are nothing but traits of a culture complex that accompanies the *market institution.* To the extent that market elements are present in the economy, the society strikes us as modern. Therefore all we need to guard against is to hypostatize the presence of *market* elements when such are not present. *And this, precisely, is what the substantive definition of "economic" can do for us.* For it permits a *redefinition* of the main *economic institutions* that *does not take as its frame of reference the market.*

In formal economics, *trade, money and markets* are elevated into economic institutions *kat'exochen* – but *one* of the three, the *market,* is pivotal to the system. The other two are mere aspects of the process implied in the market system. Once a *market,* in other words an institution embodying a supply–demand–price system, is assumed, *trade* is merely the physical aspect of the goods moving through the market, and *money* a device employed to facilitate the transit; or, even more simply, if market is the *locus* of organized exchange, money is the means of exchange, and trade the movement of goods exchanged. It follows that, where trade is in evidence, markets can be assumed, and where money use is in evidence, trade – and consequently markets – can be assumed. No wonder that nonmarket trade is overlooked, or at least minimized, and that the nonexchange uses of money are regarded as a bastard development. It demands a veritable conceptual wrench to realize that the assumed logical triad of trade, money, and markets is a mere arbitrary construct, that they may have independent institutional origins, and indeed that the various *money uses* and the different factors that subsequently congealed into *trade* may have originally been institutionalized *separately from one another.* The substantive meaning of "economic" thus opens up the road to an institutional analysis that eliminates the market assumption from the picture – and therewith also its modernizing and economistic associations.

Money

Take the origin of money institutions. Under the influence of marketing habits it was assumed that money is a means of exchange, which, once established in this capacity, can also be used for the purposes of payment, standard, and hoarding. Professor Raymond Firth, Malinowski's successor at the London School of Economics, still defined primitive currency in the *Encyclopaedia Britannica,* 14th edition, as follows:

In any economic system, however primitive, an article can be only
regarded as true money when it acts as a definite and common medium
of exchange, as a convenient stepping stone in obtaining one type of
goods for another. Moreover, in so doing, it serves as a measure of
value, allowing the worth of all other articles to be expressed in terms
of itself. Again, it is a standard of value, with reference to past or
future payments, while as a store of value it allows wealth to be con-
densed and held in reserve.

As a matter of fact, the true characteristic of primitive currency is
almost the opposite. Far from being *all-purpose* money, as currency
in the nineteenth century tended to become and as Ricardian economics assumed all commodity money to be, primitive money is
special purpose money, employing often different money objects for
different *uses*. By such "uses" we mean operations performed on, or
with a reference to, quantifiable objects in a sociologically defined
situation.

This permits a partial answer approach to the *question of institutional origins*; for the different *uses* were largely institutionalized
independently of one another. Some objects were used for payment
while others might be used as a standard and still others might be
used as a medium of exchange, if exchange *existed*. The "if" is significant. For such an exchange use *need* not have existed, and as a
matter of fact it usually did not exist.

Again, some definitions are unavoidable. For the purposes of the
social sciences in general, money should be defined as a *semantic
system* roughly analogous to language, writing, or weights and measures. In a narrower sense it means quantifiable objects used for
payment, standard, hoarding, exchange.

1 *Payment* is the use of quantifiable objects for the discharge
   of obligations. The sociological situation is that of being under
   an obligation; the operation is the handling over of the possession of goods (if payment is made in some ideal unit – a
   frequent occurrence in primitive society); some operation involving the transfer of an asset from the debtor to the creditor is
   performed.
2 *Standards of value* are required if *barter* is to be generally practicable, in other words if, on the two sides of the barter situation,
   a number of items are to be added up for the purpose of equation.
   Another source of standards is the *administration of staples*,
   which requires their equation in order to keep inventory, to plan,
   dispose, and so on. A third source of standards lies in the grading

of bride price, blood money, fines, and the like. It is to be noted that these sources of standards are *not* dependent upon the exchange use of money. In effect the existence of these uses makes exchange use unnecessary.

3 The *hoarding* of quantifiable objects may be merely for future uses, and in this case it can be hardly said to endow the goods so employed with the character of money. On the other hand, money objects – that is, objects used for some other money use – are often *hoarded* as treasure.

4 The *exchange* use of money is the most specific one and only rarely occurs outside of organized markets. But, even when money is so employed, other "money uses" are quite often left to *other* money objects.

Now let me illustrate this from Hammurabi's Babylonia. Broadly, taxes, rents, wages were paid in barley; the standard in which equivalents were expressed was silver; as to a means of exchange, it appears that no single object had preferential status – barley, oil, wool, silver, dates, and suchlike being equally popular, none of them being much employed. Everything centered on the vast storage system of temple and palace, with its staple finance. No markets [‡]. . .[‡f] any consequence are in evidence. All transactions were "in kind" (as we would say), and the administratively established equivalencies between the main staples were maintained stable over centuries (over the third millennium according to Father Deimel, who transliterated the Sumerian temple material). This was achieved by changing *measures* over longer periods such as reigns, and thereby adjusting the published equivalencies to the supply. (The latter corresponded closely, in alluvial soil, to the amount of water available – which, again, was mostly a direct result of the extent of irrigational works undertaken by the king.) Some of the most baffling features of Babylonian economy thus fall into place. The amazing stability of prices and of the basic measure of volume (the latter literally over millennia) was achieved by changing periodically the unit content of larger units without, however, disrupting the metrological system – that is, the rough proportions of the consecutive units of measurement. Taxes and rents automatically increased with the larger volume of measures, the tax of the unit of land being fixed at 1 shekel of silver = 1 gur of barley. In times of large crops the unit content of the gur was greater. But the financial system continued to calculate revenue and

[f]Editors' note: This entire sentence is added in handwriting and almost illegible.

expenditure in shekels of silver, unaffected by the increased equivalent in kind. In other words, budget figures, *if they had a budget*, remained unchanged.

With regard to Babylonia, it is a precarious matter to advance such *interpretations* for those who may be restricted[g] by their ignorance to the use of translations of the cuneiform scripts.

We can still study redistributive archaic economies in West Africa in a close-up. Measures that are changing according to season or social status are quite frequent there. Stabilization of prices is generally the aim. In one case the retail span is organized into the wholesale retail price system with the help of a *monetary device*. In the Niger Bend, the cowrie shell currency has two numerations. Of the four brackets between 1 and 100,000, the double numeration is restricted to the lowest and the highest brackets. Thus, in the one numeration,

8×10 equals 100;
10×100 equals 1,000;
$10 \times 1,000$ equals 10,000;
$8 \times 10,000$ equals 100,000.

In the other, the normal decimal system runs. Now the wholesaler receives on 100,000 only the *lower* amount, while the retailer collects from the ultimate consumer the *larger* amount. Thus, if he buys for a nominal 100,000, he only pays 64,000, while he collects from the consumer the full 100,000. It is noticeable that the middleman is discouraged: there's no span for him.

This kind of device explains how in the Niger region an elaborate market system is built into the redistributive system without danger of disorganization.

Such inconspicuous devices may offer a key to much larger problems – such as the stabilization of social classes with the help of objects circulating as elite money only. Gold, except for gold dust, circulated in archaic Greece only among kings, chiefs, and gods. Horses, an elite good, could be bought only for slaves; ivory for slaves. Evidence has been found for different sizes of copper wires used as money, the one buying *millet*, the other *wheat*. In these cases

[g]Editors' note: Instead of the normal "for those who may be restricted" Polanyi uses here one of his idiosyncratic turns: "for such as are restricted." This is his favorite way of rendering the indefinite element in quantifiers ("for those, however many they be, who . . .") and we have always reproduced it; but here this use, apart from sounding rather quaint, threatens intelligibility.

money served as a device for the maintaining of class standards of nutrition.

With regard to trade, the substantive definition of "economic" shifts the emphasis away from gain toward the acquisition of goods from outside the community. Since the external origin of trade is hardly in dispute, this results in a surprising new light on *price fixing*. Moreover, it appears that the main history of foreign trade runs along the lines of conventional rates of exchange, as practiced in primitive society (e.g. with the Tikopia). Since archaic trade consists in the exchange of a very small number of trade goods, this happens in "ports of trade" – administrative centers of foreign trade. Trade is in principle 1:1, a unit of one trade good against a unit of the other.

The problem of economic history is to trace the ways in which fluctuating prices came into being – whether they were what we would call genuine fluctuating prices, that is, market prices, or pseudo-fluctuating prices, that is, institutional prices smoothly adjusted to the supply situation and other factors of the administrative price.

Haggling in such markets is no proof of fluctuating prices. Everything is being haggled about, except prices: measures; quality of goods; rates in which different goods are to be taken in payment; the assortments, in other words the conventional mixture of various trade goods; and, ultimately – profits. If prices are fixed, the question remains whether there should be change from the 1:1 relationship for the benefit of either party, in what direction, and how much. I first came across this in a passage of Cadamosto (1455), a Venetian in the Portuguese service and a prolific writer on early African West Coast trade. He says: ". . ."[h]

Clapperton and Denham, writing about the neighboring Central Sudan in the first quarter of the nineteenth century, complained of the women of Kano. The caravan needed dates and millet in an out-of-the-way place. The women thronged the camp but were prepared to sell for Toba only at 10 percent profit. In another instance he mentioned 15 percent. I still didn't understand. However, he mentioned the prices of the sheep, goats, and so on. Clearly the price *in Toba* was put up to 2½ times the standard conventional price.

In the seventeenth century, Tavernier, the French diamonds merchant, sold jewels to the Shah of Persia in Ispahan. "At last the king said: I'll take all your jewels at 25 percent profit, but you sell your pearls in India where you'll get more."

[h] Editors' note: Obviously Polanyi intended to place here a quotation from Cadamosto, but he never did.

To cut it short: The traditional long-distance trade was carried on traditional prices – like the 150 shekels for a horse of Salomon.

In concluding, let me remind you of the meaning of *modernizing* in this context. It is a reference to nineteenth-century conditions, in other words to conditions obtaining approximately up to *World War I*. The modern times have passed. No one knows that better than the economist. The traditional definitions of trade and so on have become inapplicable. Once trade was a gainful, two-sided, peaceful exchange of goods. Today we speak of an international trade organization even if it is not conspicuously gainful, only moderately two-sided, and only prospectively peaceful. In the same line of thought, almost all economic problems have suffered a see change. Money, trade, markets are offering today problems of a nonmodern type. Last but not least, it may be economic theory that will benefit most from the contributions of institutional analysis.

6

The Nature of International Understanding*

I am taking a gloomy view of the outcome of my supposedly enlightening talk on the nature of international understanding. Having thought long and deeply upon the subject, I have come to the conclusion that I am about to deal a sequence of the most hackneyed commonplaces that an intelligent audience has ever been treated to by an unfortunate lecturer.

In effect, I will find myself trying to convince you that to achieve international understanding we must exert both idealism and common sense; we must have regard both for our interest and for that of the world; we must satisfy the demands of both expediency and principles. Now, to hand out maxims such as these to a people whose national institutions include unwritten constitutions, an Erastian church, an inveterate habit of compromise, almost amounts, when addressed by me to you, to a Gilbertian exhortation to resist all temptation and to remain Englishmen . . .

So I will have to limit myself to saying something about the kind of idealism that does *not* help toward international understanding and about the kind of commonsense realism that does *not* do so either.

*File 17–29, Karl Polanyi Archive: undated typescript, full of corrections in the author's hand. The structure, headings, and paragraph division have been added by the editors. The original contains numerous lists that look like notes copied out from index cards: we see here the author in the process of thinking and constructing his argument.

There is the kind of idealism that preaches that, if we are only sufficiently idealistic, wars can be avoided altogether. Then there is the kind of realism that says that wars cannot be avoided anyway.

Let us take the latter first.

That wars have always existed is not true. (1) Very primitive society, like some Australian aboriginals, is at a *sub-war stage*, if for no other reason than that it is unable to organize the discipline, the coordination, and the other prerequisites of a sustained moral and material effort such as is involved in the planned collective undertakings of war. (2) Some fairly developed societies, like that of the Eskimo, know not war. They somehow manage to get on without it (the poor wretches). (3) The abolishment of war in vast areas is a common experience, usually described as the *foundation of empires*. This invariably meant the *elimination of war* over large territories and with respect to enormous populations, thus restricting its occurrence both in time and space. There is nothing to support the pseudo-realistic prejudice that, of all our institutions, war is the one that is coterminous with mankind.

There have been times in the past without war; there may be times ahead of us that will not know war.

But, to turn from pseudo-realism to pseudo-idealism, the increase of idealism alone will not achieve this result. Or rather the *kind* of idealism that implies such an expectation will most certainly *not* bring it about. Indeed, since this kind of idealism was more frequent – very much more frequent – in the last thirty years than ever before, it might be argued that it is precisely this kind of idealism that has something to do with the unprecedented scale of world wars in our time. Conscientious objections are practically unknown in modern history before World War I.

This is not the idealism we need. The idealism that (1) denies the institutional functions of war, that (2) regards war as an aberration of the mind or temperament, that (3) believes it to be a bad business deal, in other words something that is intended to be profitable, though its profitability is a "great illusion" – this kind of idealism, which is idealistic in the philosophical sense of abstracting from all the basic facts, is a danger today.

It has several variants:

1   The "governments not the people" myth is one of the cheapest and most dangerous variant. This theory is essentially untrue.
    a   The democratization of the state in the French Revolution introduces the age of conscription and mass armies. The

National Convention[a] initiated the *levée en masse* . . . And
the more democracy we have, the bigger and better wars we
get. The USA produced the first large-scale war of modern
history in the American Civil War.

b   In the USA, Gallup polls prove that, in this war, the masses
urged the government to take drastic steps. Even in this
country,[b] in 1940 and 1941, the pressure for conscription, for
direction of labor, for rationing all along the line came from
the people . . .

c   But even if government and people are only two facets of the
same crystal, *for the youth leader* the demagogic exoneration
of the people is *the* thing to be *avoided*. That way "mob rule"
lies . . .

2   [The second variant assumes that][c] wars were caused by people's
passions, by outbursts of emotion, by errors of judgment due to
overpowering sentiment, the result of hatred and envy, by the
blind urge of uncontrolled instincts, the beast in man, primeval
man, the cave man: these terms are to be taken not in the endear-
ing sense but in the pejorative sense.

a   Actually, under almost all systems of organized society we
know, the council of state, which takes the decision on war
or peace, is surrounded by all the *institutional safeguards
of responsible statesmanship*. This is true of the war council
of the Red Indians as much as of that of Tudor England, of
the Prussian council of state, or of the Machiavellian council
of Italian Renaissance states; in effect Greeks and Persians,
Chinese and Arabs equally excel in these institutional safeguards. And the main point is universally the same: the
elimination of emotion and passion, of all ephemeral sentiment from a decision that is regarded as of utmost importance. The *dynastic* wars of the seventeenth and eighteenth
centuries were decided by cabinets and (perhaps) by cabals
that certainly did not act on emotions but on so-called *reason
of state*.

[a]Editors' note: Polanyi uses here the word "Convent." But this is not really the English
word "convent"; it is an anglicization of the German word *Konvent*, which means
"convention" – *not* "convent." The German *Konvent* would be correct as a name
for the French "Convention Nationale" of 1792–5, but the English "convent" has
the wrong meaning, hence this substitution is particularly misleading.
[b]Editors' note: England.
[c]Editors' note: Words added by us, to make the sentence more comprehensible and
coherent with Polanyi's thought.

b   The opposite is a *purely modern phenomenon*, and is actually
a result of modern mass democracy, which makes the participation of the masses necessary in war. It is very doubtful
whether the emotions roused by war are the cause of war even
today. But it is certain that they were not the causes of war
in the past. Most wars in the past actually happened with an
extremely small participation of the population (except in the
case of some nomadic societies, where the position was somewhat similar to modern *total war*, except that the actual fighting was still mostly restricted to the "warriors").

3   The theological explanation of war is another form of the idealistic fallacy. Luther and Calvin taught that the state, its laws and
prisons and executioners were caused by "original sin," which
made man unruly and disorderly. In this sense *all* human institutions in the field of law and order are due to original sin. In the
same order of things, marriage is justified by the human propensity to give way to the temptation of promiscuity and lust. Good
and evil are equally explained by original sin. That's why it does
not "explain" any one institution as distinct from another. Not
only war, but also peace is due to "original sin"; not only the
atomic bomb but the United Nations Organization as well.
Gravitation does not explain only the fall of the apple but also
the swimming of the ship, the flying of the plane. In other words,
original sin is much too general a phenomenon to be adduced as
an explanation of any *one* institution, I am afraid; even when we
will have succeeded in abolishing war, we will still have not heard
the last of "original sin". . . .

Neither the blaming of governments and idealization of the people,
nor the warning to keep our emotions under control, nor reminders
of man's fallen nature will help us to abolish war; every one of
these idealistic fallacies tends to increase the danger instead of
diminishing it.

The basic realities of the institution of war, its problems and
dangers, should be as removed from the range of an immature idealism and an equally immature realism as the problems of *sex*. These
also have a vast negative and a vast positive importance for almost
every realm of human existence. Yet remember the Victorian period
and its supercharged idealism and just as supercharged anguish with
respect to sex. The romantic and sentimental idealization of sex,
and the unreasoning horror mongering with respect to sex. One
proved as unhelpful as the other. Its idealistic and realistic distortions
did not help but hindered the solution of the problems of sex, as

parents and educators have realized. They made the unavoidable problems of sex even more tragic, while increasing the number of the avoidable ones and decreasing greatly the number of sane and self-respecting lives. Furtiveness and dishonesty permeated life and undermined the true forces of morality and personality. Neither romantic idealization nor unreasoning disgust lessened the perils of the complications accompanying sex, while the deep-seated forces of a healthy personality remained underdeveloped – forces that alone are capable of weaving the weft of the impersonal element[d] in passion into the woof of a personal relationship of incomparable wealth and variety of values.

Of course, the parallel is faulty, for sex is more basic than war: sex is actually coterminous with man's biological life, while the institution of war, as we said, is not. At this point the pseudo-idealist stages a comeback of a rather dangerous character. He points to the fact that war is an institution, a human institution, and consequently its existence is dependent upon us. Who declares war but ourselves? Who else but ourselves fights in it? Consequently it depends only upon us to abolish it.

Now this is a fallacy, and a very dangerous one. It is *not true that, because something is a human institution, it depends only upon us whether we will have it or not.*

Can we abolish it? Only in a narrow and superficial sense.

Take the institution of marriage. That is, we cannot abolish it without putting some other form of ordered relationships in its place. We can have this form of marriage or another form of marriage – they may vary greatly; the one thing we cannot have is to forego some form of approved relationship between the sexes, which is precisely what marriage in the broad sense means.

This seems to contradict what I said about the lack of analogy between sex and war. Not at all. It is not sex and war we are putting here on the same footing, but sex and the conflicting interests of human groups. These latter are as universal a fact of group life as sex is of human life. And war (like marriage) is an institution that solves the problems raised by the underlying facts (of group conflicts in the one case, of sex in the other). Just as one form of marriage cannot be abolished without being replaced by some other institution that would serve the same purpose, *namely of whittling down such conflicts of group interests as cannot remain permanently undecided if communities are to function normally.* (Incidentally, this is precisely

---

[d]Editors' note: This is a word added in handwriting, and the reading is not entirely secure (it could be *character*?).

the reason why marriage, in one form or another, is an inevitable institution; for sex raises issues of public approval that cannot remain undecided if human beings are to function normally.) So the idealists' last refuge has proved untenable. That war is an institution, far from proving that its existence is a mere function of our volition, really explains the fact of why it is *not* possible to abolish war without replacing it by some other institution, which will perform the same vital function.

Take the most frequent reason for a conflict of group interests: it refers, in the case of territorial groups, to *frontiers*. To the liberal idealist, nothing seems to prove better the purely illusionary character of war. Firstly, he says, it decides something that is entirely *inessential*. After all, unless the people study a map, they would mostly not even realize what all the pother is about. Secondly, war settles nothing, and so the whole terrible process has not only fictitious reasons, but also fictitious results.

This is like arguing – as some anarchist free-love pseudo-idealist of the more immature type did – that the personal aspect of love is a purely conventional fact, and anyway that marriage settles nothing, since the same issues continue to exist unchanged.

Actually the liberal idealist is mistaken about frontiers, and the simple people who cannot get over the issue of unsettled problems are right – for the good reason that no human community can develop any of its vital functions without having settled, at least for a generation, *who does and who does not belong to the community*. For communities are organized in states; and, without some loyalty to the state, the community cannot function satisfactorily. But how is it possible to produce *loyal citizens* (or even to expect them to be loyal) unless one can point out who belongs and who does not belong to the community? And this, in the case of territorial groups, is determined by *frontiers*. In other words no community of this character can produce law and order, safety and security, education and morality, civilization and culture unless its frontiers are settled and there is no reasonable danger of their becoming unsettled. Any threat to their frontiers, ever so distant, must inhibit the normal functioning of the community and stop all higher forms of life. Incidentally, this will usually be true of both communities involved, since frontiers effect them both. There must be decision – at all cost. And, if no other institution is available, war must be invoked if higher forms of life would be allowed to continue.

An idealism that *obscures this basic fact* makes it impossible to find a substitute for war. For no such substitute is conceivable that does not involve *new loyalties* and would not demand them to achieve the evoking of tremendous energies of a moral order. But how should such moral energies be generated unless mankind is faced with a real task, involving the solution of real problems? The idealist pacifist's contention is that all we need is to rid ourselves of prejudice, to dispel some illusions and to join him in his enlightened enthusiasms. Is it surprising that nothing but failure lay that way?

War is an *institution*, and to this extent it is *impersonal*. Even soldiers rarely hate their enemies personally, and the higher the rank of the solider the less is this usually the case. The idea that personal hatred is the cause of war is utterly beside the point. But why regard war as a personal matter at all? Personal facts are personal only as long as we do not have to think of them as institutional. Who should expect a judge to be anything but impersonal in his dealings? This would be true even of the postman – who would refuse to deliver to you letters meant for another, even though he might personally prefer to have dealings with you rather than with your neighbor, to whom they happen to be addressed.

All this should seem fairly obvious. But, faced with the fact of war, we tend to forget it and start arguing on an entirely different note. After all, is it not something that happens between human beings? Is it not of our own doing? If we only knew the man personally, surely we would find that we had no grudge against him? International understanding is an understanding between nations, and nations consist of individuals; consequently, if only we can manage to have understanding between individuals, we would also have understanding between nations. This means to disregard completely the nature of an institution, and in war, which is itself an institution, the reference is exclusively to institutions such as armies, states, governments, and so on. It is a sad state of affairs, when man finds himself reduced to so utter helplessness that he disregards obvious commonsense facts and sets his hopes superstitiously on a supposed "personal" element in international relations! Yet to misdirect our efforts in this way wrecks our *only chance* of establishing institutions that would make war unnecessary.

To clinch my argument, I might have to show that wars do not necessarily come about through human frailty, through envy, mutual hatred, or other forms of error or misunderstanding – though numberless wars have been caused that way – but that there is such a thing as *unwanted war*, indeed that this may be the true peril of our time.

For the sake of argument let us make a big assumption. Let us assume two great powers single-mindedly determined to keep the peace. They have become convinced that this is what they need; moreover, they are of the opinion that there is nothing they could reasonably fight about. Let us assume that these two countries regard their duty to safeguard the security of their territory in the strict sense, in which this is not a cloak for aggression but a sincere desire for safety, no more. Let us finally assume that these two great powers are not neighbors, possessing no common frontiers.

In this thoroughly angelic situation, let us construct the following experiment. A great empire, which hitherto separated the two great powers from one another, suddenly collapses. The vast populations of that (collapsing) empire and its vast territories find themselves overnight masterless, without organized government and orderly administration, a black void in the middle of the map. This is what we call a political vacuum. *From the point of view of power, the two great powers have become neighbors*, since no power separates them anymore from each other.

Now, I maintain – and most students of politics would agree – that there is now a grave danger of war between the powers, a war that might be avoided for some time but is ultimately certain, *unless* they can agree *either* to build up jointly the vast empire destroyed *or* to prevent jointly its reconstruction. Both feats are extremely difficult to perform. Yet, unless they succeed in this act of statesmanship, an *unwanted* war between them is unavoidable. Why?

(a)　The population of the vacuum is active, its domestic factions are fighting one another, and they may find an interest, for *reasons of their own*, in strengthening one or the other power (land or maritime, racially akin or stranger).

(b)　Consequently, it is imperative to keep informed about things, that is, to keep in touch with internal forces, which

(c)　means some help to some people and some control over them.

(d)　Assume this to be happening over a time, one gets *penetration*;

(e)　if this happens from the north and south, the powers must meet somewhere in the empty space, *on no boundary*, in the dark, increasingly fearful and playing a game of blind man's buff, which must end in a clash.

This is entirely independent of their intentions, apart from genuine concern for their safety. No envy, greed, or unreasonable suspicion enters. The *unwanted* war will emerge . . .

Such a situation is coming about in the Far East, but America and Russia are appearing to make great efforts to join in rebuilding a united China, *in order to avoid unwanted war*.

The key to peace thus lies in *policy*. The means to international understanding is policy. It is the *laws of policy* that we must study.

1 The first aim of policy must be to avoid *unwanted war*. This, in a time like ours, may be a very great task. For almost three quarters of the globe have turned into a *vacuum*.
2 The second aim of policy must be to eliminate war altogether, for the release of *atomic energy* has made war undoubtedly a danger to this planet and all life upon it.

Here idealism versus realism comes up again.

Policy is about the means of meeting a situation, of safeguarding interests in that situation. The decisive questions are: Whose interests? In what *situation*?

This is the moral problem of policy. *Who* is the unit? What does its survival imply? Bare survival is *not* a definition of survival in the case of a community. It's the way of life that defines its identity. But the same is true of the *situation*. To judge the world is to judge myself. The US world outlook is different from the Russian and from the British. Policy implies the definition of some persons' interests in some situation and implies a decision. At both ends moral problems are decisive. Not selfish or unselfish policy – this is a contradiction in terms. But *whose self*? That is the question. And *in what world*?

The great problem of politics is the right appreciation of our interests as a country and the right appreciation of the forces at work in the world.

Then only[e] will one be able to formulate policies that do the necessary thing:

(a) *unite* the nation at home;
(b) *secure allies* abroad.

No selfish interest is ever supported by others; and only through the support of others can strength accrue to the community. That was the secret of nineteenth-century British politics. The same is still the case; and the same answer is required.

---

[e] Editors' note: I.e. upon achieving such appreciation.

Sane realism is a realism that takes the moral and spiritual facts as *realities*. They are basic realities in politics. Sentimental idealization mistakes the facts. We do not love a person less because we understand his or her problems. We do not love our country less because we understand its problems.

I warned you that I would leave you with the usual generalities. Still, it was perhaps worthwhile to think them over again. This, too, promotes international understanding.

7

The Meaning of Peace*

The Postulate of Peace

To assert that war is the central problem of our time is to go straight to the heart of the crisis of our civilization. For such an assertion implies two basic assumptions: (1) that, unless war is abolished, our civilization must perish in and through wars; and (2) that the obstacles to the abolishment of war are bound up with the fundamental political and economic institutions of our society. To declare war the greatest evil and its abolishment our chief task is, therefore, to formulate a revolutionary principle.

This has been clearly recognized by the consistent upholders of the present system. "A doctrine which is founded upon the harmful postulate of peace is an enemy to Fascism," declared Mussolini in his statement on fascism in the *Enciclopedia italiana*.[a] The postulate of peace is the dividing line between two worlds today.

What, then, is the exact content of this postulate, and what precisely are the premises on which it is based?

---

* File 20–13 Karl Polanyi Archive: composition from 1938. According to the archival account, it was reproduced in the draft typescript of the Christian Left Group's *Bulletin*, No. 3, of August 1938. The same file hosts two other versions of the same piece, while file 18–39 preserves a draft from 1932.

[a] Editors' note: Benito Mussolini, *The Political and Social Doctrine of Fascism*, trans. Jane Soames (London: Hogarth Press, 1933), p. 588: this little study was published in book form by Leonard and Virginia Woolf at their own press. The Italian original had been published the previous year in vol. 14 of the *Enciclopedia italiana*.

Postulating peace, or, in common English, insisting on a peaceful world, is simply to assume that we could carry on today without the institution of war. But let war cease to be a paramount necessity of human existence, and it becomes the negation of humanity by humanity itself. Once it is not inescapable, it must be abolished at all costs; and no other task can claim priority over this one. This is the content of the postulate of peace. Its validity depends upon the truth or falsity of the premise, namely the assumption that the need for war as a condition of human society has passed away.

War was "destiny unshunnable, like death."[b] To participate in it was the common lot, from which such only could contract out as were prepared to accept personal safety at the price of breaking away from the community. But neither the Old Testament nor the New, neither Greek nor Roman philosophy saw as much as a moral problem in the institution of war. The common people refused to regard it as a crime. The acceptance of the postulate of peace by the broad masses of the population is an entirely new development. It is the most significant change that has come to pass in the consciousness of modern man.

The Institution of War

That war is no longer necessary by no means implies sharing in the delusion that war is an atavistic remnant, which has come down to us from the caveman and which our enlightened age has discarded at last. It is improbable that our cave-dwelling ancestors knew war; they had neither the reasons nor the means for carrying on such highly organized activities. The need, the instruments, and the capacity for waging war developed probably in mutual interdependence, once a certain level of civilization was reached. War is neither "as old as mankind," nor will it "last as long as human beings do not change their nature."[c] Dogmatic statements about the psychological nature of war are meaningless.

Human institutions, it should be recognized, are not explained as a rule by pointing to the psychological motives individuals may have

---

[b]Editors' note: Shakespeare, *Othello*, Act iii, Scene 3, line 279.

[c]Editors' note: Concerning the first quotation here, the full sentence attributed to the nineteenth-century jurist Sir Henry Maine runs thus: "War appears to be as old as mankind, but peace is a modern invention." See the opening of Michael Howard's *Mind the Peace* (New Haven, CT: Yale University Press, 2000). As for the second quotation, its source is unidentified.

for making use of the institution in question. The existence of courts of justice, for example, is not due to the motives for which individuals appeal[d] to courts once these are in existence. And the need to decide on conflicts between members of the community without recourse to private warfare has nothing whatever to do with the motives of such conflicts in individual cases. These motives may be good or bad, permanent or transitory, conscious or unconscious, emotional or rational; the validity of the motive for establishing the law courts themselves bears no reference to these features.[e] The advantages (or disadvantages) to the individual that derive from the existence of the court are of an entirely different character from the advantages (or disadvantages) deriving from the existence of the court to the community and, incidentally, to the individual as a member of the community. In this capacity the individual reaps the benefit of internal peace, while in his capacity as a litigant he may be securing for himself (or having to suffer) the various advantages (or eventual disadvantages) inherent in his personal contact with the law.

Similar is the case of war. It is an institution the primary function of which is to decide on issues that arise from various territorial groupings and cannot otherwise be decided, and that cannot remain in abeyance without endangering the existence of the communities concerned. Such issues are chiefly – though not exclusively – territorial. States can exist only within definite boundaries; uncertainty about these reacts upon the state itself as fatefully as a permanent challenge to its sovereignty would: the state is inevitably thrown into anarchy. But, while a challenge to sovereignty is met by the action of the executive or, in the last resort, by civil war, doubts that arise with regard to the frontiers must be removed either peacefully, by agreement, or forcibly, by war. Failing peaceful agreement, war is unavoidable whenever the states in conflict owe no common allegiance to a higher sovereignty. The reasons for their quarrel may be good or bad, rational or irrational, material or ideal – this affects in no way the imperative need for a final decision, whenever there is a conflict. In certain typical cases – such as the migration of peoples, the rise of

---

[d]Editors' note: The word that appears here in the original typescripts is *repair* ("motives for which individuals repair to the courts"). This is obviously a slip of pen such as Polanyi's English registers from time to time; again, we recorded this one because it is more striking.

[e]Editors' note: The original reads here *them*, which is wrong and very confusing: grammatically, it can only refer to "motives" or to "courts," the only plural nouns in context, and neither makes sense. This type of mistake, related to the use of the English pronoun, is not unique to this passage; like the others, it would not have passed uncorrected in a paper revised for publication.

national states, the great movements of social emancipation – it cannot be reasonably be doubted that the very progress of mankind would have been impeded if, by some miraculous intervention of a super-historical authority, the motives for the dispute would have been ruled out as invalid. The close connection between civil and national wars in various periods of history should alone warn us away from lightly assuming that wars were always carried on for reasons that, in retrospect, cannot be recognized as valid.

"War exists because people wish it to exist" (Aldous Huxley).

This, in a nutshell, is the psychological theory of war. But very few institutions exist because individuals wish them to exist. It is time to cease to discuss human institutions in terms of the pleasant or unpleasant moods commonly associated with the personal discharge of the social functions in question. Judicial systems do not exist on account of the grim humor often attributed to judges, but by virtue of the need of developed societies for some institutional provisions against the breaking of laws. Similarly, wars are neither caused by people who happen to be in a "warlike spirit" nor carried by soldiers owing to that spirit. Such a spirit is rather the result than the cause of war; the people directly affected by the fighting may be in a comparatively peaceful state of mind. Handbooks of military science hardly contain more than a passing reference to hate or greed. Neither in the period of dynastic wars nor in that of cabinet wars did hate have any appreciable influence upon the decision of the government to carry on the war against the one or the other of the eligible "enemies." Even the USA went to war in 1917, mainly because it could remain neutral no longer without suffering grave damage as a sovereign state; as far as this goes, it mattered little whether the USA declared war on Great Britain (as it had done in similar circumstances in 1812) or on Germany (the alternative, in 1812, had been France). It was not hate that impelled the USA to go to war, although once peace was untenable, hate may have helped to decide who should be the enemy. War, in effect, is as little caused by hatred as the stock exchange is the outcome of the need for excitement, or the newspaper of that for litter. Wars as such are not concerned with the sentiments. If they could be waged without emotions, this might make them even more cruel; and that emotions have to be aroused today in order to wage war more effectively is rather an incidental result of modern mass democracy than of the nature of war.

It ought to be evident that no community can settle down and do its job as long as doubts about its boundaries blur the loyalty of the members of the community, drain the treasury of its income, and deprive the organized community itself of one of the attributes of sovereignty. That is why the arbitration of war was vital to the existence of human societies. Being so, it was sanctified.

The postulate of peace, simple as it seems, comports no less than a new foundation for politics. It stands for an act of faith that heralds the coming of a new age in the history of the race. The sudden emergence of the widespread conviction about the criminal nature of war is to be regarded as the intimation of the birth of a new and wider community, for which the overlordship of the sovereign states of the earth is claimed. The time has come when a power is to be set up over the nations and a sovereignty established that will achieve peacefully what war did in the past by violence: to arbitrate among the nations.

How is this to come to pass? It is at this point that the pacifist fallacy enters.

The Pacifist Fallacy

Pacifist policy is based on the erroneous belief that war had no vital functions in the past and that it can therefore be simply abolished. This is a fateful illusion, which, in case of a substantial success of the pacifist movement, is bound to arouse a reaction in which the pacifist movement itself would necessarily be destroyed. For, as long as the need for war has *not* passed away, a society that were rendered incapable of using this ultimate means of asserting its existence in a conflict would thereby be automatically deprived of one of the preconditions of its existence. No community could follow such a path to the end. The danger is that, if the pacifist movement had gained an important measure of success before it collapsed, its failure might engulf the cause of the postulate of peace as well. And almost necessarily so. For, if the forces of peace failed to realize the implications of the postulate for which they stand, then the postulate of peace might in effect become a means of paralyzing progress while condemning mankind to a futile search for peace in passivity, anarchy, and decay.

The Tolerance Analogy

Yet the principle for which the pacifist stands is a true one. How, then, can that which appears as its consistent practical application inevitably lead to its refutation?

A similar dilemma faced the early protagonists of the principle of tolerance in this country.[f] The principle of religious tolerance was transferred from the realm of religious experience to the field of politics by that greatest of all Englishmen, Oliver Cromwell. The Puritan in him had developed into the independent; freedom of conscience was translated into tolerance. He set an example in modern history, perhaps in the history of the world, for a dictatorship that fought for the enforcement of liberty and enlightenment. His conflict with parliament was the struggle of a determined adherent of religious tolerance against a pseudo-representative body of religious intolerance. And yet what would the result of Cromwell's triumph over parliament have been, assuming an outcome was conceivable? In the long run, undoubtedly, the victory of Roman Catholic intolerance over his own tolerant Protestantism. For, if Cromwell and the army had had their way and England had embarked in the 1640s on that regime of religious tolerance that was to be, ultimately, the outcome of the Great Rebellion, the result could hardly have been anything other than the triumph of the counter-Reformation. This can easily be shown. The church and the state had not yet been disentangled. Thus religious tolerance on the part of the state would have resulted either in the immediate victory of an intolerant religion over the state or in chaos. For, unless the state had eliminated religious sanctions from its own legislation and religion had recognized the sovereignty of the national state, the separation of church and state would necessarily have led to disintegration, England would soon have fallen under the sway of the European counter-Reformation, and the cause of religious tolerance would have been buried for many generations. (Where institutional conditions could be shaped, as in New England, tolerance was accordingly introduced without endangering the community itself.) The triumph of an intolerant form of Catholicism was thus averted only owing to Cromwell's failure to force tolerance prematurely on the country. But, assuming that our analysis is correct, does it prove Cromwell's ideas false? Hardly; for the true reference of his religious experience lay in the prophetic recognition of a time when the state would allow freedom to all religions and religions would accept freely the sovereignty of the state – a state of affairs, however, that could be brought about only after manifold and far-reaching changes in the institutional structure of society. Cromwell's fate was that of a commanding officer in power; he had mistaken his prophetic vision for a political mandate.

[f]Editors' note: England.

What Is to Replace War?

What, then, are the institutional changes that will make the postulate of peace actual reality?

If war is to be abolished, international order must take its place. But no international sovereignty is conceivable without a new international economic order to replace that which is passing away. This order, of which the international gold standard formed a part, with its free movements of capital and labor, of commodities and payments, can never come back again. But, unless the international division of labor is maintained in some form or other, a general fall in the standards of life is inevitable; and, even if such a fall can be avoided, a great increase in the standard of life will always be attainable in the future through the simple means of re-establishing the international division of labor. Whatever the immediate future may have in store for us, internationalism will remain an irresistible driving force of history.

Another fundamental feature of our period derives from the fact that a new international economic order must involve far-reaching economic readjustments, not so much between the haves and have-nots as between all the various countries of the globe – and in a great number of ways. Accordingly, the chief task of domestic politics will be to equip the nations with a social organization that can stand the gigantic strain of – in fact inseparable from – any major readjustments in the international economic field. In the last resort, it is the class structure of society that will prove to be an obstacle to international economic readjustment; for massive economic sacrifice can be borne willingly only by communities that are closely united in the service of transcending ideals. This is the abiding source of the forces that make the coming of socialism inevitable in our age.

The setting up of an international peace order cannot therefore be brought to fruition through a simple refusal to fight, but only through the actual achievement of the institutional basis of such an order. The first step toward achieving this end lies in the transformation of our capitalist nation-states into actual communities by means of bringing economic life under the control of the common people and of thereby abolishing the property cleavage in society.

The Reform of Consciousness

Insofar as it is possible for us to reconstruct the meaning of the New Testament ethics in terms of institutional life, its tendency was undoubtedly both pacifist and communist. The practice of the early church reflected these tendencies, which implied the rejection of society as a set of permanent institutions.

Human consciousness itself had been reformed in the gospels through the discovery of the personal nature of human life and of the essential freedom of personality. Accordingly, a negative attitude toward institutional society was implicit in New Testament ethics. Neither institutions nor customs nor laws were the substance of social existence, but the community as a relationship among persons: an interpretation of the nature of institutional society that amounted to its rejection.

In terms of the modern world, the social philosophy of Jesus was anarchist. Its pacifism and communism were based on the denial of the inescapable nature of institutional society. Power, economic value, coercion were repudiated as evil. The discovery of the nature of personal life was thus linked with the refusal to accept the need for permanent forms of social existence.

In our epoch, human consciousness is being re-formed again. The recognition of the inescapable nature of society sets a limit to the imaginary freedom of an abstract personality. Power, economic value, coercion, are inevitable in a complex society; there is no means for the individual to escape the responsibilities of choosing between alternatives. He or she cannot contract out of society. But the freedom we appear to lose through this knowledge is illusory, while the freedom we gain through it is valid. Man reaches maturity in the recognition of his loss and in the certainty of ultimate attainment of freedom in and through society.

The truth about human life discovered by Jesus asserts itself today, in the recognition that, in our present society, man is in a condition of self-estrangement and that the socialist transformation is the only means of reclaiming personal life in a complex society.

Pacifism and the Working-Class Movement

Proverbially, the Wesleyan revival saved England from a revolution. Social pacifism – the rejection of class struggle in every sense of that phrase – was established as part of the Christian way of life. So far as the working class is concerned, modern pacifism merely meant extending the application of this harmonistic creed from home to foreign affairs. The responsibilities with which members of the ruling class itself were invested naturally prevented them from putting such doctrines into practice.

On the whole, nonconformity tended to foster an idealist philosophy, which persisted even after the religious concept originally associated with it had faded away and been replaced by secular ones. Thus, in spite of the decay of religious life, the world of ideals remained a separate world; ideals were simply divested of their supernatural setting and became attached to secular contents – the fateful gap that had opened up between ideality and actuality outlived the change. The ideal of social justice, under the name of righteousness, became separated from the institutions that could alone embody it. Similarly, after the war, the League of Nations as an ideal became separated in the minds of people from the League of Nations as an institution. It is in the religious history of the working-class movement in this country that we must seek an explanation of a development that has made pacifism into a chief obstacle to the fulfillment of peace.

8

The Roots of Pacifism*

Mr. Chairman,

May I state in what sense, and in what sense alone, I could consent to be called a pacifist? Mussolini stated the position of fascism to pacifism thus: "A doctrine which is founded upon the harmful postulate of peace is hostile to Fascism."[a] What Mussolini here denounces as the "harmful postulate of peace" is the doctrine I stand for; it was not an idealist or sentimental contention such as peace is "good," and therefore it "ought to be" – or any other equally meaningless assertion – but this postulate implied a definite political and economic diagnosis of the present crucial stage in the development of human society. *It is to this specific diagnosis that I subscribe*. According to this diagnosis, at the heart of the present struggle between fascism and democracy, as between capitalism and socialism, there is the problem of war. If to uphold such a belief makes one a pacifist, then I am a convinced pacifist. I will have to deal with this at length tonight.

If, however, pacifism implies the acceptance of the command "not to fight," then I am emphatically *not a pacifist*. My specific diagnosis implies, on the contrary, that, perhaps for a long time to come, human beings will have to fight if the institution of war is ever to be abolished.

* File 18–38, Karl Polanyi Archive: Gillingham Lecture, 1935–6, with numerous corrections in the author's hand.
[a] Editors' note: See above, Ch. 7, p. 77.

What is the root of the danger of war in our age? It is this.

The actual forms of material existence of man are those of world-wide interdependence. The political forms of human existence must also be worldwide. Either within the boundaries of a world empire or in those of a world federation – either through conquest and subjection or by international cooperation – the nations of the globe must be brought within the folds of one embracing body if our civilization is to survive. Until peace is organized in one of these two ways wars, and wars on an ever increasing scale, must continue.

Our starting point is economic interdependence.

The reference to the material factor has in this case nothing whatever to do with so-called economic self-interest. Not incomes, profits, wages, and standards of groups or classes of the population, but the very lives of millions of human beings depend upon the material factor in question. That which would involve the deliberate destruction of tens millions of people becomes, in the nature of things, politically impracticable and morally indefensible.

Now, *but for the actually existing economic interdependence*, the nations and peoples could decide tomorrow that they will henceforth live peacefully, as independent sovereign states, in economic self-sufficiency. Passion and prejudice might prevent them from following this course; but politically and morally it would be justified. But for one factor, precisely: the economic. The establishment of the universal self-sufficiency would necessarily and inevitably cause such a sudden and fateful drop in the material resources of mankind as would reduce the population of earth to a very considerable degree. For the enforced return to primitive conditions of production would involve the starvation and death of vast masses of human beings. *For this one fundamental reason the solution of the problem of war by the method of universal self-sufficiency is inacceptable.*[b]

Most important consequences follow. If universal self-sufficiency offers no solution, we must attempt to secure at least that measure of international economic cooperation that existed until recently. The question is: How to achieve it?

Our thesis is that this cannot be done in the traditional forms of economic cooperation. These have broken down for good and all and cannot be restored. New forms of economic cooperation will have to be created. And it is the necessity of creating these new forms of economic cooperation that compels us to establish new forms of political organization on an international scale. It is precisely in the imperative need for new forms of international life that we must seek

[b]Editors' note: Unreadable sequence added here in the margin, in the author's hand.

the ultimate cause of all the strain, stress, and suffering that mankind has to undergo at present and may yet have to undergo in the future.

It might be objected: Why could the traditional forms of economic cooperation not be restored? And why should the creation of new forms of international economic cooperation necessarily involve the tragedy of fratricidal wars and civil wars?

Our two main problems:

The traditional forms of international economic cooperation have broken down. An international gold standard, an international capital market, an international commodity market, based on the free exchange of goods and payments, have passed away. The system hinged on the international gold standard. It cannot be restored, because it has become apparent that the closer the interdependence of the nations, the greater the sacrifices needed in order to keep the system going. Why? The working of the international gold standard implies the readiness of all countries concerned to allow their internal price level to move up and down according to uncontrollable changes in the international balance of payments. As long as the swing of the prices is upwards, governments might agree; but a permanent fall in the price level means a slowing down of production, a drop in the consumers' wealth produced, it means mass unemployment and the consequent danger of the dissolution of the social fabric itself. No government can deliberately bring about such a state of affairs; no society could maintain itself under such conditions.

The alternative to the present forms of international economic cooperation is the setting up of new forms. *Why can these not be established right away?*

At least in the stage of transition – and this stage covers a long period – massive economic sacrifices would have to be made by all countries concerned. Under our present economic system the people of no country will voluntarily embark upon such sacrifices. The reason is obvious. A genuine community might very well resolve to make heavy sacrifices for the sake of a great purpose and persevere in its endeavor as long as necessary. But under our industrial system society is not a community of that sort. Our property system divides it into two separate sections: the people who are responsible for the actual carrying on of industrial production, as owners and managers of the means of production; and the people who have no such responsibility.

The latter cannot be seriously expected to shoulder the economic burden of wage cuts and unemployment consequent upon a general policy the actual costs of which they are not in the position to assess. For this simple reason it is impossible under our present system to make the whole of the population act as a single unit where economic questions are concerned. This is the ultimate reason why our nation-states, as at present constituted, are inadequate to the task of setting up a new system of international economic cooperation.

Incidentally, I wish to give you an example of the economic reasoning of our outstanding pacifists. The point at issue is no less than whether or not economic self-sufficiency is possible. Decisive for this, as we have shown, is the one and only supposition under which human communities, *as at present constituted*, could settle down to peaceful existence in independent sovereign states. This is what Russell says on the possibility of self-sufficiency: "I do not think it can be doubted that by the application of existing knowledge Great Britain could, within ten years, become capable of producing the amount of food necessary to support life for its own population." It would be "much easier than usually supposed to develop our domestic supplies."^{c} He proceeds to quote at length an article of Dr. O. W. Willcox from *The New Republic* (of June 3, 1936), in which this American writer on agro-biology refers to the work of Dr. W. F. Gericke of the University of California. Dr. Gericke asserts that he has produced 217 tons of tomatoes per acre and has grown 2,465 bushels of potatoes per acre, that is, some 20 times the national average of the USA. *The plants were not set in earth at all.* Shallow tanks, filled with liquid chemicals were used, into which the roots of the plants were dipped. The liquid chemicals were heated by electricity. "Already we are hearing stories," Dr. Wilcox concludes his article, "of an occasional scientist who is said to grow a years' supply of potatoes for a large family in a tin pan under the kitchen table. There is, as a matter of fact, no reason why we should not have skyscraper farms on which the rows of shallow pans would be stacked one above the other to the height of a hundred – or a thousand – feet . . ." Personally, I do not doubt the possibility of scientific agriculture. Indeed, ever since agriculture existed, it has been more or less artificial. But the socialist construction in Soviet Russia offers the best example of the economics of such a venture. Great capital outlay means a check on the standards of life. Does Bertrand Russell realize the amount of capital outlay involved in schemes of this kind, if they are planned on anything approaching a national scale? This capital outlay, in terms of labor and commodities, means the enslavement of the people of this country for something like a generation. Obviously there would also have to be tin pans for cotton, coffee, and tea plants,

^{c}Editors' note: Unidentified source.

tin pans for rubber, orange, and lemon trees, and even tin pans for pigs, sheep, and oxen in order to procure the meat.

But Dr. Willcox's discovery has not been overlooked in other quarters, where the scientific mind is even more in evidence than in Russell's case – who is at least a great scientist in his own sphere. I am alluding to Aldous Huxley's recent book *Ends and Means*.

"Dirtless farming" devised by Professor Dr. Gericke holds pride of place in the book, although, as Huxley cautiously adds, "it is still in the experimental stage." Dr. Willcox's book *Nations Can Live at Home* has convinced Aldous Huxley that the English can live at home, without the assistance of other homes. "To what extent is overpopulation a valid excuse for militarism and imperialism?" asks Huxley. "It is probable indeed that dirtless farming will produce an agricultural revolution compared with which the industrial revolution of the eighteenth and nineteenth centuries will seem the most trifling of social disturbances."

Now one of the results of this trifling disturbance was that the population of England increased sixfold between 1700 and 1900. If "dirtless farming" results only in another sixfold increase of the population, the population of the earth may easily grow from 2 to 12 thousand million. However, Huxley wisely provides for this by expressing his hope that "the birth rate does not sharply rise." Still, he finds it "profoundly significant that no government has hitherto made any serious attempt to apply modern agro-biological methods on a large scale, for the purpose of raising the standard of material well being among the subjects and of rendering imperialism and foreign conquest unnecessary." This fact alone, Huxley says, would be a sufficient demonstration of the truth that the causes of war are not solely economic, but psychological. Only a fool would assert that the causes of war are solely economic. But has Huxley completely forgotten that the universal complaint against imperialist and militarist states is precisely that they do, by all artificial means, try to increase their food supplies and enlist the help of science to achieve the impossible in this respect? Mussolini's scientific "battle of grain" and Göring's dirtless butter seem to have escaped his attention. Even peaceful Czechoslovakia has diminished her agricultural imports by not less than 74 percent in 13 postwar years. But it is precisely the ghastly costs of these uneconomic pseudo-scientific efforts that impoverish the nations, depress their standards of life, and make them ripe for the psychosis of expansionist imperialism.

So much for the reasoning of "ends and means"; the most charitable thing to say about them is, I suppose, that they derive from the maxim that the end *does* justify the means.

We have given so much of our time to Dr. Gericke's argument in order to show up the levity with which serious pacifists sometimes treat these questions. Characteristically, it is not the *religious pacifist*, but a *rationalist*, like Russell, or someone *psychologically* minded, like Huxley, whose arguments are conspicuous for their irrelevance. The religious pacifist alone can make out a consistent case. I need not say that, in my conviction, he is wrong.

But let us return to our argument. Mainly for economic reasons, the international organization of life must be restored. This can*not* happen on the traditional basis; for governments can and will not allow the economic system of their countries to be the football of uncontrollable international forces. It *cannot happen on a new basis as long as our present economic system lasts*. For our modern class societies are lacking in that degree of unity in the economic field that would enable them to shoulder the massive sacrifices involved in the establishment of a cooperative international. Only true communities can generate the moral forces of a historical heroism without which no such efforts are likely to be undertaken, to prove successful in the face of almost insurmountable obstacles.

We find ourselves in the following situation: In the international sphere, the necessarily slow process of establishing a world federation cannot cease before it reaches its final consummation. In the national sphere, our present economic system will have to be replaced by a real economic commonwealth, precisely for the reason that only such a commonwealth will be able and willing to pay the heavy economic price that must be paid for the establishment of a world federation. This is why, in the period lying before us, foreign affairs must continue to dominate over home affairs.

The powers opposed to international cooperation will force their imperialist wars on the other countries. The powers that, for whatever reason, favor an international system will tend to oppose them jointly.

It will be in the course of this prolonged and painful attempt to evolve a cooperative solution that the inherent weakness of the present economic system as a unit of planetary cooperation must bear its fateful fruit. For no international system can prove workable that does not provide for the exigencies of genuine economic cooperation on an international scale. Thus no measure of human suffering will bring us any nearer to the desired international political order, except to the degree that the nations themselves will be transformed – during the course of wars, painful defeats, and no less costly victories – *into a true economic commonwealth*.

9

Culture in a Democratic England of the Future*

Mr. Chairman,

I was faced with the choice of doing one of two things, the first of which I believed to be intolerably boring. Discuss the meaning or meanings of the term "culture" and the correlative meaning or meanings of the term "civilization," and of course the difference or differences between them; or else try and say something about the less abstract subject of English culture and its present problems. I decided for the latter. I hope to gain your approval for this departure. Indeed, I went one better and decided that, of all present problems of English culture, the most interesting appears to be that of the *culture of a democratic England of the future*. Accordingly, I decided to choose this as my subject. Again, with your subsequent approval.

Civilization is about the availability of knives, forks, and spoons; culture is about the use of them. Civilization is about the availability, say, of libraries and marriage laws; culture is about the use of them. That is one reason why civilization and culture do not coincide. One may possess the civilization, but not the use of it. Civilization refers to external matters – like tools or institutions – available in a society; culture is a more internal and personal aspect of that civilization. Whether the ancient Greeks, who were hardly better than barbarians, possessed a culture or not cannot be determined through the mere presence of knives, forks, and spoons – or even of marriage laws – among them (at least with their gods and goddesses adultery was the

*File 17–30, Karl Polanyi Archive: undated lecture.

rule). Homer and his literary set may have possessed a poetic culture, but the goddess Hera certainly did not indulge in a hygienic culture. Otherwise the poet would hardly have made a point of the fact that, on the memorable occasion of her taking a bath, she got rid of "*all the dirt*" (*rupa panta*). As for the use of soap, as late as 1801 English doctors noted that "ladies neglected washing their bodies from year to year." Yet who would doubt that Jane Austen, and certainly her heroines, were cultured beings . . . But cultured in what respect? Shakespeare – and Bunyan, too – possessed a culture; but in what respect? The latter closed his own Preface with the words: "I am thine, if thou be not ashamed to own me, because of my low and contemptible descent in the world, John Bunyan." Bunyan was a gipsy – as he put it: "I was brought up at my fathers house, in a very mean condition." The Preface was altered in the subsequent edition to this "I am thine, to serve in the Lord Jesus John Bunyan." Yet the poetic culture of the Elizabethan period was no less real that the religious culture of the Puritan period, which permitted Bunyan to produce a monument to that religious culture unequalled – except by Shakespeare – in its importance for the mental sanity of the English people.

Culture, though essentially a personal trait, does not belong to an individual. It implies the existence of a group, for the simple reason that it refers to *accepted* values, and not to the creation of *new* values.

An individual may be exceptionally cultured, but not even exceptionally can he produce a culture of his own. As Eddington once said: "You cannot take the King of Spades and shuffle him."[a] Culture is a reference to accepted values, but *accepted by whom*? There's the rub. The smaller the circle, the more the "culture" may tend to emanate the esoteric effluvium of snobbery. Yet the only "culture" that is immanently and intrinsically snobbish is the culture of class privilege, since such a culture cannot in the nature of things become universal. Christianity is radically opposed to "culture" in this sense (except, of course, for Dean Inge, who denied that a man might have to chose between his capacity as a Christian and that of a gentleman, while adding that, if nevertheless such a choice had to be made, he for one would prefer to remain a gentleman).

Thorstein Veblen, of Scandinavian parentage, put forth the theory that in a class society "culture" is necessarily the expression of class

[a] Editors' note: Arthur Stanley Eddington, *The Nature of the Physical World: The Gifford Lectures* (New York: Macmillan, 1927), Ch. 4: "The Running Down of the Universe."

distinction. Bluntly, the position is this. Certain forms of culture are possible only if some people are exempt from toil. Veblen's thesis is that in a class society exemption from toil tends to become not the *condition* of culture, but *synonymous* with it. *Culture then becomes a sublimated form of class superiority*. Since exemption from toil is expressed mainly in wealth and leisure, consumption of time and consumption of goods are the measure of reputability. Reputability is thus a function of *conspicuous waste* and *conspicuous leisure* camouflaged by alleged cultural values. Peacocks strutting on the lawn are a sign of culture, while grazing cows are not; for the latter do not present a convincing spectacle of waste, while the former do. Servants, if there be any, must preferably be employed in useless occupations, in order to display "vicarious leisure." But the matter does not stop here. Ruling-class culture will permeate the classes that are not naturally leisure classes. In modern civilized communities, Veblen wrote,

> the lines of demarcation between social classes have grown vague and transient, and whenever this happens the norm of reputability imposed upon by the upper class extends its coercive influence with but slight hindrance down through the social structure to the lowest strata. The result is that the members of each stratum accept as their ideal of decency the scheme of life in vogue in the next higher stratum, and *bend their energies to live up to that ideal*. On pain of forfeiting their good name and their self-respect in case of failure, they must conform to the accepted code, *at least in appearance*.[b]

Such a leisure class "culture" – the chances are that it is none[c] too valuable even to the class that generated it – becomes positively harmful in its effects on other classes. Instead of culture, snobbery becomes general. For a culture that is not in conformity with conditions of life is worthless. A culture of a conspicuous waste is not of particular value even to the class that can afford the waste, since it may be merely a sublimated form of class superiority. But, for the class that cannot afford it, it is a crippling moral disaster, for, instead of making life more abundant, it stunts, frustrates, and distorts it. The prime condition of all true culture is that it correspond to the

---

[b]Editors' note: Thorstein Veblen, *The Theory of the Leisure Class: An Economic Study of Institutions* (New York: Macmillan, 1899), Ch. 4: "Conspicuous Consumption," p. 84.
[c]Editors' note: uncertain.

social realities of those who shape their way of life in conformity with it.

The problem of English culture is, broadly, this. The strength and beauty of English culture is that it is rural. It grew out of the rural environment of a feudal society and is, in its very essence, a class culture. Yet it succeeded in permeating the whole of the middle class, and even much of the lower middle class. Thus the forms of life of the countryside became the universally accepted ways of the nation as a whole.

But the *absence of an urban culture* worked out as a grave weakness after the advent of the Industrial Revolution, for it left the industrial workers beyond the pale of national culture. They had lost the rural culture of their original homesteads, but acquired no other cultures in their new surroundings of mushroom towns and wastes of slums. It is hardly conceivable that a democratic England of the future should not seek its strength in a working class that reincorporated the national culture. But how can this come about, unless *urban life* develops in this country valid and dignified forms such as deserve the name of culture? This is not the only cultural problem facing English democracy in the present. But it is an epitome of English culture.

•••

British people are intensely conscious of their insularity, but it takes a continental to realize what it consists in. It is a very simple matter. On the continent civilization was a product of the towns. The Roman Empire was a world of cities and established an universal urban culture. As long as the empire lasted, the Romans continued to found cities, and as long as these isles formed part of the empire, the Romans never wearied of founding cities over here. When the empire collapsed, the cities everywhere submerged and civilization ceased to exist in the West. The return of the cities heralded the return of civilization on the continent of Europe. Revival came first where towns have survived, as in northern Italy and in southern France. This was followed by the rise of towns in France, Italy, Germany, Belgium, and Holland. This, again, meant the rise of a new privileged class, *the bourgeoisie*, which took its place alongside of nobles and priests. Almost everywhere the bourgeoisie had a revolutionary origin. "Like the clerk or the noble" (to quote Pirenne), "the burgess escaped from the common law; like them, he belonged to a particular estate (*status*).

In the towns of the Languedoc the petty bourgeoisie achieved their rights in the communes of the twelfth and thirteenth centuries."[d] Italy, Southern Germany, the Rhineland, and the Low Countries were crowded with city-states. Florence bought estates in Tuscany and devoted itself to the development of agriculture under the control of the city. The towns actually carried on a *cheap food policy*, in the interest of the burgesses. As Pirenne put it: "For the burgess the country population existed only to be exploited."[e] In Florence the people compelled the nobility to move to the city and take up residence there. The nobles gained the franchise only after having joined a craft gild and proved that they were actually playing the trade. In Germany also the civic control of food supplies and raw materials became the function of towns.

Venice, Ancona, Bologna, or Ferrara in Italy were regular city-states; similarly Ulm, Basel, Bern, or Strasbourg on the Danube and the Rhine, or the three great cities of Bruges, Ghent, and Ypres in Flanders. Urban life became the civic life. It was there that the political spirit was first developed. In the view of Thomas Aquinas, a typical Italian, man was naturally a town dweller, and St. Thomas regarded rural life only as the result of misfortune or of want. Of course, the town of which Thomas Aquinas wrote was itself strongly agrarian and supported itself through a system of ordered exchanges with the surrounding country, which was under its rule. The Angelic Doctor described agriculture as "dirty and miserable." No doubt that it was the town that first brought in real Christian lay civilization; it was the place where the cathedrals were set up. The Christian social ethic of the middle ages was patriarchal but not feudal; it was urban, not rural. The Waldenses and the Albigenses – sectarians, precursors of Savonarola – were an expression of the fervent religious conscience of the towns. Urban sites were the birthplace not only of commerce and trade, but also of arts and crafts, religion and learning, statecraft and politics on the continent. And above all they were the home of the bearers of urban culture, the proud, wealthy, and soldierly citizens of these famous cities, the sword-bearing patriciate of the realm.

Nothing even faintly similar ever happened in England. William the Conqueror set up within an almost incredibly short time a centralized efficient administration, the first and for a long time the only one to be established in Europe. Even after the country was governed by the crown and its officials, until the seventeenth century,

---

[d]Editors' note: Henri Pirenne, *An Economic and Social History of Medieval Europe* (Abingdon: Routledge, 2006 [1936]), p. 57.
[e]Editors' note: Ibid.

the parliament took over the job. Apart from rare periods of civil strife that did not compare with the permanent state of international war on the continent, peace reigned in England. Now towns are military establishments, and extremely costly ones at that. The upkeep of a walled town and the maintenance of civic order within its narrow confines are the rationale of urban existence. Hardly had the Norman nobles erected their castles and withdrawn to their donjons, when their horse took over the policing of the countryside from the townspeople, who became simple tradesmen and farmers and never again turned to soldierly occupations. The enfranchisement of the towns was a peaceful process of *purchase*, not a violent one of risings and rebellions. After the War of the Roses many towns decayed and the Tudor laws against "the pulling down of towns" were of no avail.

In the sixteenth century it became increasingly difficult to induce men of substance to undertake the burdens of municipal government. Often they ceased to reside in the town, even when they continued to trade there. When they had made money they invested it in land and turned themselves into squires, as Professor Meredith notes. Not even London – the only city to have retained her walls ever since Roman times and never to have relinquished her military privileges – was a real exception. True, the city was, almost all throughout English history, a political power of the first rank. As Macaulay wrote, London vanquished Charles I and London restored Charles II. But even by that time the noble families of England had long migrated beyond her walls. Except for Shaftesbury, whose palace stood at Aldergate Street, and Buckingham, who lived near Charing Cross, hardly any aristocratic name is attached to London. Sir Robert Clayton lived in the Old Jewry, Sir Dudley North in Basinghall. Charter House, Christ's Hospital, Gresham College, Dulwich College, or the College of God's Gift show the concern of middle-class philanthropists, but most of them were no citizens of London. When Richard Johnson, in 1612, writing to extoll the citizen heroes of London, selected nine worthies, none of them was of much account: Sir Henry Pritchard, the vintner; Sir William Sevenoaks, grocer; Sir Thomas White, merchant tailor; Sir John Bonham, mercer; Sir Cristopher Croker, vintner; Sir Hugh Caverly, silk weaver; Sir Henry Malevert, grocer. One only has gone down in history: Sir William Walworth, the fishmonger, major of London, who slew Wat Tyler when Richard II met the peasant leader at Smithfield. It was a characteristic episode. At a time when the arrogant bourgeoisie of Ypres was putting the queen of France to shame by the sheer splendour of its dress and jewellery, at a time when the Swiss peasant hero

Arnold Winkelried died a hero's death in the battle of Sempach and the proud knightly armies were put to flight by simple commoners, the Lord Major was on the side of the knights and barons against the revolting peasantry. It was an almost unbreakable rule that, whenever a burger was raised to the knighthood, he stopped practicing this trade, and indeed was made to do so. Perhaps with the lone exception of the Chamberlains, whose repute was linked with Birmingham, no English historical family ever came from a town or city, or, if so, remained there.

The institutional origins of English culture sprang from the genius of Charlemagne. He and William the Conqueror were the co-founders of Norman England. If we can believe the account of William Cunningham, that great scholar and great mind, the *Capitulare de villis* issued by Charlemagne was the strictly followed model on which the Norman manorial system was run. (The origins of the manor as an economic unit go back of course to Anglo-Saxon times, but it is the manor as a cultural center that is in question here.) The Frankish Empire of the ninth century was the link between the Roman Empire and the France of the High Middle Ages. Charlemagne's initiatives were more recently being described as "a flash in the pan," a brilliant interlude in an age of darkness – the darkness that, in Western Europe, separates the Roman Empire from the High Middle Ages. In this period of anarchy and decay, when cities and towns had practically disappeared, Charlemagne conceived the idea of highly organized cultural centers based exclusively on a natural economy, without money, commerce, trade, and other emanations of urban life. The elaborate regulations of the *Capitulare de villis* seem to have been taken by the Norman conquerors as the model on which they established economic and cultural life in this country. Cunningham, an ardent believer in the unique cultural value of a great rural center, may have exaggerated the wealth and variety of life that sprang from it. Personally I do not think so. I happen to be myself a believer in the virtues of an existence close to nature and the more obvious hints to happiness that nature vouchsafes us.

English insularity – I hope so much has become evident – is only partly a gift of nature: England was an island before the Norman conquest, but it was not insular; it was not politically unified and was therefore a veritable thoroughfare of invading peoples. Only after the Norman conquest had unified the defence of the island and at the same time centralized its administration, thus establishing domestic peace, was it possible to start out a line of development utterly foreign to the continent, namely of discarding the walled civilization of fear for the open rural civilization of the manor and the cottage, the endless wonders of which are the glories of English insularity. The Angelic Doctor, on whom Dante mapped his trajectory through the universe, never knew the English countryside from which Shakespeare and Keats sprang.

English insularity is the lengthy story of the spread of manorial culture through time, space, and social groups, until it almost comprised the nation as a whole. While new social classes rose to the ranks of the ruling strata and gradually changed the economic basis of social rule, culturally they were assimilated to the world of the country mansion and cottage.

I am afraid I cannot go into details. Clearly a great danger was involved in this extension of rural culture to social classes of a non-rural origin, namely that these classes would attempt to accept the values of a way of life that was out of harmony with their actual conditions of life. In brief, the rising bourgeois of the city of London, its bankers and financiers, its great traders and merchants never succeeded in setting up a culture of their own; the Puritans of England failed to maintain what they had won during the Commonwealth {Charles II's portrait}.[f] In the Restoration, Puritanism was eradicated as a cultural trade from the life of the upper classes.

Such a discrepancy between approved ways of life and actual conditions of life would have been catastrophic, but for an important compensatory movement that raised many individuals of the urban class into the ranks of the traditional ruling class and at the same time shifted the financial foundations of the ruling class so as to bring it close to the new capitalist strata.

Still, England's culture may have lost in variety, while gaining in unity, when the urban patriciate finally succumbed in the cultural struggle of the second half of the seventeenth century.

A similar struggle broke out when the urban middle classes of lesser status made their bid for independent personality, some time around the Napoleonic Wars and the age of Dickens. His works are teeming with figures of striking originality of character. Mr. Mantalim, Micawber, and the Cheerible brothers, but above all the incomparable Mr. Pickwick, meant the appearance of an entirely new type of personality on the English scene.

The political and religious sectarian movements of the early nineteenth century abound in Robert Carlisles and William Cobbetts. But this stratum, again, was mediatized after *The Revolution in Tanners Lane*, as described in Mark Rutherford's novel. Again, variety and

[f]Editors' note: Marked in red ink, probably a reminder for an oral development in the lecture.

wealth of personality were sacrificed for the sake of national unity. But this time there was also an important compensating move: the lower middle class, which lost out in the struggle for self-assertion, was financially enabled to secure for itself some of the conditions of life that are required for rural existence. They did not sink to the level of slum dwellers. They possessed their houses in the countryside, their gardens, and the rural amenities that go with them. Rural culture, with them, did not become the ill-fitting clothes of detribalized natives but was assimilated to their (admittedly, somewhat subdued) existence.

But the problem of the industrial working class proved insolvable.

A veritable cultural cataclysm was bound to develop out of the sudden emergence of vast new towns and urban surroundings sans beauty or coherence, indeed lacking the rudiments of human culture. The industrial working class also made a bid for independent cultural existence, in the wonderful Owenite movement and in chartism, but it was beaten.

And this time there was no redeeming counter-movement to raise the workers into the ruling class and at the same time bring the economic basis of class rule nearer to their own conditions of life. Nothing of the sort was even approximately conceivable. The industrial worker was doomed to live in a surrounding and under conditions of life to which the values of a rural existence were simply inapplicable.

10

Experiences in Vienna and
America: America*

The American experience seems to confirm the fact that the social effectiveness of education depends in a definite manner upon social reality.

My American experience is very much more limited than the Austrian. A six-week stay in the Middle West, an eight-week tour of the central and eastern South, as well as a few weeks spent in the East, that is all. But I had the opportunity of short stays at some 30 colleges and universities, as well as of interviews, visits, and so on at high schools (senior grade schools). Incidentally, I was asked to advise on "study plan on social sciences" at a progressive high school in the Middle West and had some official contacts with the Office of Education of the USA in Washington, which introduced me to the federal agencies dealing with the relief of the youth with Civil Conservation Corps and so on.

The well-known and somewhat perplexing paradoxes of the American education may be summed up thus:

(a) fundamentalism – religious tenets enforced by state legislation – complete lack of religious education or teaching in state institutions of any kind whatsoever;
(b) idealist "uplift" – materialist practical philosophy; extreme constitutional traditionalism;

* File 19–26, Karl Polanyi Archive: undated conference, titled "Experiences in Vienna and America."

(c)   experimental creative attitude;
(d)   a measure of superficiality – a very high national average of
      education.

Some Striking Features of the Situation

(A) The complete separation of church and state, enforced in order
to safeguard religious liberty in a deeply religious community, led to
highly paradoxical results in the United States.

Though in some of the fundamentalist states of the USA anybody
is liable to instant dismissal for a mere mention of Darwinism, at the
same time in teacher colleges every vestige of a religious atmosphere
has been removed through a ban on religious teaching enforced by
state authorities. This ban was meant as a safeguard against religious
freedom from secular encroachment, but has resulted in a complete
freedom from religion in the educational field.

Education is thus, in America, practically more secularized than
under the social democratic school reform in Vienna. Conjointly with
a very marked development toward departmentalism in religious
belief, this explains the striking secularization of the thoughts, work,
and life of the whole community, without distinction.

(B) Although throughout public life a very high degree of idealism is
professed, and often practiced, education is *confessedly aimed* at the
purely practical purpose of enabling the young to earn a living as
quickly and efficiently as possible. The "job" is not only the main
concern but also the chief hobby of the young in vacation time. In
fact young boys are traditionally as keen on *jobs* as the grown-ups
are in the depressed areas of England. (Incidentally, imagine the shock
that unemployment must have meant for a school system that sees
its only justification in helping to get jobs for the youth. For what is
the purpose of the school, once the boy cannot get a job, anyway?)
In fact the American educationalist often cannot answer satisfactorily
the question of why a definite subject – a definite mater of no definite
practical value – should be included in the curriculum.

On the other hand, as you will see later on, the idea that school
and education must have a *practical* value works as a strong motive
toward the use of the school as a vehicle of *social cooperation*, an
instrument of developing *new organs* of conscious adaptation to
environment, and so on – and not similar social values of a higher
type.

(C) The task of setting up social *equality* does not fall to the school
in the USA. In common human appreciation, both on the side of the

rich and on that of the poor, *equality is a fact*. So is equality in *speech*, *manners*, *behavior* for some 80 percent of the population (excluding the Negroes). The rich man does not feel socially superior to the not rich, the common citizen does not feel socially inferior to the rich. (Exceptions are of course numerous but do not affect the fundamental facts.) *Thus equality is achieved*; setting for the schools the task of establishing equality would be beside the mark.

On the other hand, the differences of income between different individuals and groups do mark definite social differences between them. Such differences of "belonging to this or that set" are numerous; they correspond to the English social strata. But they are different in character from these.

They are not marks of descent, upbringing, breed, and breeding, but marks of income. You move into a set when your income rises, and you move out of it again when you lose your income – moving into the set corresponding to your present income. Thus *cash* brings the groups together and also separates them again (in a sense). This kind of group distinction is *less deep* and yet *more* brutal and *harsh* than any other. But it is *very much* mitigated by the *fact* that the ups and downs of income are *frequent*, the different members of one and the same family often living at different social levels, according to the set into which their earning capacity falls during a given period.[a] The youngest brother would be a university professor while the oldest one would be a miner, another five or six between them ranging on a sliding scale of income grades and corresponding social sets. Thus friends are often separated by a change in their social sets, but the cleavage is *factual* more than one affecting self-valuation – while in England social cleavage is so deep that, for the sake of appearances, it must in many ways be artificially bridged.

Here again, as in case of the effect of unemployment on the ideals of education, the influence of *actual economic and social conditions* becomes strikingly apparent:

- *actual* unemployment refutes in practice the idea of job-getting school;
- the *actual* frequency of changes in income mitigates very considerably the effect of social differences based on variations in income;
- *actual* employment and an ever-rising standard of life for practically everybody means a justification of the general belief in an

---

[a] Editors' note: Corrected by us from "according to the period into which their earning capacity fell."

order of society that claims to be the freest and most equal and most fair ever conceived.

The understanding of American social thought is impossible without relating it to the actual social conditions obtaining during the period in which this concept of social life was developed. This is the clue to perhaps the most essential trait in the American attitude to society. Thus:

(D) It is only superficially true that the American attitude toward society as a whole is "materialistic" – in that sense where "materialistic" designates a valuation divorced from advancement. In fact the opposite is true. The American is convinced of the fundamental righteousness of the social order. He believes that it has produced the highest degree of material welfare for all, that it affords opportunities for all, in fact that it makes everybody free and equal. In a sense this is true. Thus the American, *disregarding the very important qualifications of this truth, believes* in his society and upholds it as the highest fulfillment of God's purpose on earth. He does this, in a sense, irrespectively of whether he believes in God or not, for his belief in society transcends religion in a paradoxical sense; it is a *direct expression* of his faith in life. His views and opinions about the whole of society must therefore be regarded as equivalent to religious convictions.

The Webbs call the communist regime in Russia a creedocracy. The USA too is, in a wider sense, a creedocracy – only one of a different creed.

(E) The Covenanters founded a *society*, not a *state* or a *nation*. In the USA the *political state* is banished by the constitution to a remote corner in society. It exists only on sufferance and on condition that it will on no account try to gain powers and competences similar to those enjoyed by the European states. Thus society in the USA exists without the props of the political state. The American does not think of society as being supported by or based on the power of the state or of any kind of force whatever. The US federal government has no police powers in home affairs whatever. There is no police. Society is supposed to look after itself. *Anarchy* is here realized.

Social reality is at the back of these educationally decisive social ideals. The general belief in the ultimate validity of the principles of this society is its only support. It is delivering the goods: an unprecedented standard of life and a great equality of chances. After all, there is not more than a small percentage of very rich and more than a moderate percentage of down and outs in the United States, and those are almost all recent immigrants. The rest, the vast majority, are the best fed, best clothed, best housed, and (on average) certainly best educated people in the world. (The economic crisis, although it has made an indentation in the minds and thoughts of the people, has not yet decisively changed this appreciation.) This is the outcome of the experiment started by the Covenanters. It has not yet come to an end. It still continues. This is the meaning of the well-known phrases: "How do you like America?" and: "We are a new country." In America, in these past 150 years, these phrases have meant what they mean in Soviet Russia today and probably in the next two hundred years, namely the attitude of a people taking part in a vast experiment – only with the curious difference that, in the USA, there is a very distinct element of vagueness and uncertainty as to *where all this will lead to*, while in Russia the aim and end seem to be known and fixed (in a manner) *beforehand*. On the whole there is no country more similar to Soviet Russia than the USA – the only other country in modern history that is the outcome of a conscious and deliberate determination to found a society. The real difference between the two is that the Russian effort is on an altogether higher plane.

Yet the USA should not be underestimated, as happens so often in this country.[b] Its obvious weaknesses *are* partly due to its being a "new country." Although the lower layer of educational attainments is low indeed, the average level of the educational attainment of the masses is unprecedentedly high. The experimental attitude, for example, is often regarded as a very much misplaced application of a technologically fruitful principle to the cultural field. But this experimental attitude is only partly due to the American tradition of starting everything anew; partly it expresses a highly positive relatedness of the school to the *task of society building*.

Here we are touching on a very important aspect of the educational task under the conditions given in social reality in America.

1   It was in the nature of the society founded by the Covenanters that the relationship of *individual life and society should be direct and immediate*. The individuals thought of themselves, without the intervention of any kind of authority, bureaucracy, political state, or government. *This is the origin of the extreme plasticity of American society*. There is nothing between the individual and society.

[b]Editors' note: England.

2   Rapid and constant *change* is an outstanding feature of American
    social history. As a rule, the environment changed inside 20 years
    to such a degree as to transform the economic and social function
    of every single element in it completely.

*This is the reason why Americans know more about social change
than any other people in the world* (excluding USSR).

These two facts account for the *constant concern of the American
for the role of the individual* and of the small group of individuals
in the change of the new environment. The plasticity of society and
the fact that *change was the only constant thing* in his experience
account for it. The American knows incomparably more about the
role of the individual and of the small group in social change than
we do. If one day the Americans ceased to believe in their society and
therefore to run it, it would instantly change – for there is nothing
to prevent it from changing.

This is the social background of the belief in the formative value
of education in society in the USA: insofar as education *indoctrinates*
(as the American phrase runs) the child with these ideas and principles, it is, more than in any other country, the *direct formative and
supporting force in society*.

Thus the achievements of American education, from the point of
view of American society and its improvement (if only in the American sense), depend for their effectiveness on two preconditions: on
the existence of given *social ideals*; and on the environmental factor
of *social reality itself*.

Whether we take the Austrian case of an education aiming at a
transformation of society or the US example of an education that,
although progressive, is essentially conservative, the result is the
same.

The possibility of socially effective educational efforts in the
abstract, detached from the concreteness of society, is an illusion.

Part III

How to Make Use of the Social Sciences

11

How to Make Use of
the Social Sciences*

Such a question seems to involve the following points for consideration:

Firstly, what is it in the nature of the sciences that makes it impossible to pool their results in a general scheme of knowledge, on which we could draw whenever there is a need?

Secondly, is there anything in the nature of the social sciences that accounts for the difficulty in making use of them in the same way as we make use of the natural sciences?

Sciences Cannot Be Pooled

The reason for this fact is simple:

Man's innate[a] interest in his environment is the starting point of all the sciences. But every science necessarily restricts its subject matter to such elements in the context of its environment as are susceptible to its method. Consequently the subject matter of the sciences will deviate from the original subject matter of the innate

---

*File 19–1, Karl Polanyi Archive: undated typescript, probably written after 1939 (the publication date of Lynd's book from which Polanyi quotes here establishes a *terminus post quem*). The lateral sides of the typescript have deteriorated and quite a few words have been lost in a tear, but in most cases their reconstruction is fairly certain.

[a]Editors' note: Throughout this essay Polanyi constantly uses the word *native*; but it's clear that his intended meaning corresponds best to *innate* – and in a few places it also comes close to *natural*.

interest – the matrix. That is why physics, chemistry, and psychology[b] do not "add up" to the model of a cat; nor can mathematics and botany, between them, produce the complete pattern of a meadow.

It is an intriguing question how the various sciences can deviate from the matrix in different and undefinable directions and yet describe true facts. But the origins of science in an innate interest account for this, too; man seeks guidance for his conduct in many different ways and in relation to many different aspects of his environment. In other words, both the innate interest and the matrix are composites. Scientific interest and scientific subject matter are the results of a process of mutual selective adjustment between the factors comprised in innate interest and the elements that form the matrix. Eventually a method is evolved through which some elements of the matrix are ordered in such a manner as to satisfy some factors of the innate interest, either through convenient classification or through direct prediction. In the course of this process of adjustment the sciences tend to become increasingly "selective" – or, with a more usual term, abstract, restricting themselves to elements adapted to their methods. Although [c]. . .[c] of them represents true facts, the various segments of the truth tend to resemble one another less and less.

Method is the key to what science can do and what it cannot; it is the general rule applicable to the operations constituting a particular science. That which is selected as its subject matter and that which is eliminated from it as "unscientific" matter are differentiated by method. It is to method that sciences are indebted for their definitions, and therefore for their grip on the elements selected, as well as for the rejection of that part of the matrix which now appears as "metaphysical."

Science is, by method, out of matrix.[d] The birth of a science destroys the matrix in which it was conceived. Metaphysics is the remnant of the matrix surviving in incomplete science. To become a science, mathematics, for instance, eliminated the magic of numbers; physics rid itself of "matter"; chemistry shed[e] alchemy; physiology eliminated the "life force"; logic divested itself of "truth." To the

[b]Editors' note: Conjectural. This word starts with a typo of a frequent type (the possible inversion *pys-* for *psy-*), and the rest is lost in a lacuna.

[c]Editors' note: Lacuna in original. This page corner is unfortunately lost, and the first letter (very smudged) of what's missing here could be *o*, *s*, or *a*.

[d]Editors' note: This cryptic sentence probably means that science evolves out of its matrix with the help of method.

[e]Editors' note: Our conjecture – only the sequence *she* visible.

extent that sciences are able to achieve this feat, they rank as theoretical sciences. The more mature they become, the farther they wander from the matrix.

Now, while all this has for some time been recognized in relation to the natural sciences, it appears much less obvious with respect to the social sciences. And yet the development of some of these sciences is strikingly similar to that of the natural sciences. The social sciences also start from our innate interest in the job of living, and only gradually attain that stage of development at which interest and subject matter are mutually adjusted through method. In the course of this process of adjustment those elements of the matrix that are intractable from the point of view of the method fade out, leaving only those elements that form part of the "situation," as determined *not* by innate interest but by the strict application of the method in question. It may then appear that psychology is not concerned with subjective states of mind; that economics is not about production or gain; that politics is not the art of government. In this manner psychology may cease to be the science of the human soul; economics may cease to be the science of wealth and value; politics may cease to be the science of sovereignty.

Soul, value, sovereignty – these remnants of the matrix have no place left for them. Psychology may now redefine its field as that of behavior; economics, as that of choice; politics, as that of power; and so forth. The completed sciences will sometimes have no more than a historical reference to the original matrix. Moreover, after slimming almost to vanishing point, they may expand again in unexpected directions. Psychology may incorporate the behavior of animals and plants; economics may apply to ethical, esthetic, or religious situations indifferently, as long as they contain the crucial element of allocation of scarce means; politics may comprise any group in situations that give rise to power. And here, also, the more advanced the sciences are, the more completely they will tend to separate the various elements of the matrix from one another. Thus the social sciences as much as the natural sciences, in order to be effective, get differentiated from one another and distort methodologically the picture of the environmental universe to which man adjusts in the immediate task of living.

Incidentally, we did not trouble to define the natural and the social sciences more particularly but simply accepted the usual grouping of the disciplines. That distinction should always be regarded as relative to the question under discussion. The most stable line of demarcation between various disciplines appears to be that between purely historical sciences, which deal with the unique and nonrecurrent aspects of nature *and* society, and sciences dealing with generalizations such as laws or other abstractions. An even more important division, but of a broader kind, refers to *all* human experience. It would tend to put science on the one side and all nonscientific awareness of our environment, as it occurs in the course of living, on the other – whether such awareness would otherwise be described as artistic, moral, poetic, religious, personal, or simply as naive experience. Neither of these distinctions is, however, vital at this stage, as our introductory analysis of the nature of science has sufficiently shown why the cooperation of the social sciences, just like that of the natural sciences, cannot be sought through *fusion*, on the line of popular demands[f] such as "economics should be more political, political science more economic." The widely held view that the various social sciences should be "less abstract and one-sided" and should thus help to link the different spheres of practical interest is a serious fallacy, not uncommon even among eminent writers. Thorstein Veblen, himself an ardent positivist, actually reproached the economists for *not* being interested in value, an obviously metaphysical concept. More remarkably still, two decades later Robert Lynd still quoted Veblen's stricture with approval! In the natural sciences consciousness of method was achieved very much earlier. The elimination of metaphysics progressed greatly during the second half of the nineteenth century, in the period separating Robert Julius Meyer from Ernst Mach, but no serious scientist is known to have clamored for the reinstatement of the metaphysical concepts of "matter," "virtual motion," or "absolute space" into the science of physics. Not fusion of the conceptual instruments of theory, but either the creation of a new science or the application of the existing – separate and distinct – sciences to a specific task is the solution. For example: economic and political motives; economic and political institutions; economic and political power can be separated only with difficulty in practice. In premodern societies economic and political institutions actually formed a unity, and even after they had been differentiated into separate institutional bodies interaction was close and continuous. But does this imply, as is being overtly and covertly asserted, that the sciences of politics and economics should somehow be *fused* – two disciplines as different with respect to their subject matter and method as law and embryology? The right answer can be found only in one of two ways:

[f]Editors' note: Or possibly *desiderata*: after "de-," the remaining part of this word is lost.

One is the creation of sciences more closely related to the subject matter of special interest than the existing ones. The relations between economics and politics, for example, are dealt with by various disciplines such as historical sociology, anthropology, and general sociology. Numerous sciences such as biochemistry or criminology came into existence in response to similar needs. There is no valid reason why this progress of scientific specialization should not proceed indefinitely. Whether a science will or will not emerge is a question of factual success, depending primarily upon how far a method can be found that will deal adequately with the circumstances concerning which guidance is sought.

Or the demand may be for an ad hoc cooperation of existing sciences by applying them to definite problems. There is, in principle, no reason why the social sciences should not cooperate in the same fashion as the natural sciences in the solution of practical problems. The use of the sciences of statistics, law, and economics in the mapping of a new branch of social insurance is an instance of such cooperation; they could be indefinitely multiplied.

To sum up, sciences cannot be pooled. This is as true of the natural sciences as it is of the social sciences. The characteristic of science, namely that it proceeds through the elimination of the metaphysical element and secures its grip on the facts by following up the peculiarity of its method, applies to *all* science. If the practical usefulness of the natural sciences has proved so much greater than that of the social sciences, this cannot be due to the lack of a "continuum of knowledge" (Robert Lynd)[g] in social matters, for the natural sciences too lack such a "continuum." From the point of view of method the social sciences are hardly inferior to the natural sciences. It is elsewhere that we must look for the reason for the greater practical usefulness of the natural sciences.

The Sovereignty of Man over Sciences

It is most plausibly argued that the practical successes of the natural sciences are simply the result of the superior validity and precision of the knowledge they yield. Certainly this is to a large extent true. And yet it is doubtful whether this explanation does not cover up rather than reveal the essential features of the position.

That the natural sciences can be used for the purposes of medicine, technology, and so on is, inter alia, due to the fact that man's attitude

[g]Editors' note: Our addition (see reference to Lynd below).

toward his material environment is directed by definite ends, which are but little influenced by the rise of these sciences. The development of mathematical physics or biochemistry has, fortunately, not undermined man's interest in his health, in the safe crossing of chasms, and so forth. Thus it is possible to pool the results of the various sciences, *not* in a "continuum of knowledge," but in a *sheaf* of different *techniques* cooperating toward the same ends.[h] Though the theory of relativity may have abolished space and time as nonscientific man understood them, he still wants to be able to cross a river without the risk of drowning. Agreement on the practical issues, a consensus unaffected by the proceedings of the sciences themselves, was the given condition of the successful use of the natural sciences in the advancement of technology or medicine.

Precisely the opposite was the case with regard to the social sciences. Man has hardly a wish or purpose with respect to his social environment that does not contain elements of ambiguity suggestive of conflicting conduct. The social sciences have in fact a *dual* function, and their usefulness must be judged by the balance of their achievements in both directions: it is not enough to inquire how far they assist us in attaining our ends; we must also ask how far they help or *hinder us* in clarifying them. Until recently, in effect, the attempt to clarify our conflicting wishes and ideals was almost the sole aim of the social sciences. It is human to crave for ends as opposite as "security and risk, coherence and spontaneity, novelty and latency, rivalry and mutuality" in one and the same "rhythm of living," as Lynd put it recently.[i] We can add that man will crave for liberty and equality, for freedom and order, and other mutually exclusive ideals while seeking guidance on matters as diverse and complex as sex and war, crime and tradition, fashion and business, education and ecstasy. It is almost a miracle that he can make up his mind at all, *even when unhampered by the unsettling effects of scientific analysis on the conventional background of his judgment*. The crux of the matter is that, while the social sciences may have enhanced man's ability to attain his ends, they certainly diminished his faculty of knowing what they are.

For indisputably the social sciences have a massive influence on man's wishes and purposes. Take the impact of the popular sciences on the popular phenomena of economics, sex, morals, and politics in our time. Some assertions tended to be actually question begging

[h] Editors' note: This last word, *ends*, is lost in the page tear.
[i] Editors' note: Robert Lynd, *Knowledge for What? The Place of Social Science in American Culture* (Princeton, NJ: Princeton University Press, 1970 [1939]), p. 42.

in a rather unexpected way, by creating the very phenomena on the existence of which they were insisting – such as a utilitarian psychology in the businessman, sex consciousness in psychoanalyzed persons, or class consciousness in social groups. Others, again, tended to be self-refuting, such as the assertions concerning the psychology of propaganda or of the slump, cancelling, so to speak, the actions of the very laws they alleged to have discovered. But the most important effect of the social sciences, we submit, lay in the direction in which their influence was cumulative, namely in creating confusion in the minds with regard to the values underlying social adjustments.

To some degree such an effect was inevitable.

The elimination from natural sciences of the concepts of force, substance, matter, of ghosts and goblins, of the magic of numbers, of the illusion of the flatness of the earth, or of the simple nature of space and time did not necessarily disturb man in his job of living; in spite of Newton, Darwin, and Einstein, he continued to behave – in relation to space, time, and gravitation, wild animals and the surface of mother earth – very much like before. We do not wish to deny that some of the suggestions made by science caused perplexity, and even confusion. Traditional responses with regard to ghosts, the shape of the earth, and the stability of animal species turned out to be intimately related to theological dogmas that had a direct bearing on social existence; consequently, major adjustments had to be made. But ultimately these social adjustments were made, as the evident practical usefulness of the natural sciences worked decisively in favor of the reorientation of theological ideas. However, that the natural sciences were as useful as we assumed proved sufficiently that man's practical purposes had been but little affected by them. Man still wished weights to be lifted; sickness healed; rivers crossed without too much inconvenience. And the sciences themselves did not suggest to him that he should wish otherwise.

The gradual progress of the social sciences toward methodological purity involved a similar elimination of metaphysical remnants from the scope of these sciences. But the respective roles played by these elements in society and nature were very different: rivers run their course whatever we think of space, time, and gravitation; changes in our concepts of nature do not affect the laws of nature appreciably. On the other hand, changes in our concepts of society affect the laws governing social existence radically. Also, while natural science does not threaten the clarity of our practical purposes, the social sciences may very well do so, unless our directive values are deliberately protected from corrosive influence as the Roentgen manipulator's hands are from the effects of X rays.

In other words: man's life is a process of adjustment directed toward an environmental universe that consists precisely of the elements of the matrix that science tends to eliminate as metaphysical. Hence the opprobrium attaching to metaphysics when it[j] can be shown up as the hopeless attempt of anti-scientific forces to compete with science through a vain conceptualization of those elements. But hence also the dignity of metaphysics in its insistence on the comprehensive character of common human awareness as the matrix of art, religion, morality, personal life, and science. In order to use science as an instrument, the matrix and the innate interest of life – or, in conceptualized form, the valuations of life – must be maintained, out of which science arose, the difficulty being that the social sciences naturally tend to influence these valuations themselves.

The implications of such a postulate must make us halt. Can the matrix of science be preserved without interfering with the progress of science, or at least with its choice of the most effective method of pursuing its aims? Should a conservation of the matrix be sought at all cost, or is it not rather to be desired that our wishes and purposes themselves should be clarified and ennobled in the light of science? How should mankind progress, if we are to exclude the influence of science on the core of life? And yet, how should these instruments of enlightenment be secured without confusing the ends of life in the process? Is a creative compromise possible, which would leave scope for progress, while protecting us from the danger of losing our way in our search for it? And, if so, what are the requirements of such a directed progress?

The answer to these questions would involve no less than the critique of a civilization practicing the indiscriminate use of science and the wholesale disregard for the essentially different ways in which knowledge affects man. The abstraction "all knowledge is good" is as vague as the maxim that "all freedom is good" or that "all order is good." One of the most recent examples of the dangers of the propaganda of science is the use made by fascism of the attitude of scientific skepticism with regard to human ideals. By a slight *leger de main*,[k] the general methodological postulate of skepticism is transformed into a material doubt of the validity of these ideals. The typical progressist is thrown into a veritable panic today by the realization of the ambiguous effects of such a use of the social sciences on all but those who have trained themselves to withstand them. The answer lies in the courageous facing up to the issue, which implies

[j]Editors' note: I.e. metaphysics.
[k]Editors' note: *Leger* is yet another word lost in the torn margin of the manuscript.

no less than the transcending of the liberal axiom of the indiscriminate usefulness of all types of knowledge.

If we know one thing about knowledge, it is the fact that some types of knowledge affect man's life radically and immediately, while other types are merely instrumental in the sense of serving his formulated ends and aims. The distinction is basic. While the broadcasting of instrumental knowledge should be fostered through all the means at the disposal of the community, knowledge that, by its nature, might be destructive of man's external and internal life should be handled under the intellectual safeguards of social responsibility where education or medicine is concerned. It is through a mature comprehension of the relation of man to science that the fascist reaction against an abstract liberalism in the handling of knowledge must be forestalled.

In a time of rapid growth and decreasing existential pressure, lack of clarity about man's end and aims in life may pass unnoticed, or may even be felt advantageous in facilitating swift adjustment. Yet, more or less unconsciously, the community is even then aware of the high price it is paying for the ease of transition and remains vaguely suspicious of the very sciences to the authority of which it owes lip service. Of this there is convincing proof. Let us suppose an emergency call on the community for a clear and categorical definition of its basic values, and the world stands aghast at the vehemence of the reaction against the disintegrating influence of the sciences. We agree with Koffka's penetrating remark on the subject: "The denunciation of the intellect which has assumed such tremendous proportions in some part of our world with such far-reaching consequences, seems to me the outcome of the wrong scientific attitude, although for that reason it is no less wrong itself."[1]

One thing is certain: whatever safeguards the mind will devise to protect itself against the dangers of the scientific handling of human affairs, their purpose cannot be to stop human progress, either collectively or in terms of the individual himself. Man will continue to change, and one of the main factors in this change will be, and should be, the impact of the social sciences. Thus, inevitably, innate interest will evolve, and man will not remain what he was.

It is at this point in our discourse that the need for a directed existence looms large. Unless man can define his destiny, he cannot hope to master it. Unless his social purpose is present in the individual man, he cannot assimilate the new knowledge without losing his way.

[1] Editors' note: Kurt Koffka, *Principles of Gestalt Psychology* (London: Lund Humphries, 1935), Ch. 1: "Why Psychology?" section "The Danger of Science."

Unless his interest in life and the universe fixes for him the direction in which his own evolution shall proceed, it is vain to expect that he can remain master of his own changing nature and not lose his grip on life.

The use of the social sciences is not a technical problem of science. It is a matter of providing such a definition of the meaning of human society as will maintain the sovereignty of man over all instruments of life, including science.

12

On Political Theory*

It might seem far-fetched to introduce the discussion of the theory of politics through a survey of scientific disciplines in general. However, I hope this will appear justified in the sequence.

All scientific disciplines, whether they be akin to physics or to politics, owe their existence to the conjuncture of three entirely independent factors: a human interest in some "corner" of the universe; a method that is suitable to form definite elements into a pattern; finally, the presence of such elements in the "corner" toward which interest is turned. The discipline registers the regularities shown by the pattern to be existing in the element.

The emphasis is on the independence of the factors. None is a function of any other. *Interests* form part of man's original equipment; most people are interested in nature, glory, love, secrets, or fate; some in mathematical series; all in matters of everyday life. *Methods* are rules applicable to operations concerned with definite elements; innumerable rules of this sort may be devised, but only few will produce a pattern. Finally, there are the *elements* themselves and their actual distribution in the universe. Obviously it is a matter of chance whether a method produces a pattern or not and, if it does so, whether the elements thus patterned out occur in a region toward which human interest happen to be directed. Yet, unless the three factors coincide, no science can emerge.

Mendelism is an example, in natural science, of method meeting the conditions that lead to unpredictable success. The crossing of peas

*File 18-40, Karl Polanyi Archive: undated typescript.

of various kinds according to definite rules of operation happened to produce a numerical pattern. Even so, the method could not have resulted in the establishment of a scientific discipline if we had no interest at all in the phenomenon of heredity.

Or take in the field of social sciences: the device of choosing from scarce[a] means according to a scale of priority. When applied to markets, this otherwise useless method produced a pattern that revealed highly complex regularities in the various kinds of prices. And yet this astonishing result would not have led to the creation of the discipline of theoretical economics were it not for the interest attached to the phenomenon of prices in a market economy. Without it, the regularities shown by the pattern would have been †hardly even of . . .‡[b]

Let us apply this to political theory. The interest that is designed to satisfy centers roughly on the body politic. The method that brought it into existence is the rule of reason. The elements that thus come into view form part of the individuals on the one hand, of the common good on the other.

We will have to show how a theory was constructed on these foundations. Throughout we will rely in our inquiry on the threefold determination of the structure of science.

Before we proceed to do so, some remarks on the nature of the three factors may be in place.

(1) Few sciences, unfortunately, respond to the direction of our *interest*. They simply do not answer the question. They merely get near enough to the object of interest or circumscribe it with sufficient clarity to satisfy *some* of our curiosity. Very few disciplines are as much to the point as that part of mathematics called arithmetic, which tells us how much 2×2 is. We should also like to know, naturally, what gravitation is. Yet physicists keep telling us that the question is meaningless. And so we put up with what they *can* tell us (which may satisfy some of our interests completely, some partially, but leaves our original interest unsatisfied).

The same may be true of political theory. Nothing is probably more natural to man than interest in his position in the community, in the good and evil that comes from government, in right and wrong in public affairs, in the prospects of communal welfare and of his

---

[a] Editors' note: This conjecture is not very certain: the word typed here is not very legible and probably has a typo (it looks like "cscrace" or "csorace").
[b] Editors' note: This sentence, added in the author's hand, is heavily corrected and mutilated; the end is lost in a tear at the bottom of the page.

own share in it. Nothing, accordingly, could be more welcome to him than reliable knowledge about what to do and what to avoid in order to make both the community and himself happier. He would like to know how to vote; how long the government will be in; what foreign policy it should support. It is better, anyway, to have to resign himself to the fact that there is no science that could tell him all that.

He must put up with a second or even third best and be content if he can gain some clarity on the nature of his position in society, learn, in brief, anything that is relevant. Even that may be useful to him. Again, what exactly is relevant depends on the precise nature of the interest – which natural science rashly assumes to be cognitive, in the sense that "we want to know something."

But neither the word "want," nor the word "know," nor the word "something" should be taken in its precise sense. Actually our interest may reflect no more than a hitch in the process of living, which cannot be formulated as a question and therefore cannot, strictly speaking, be answered. At this sub-inquisitive stage we are not yet interested in "something," nor do we "want" anything; even less would it be accurate to say that what we desire is to "know." Everything depends on the situation. Even assuming our interest to have reached the intellectual level, it still may be no more than a wish to discover some indication of how to behave so as to get rid of the cause of the interest – a very different thing from a "thirst for knowledge." The notion that a numerical statement about measurable quantities is the ideal answer to any question is simply the physicist's way of saying that any interest that is not directed toward such an answer should be discounted. Indeed, in the case of political theory, the questions themselves are ridiculed as meaningless. This, however, is only another instance of the proved incapacity of the scientific mind to understand human problems. It[c] maintains that the method, used arbitrarily, defines the body politic and leaves in effect no room for investigation. But this means to leave out the "third dimension" of science, namely interest. If "knowledge" about "something" were everything, then nothing could be learnt about such things. But the same, accidentally, would be true of mathematics, without entailing either its uselessness or its unscientific character. Actually, neither political theory nor mathematics is useless, only their uses are not always obvious.

[c]Editors' note: I.e. the scientific mind. "It" in corrected (in handwriting) from "He" (probably Polanyi was thinking of "the scientist," but this word was nowhere in context).

Political theory, however, caters not so much for interest in knowing what the body politic is as for interest in living in it.

(2) The rule of reason consists in relating individual behavior to the common good. This is implied in the postulate that the common good be the "purpose" of that behavior. When applied to an empirical society, such an assumption seems singularly vague. The common good may be taken to refer to matters as different as the glory of the nation, the survival of an existing society, the welfare of individuals, the freedom of public life, the maintenance of the covenant with God, or a favorable balance of trade. Behavior of the individuals, again, is a no less inclusive term. It comprises the whole sphere of their private and public life, viewed from any conceivable angle. Now the rule of reason demands that, in every case, the "common good" be the purpose of their "behavior."

Such a postulate would be in effect meaningless, unless it was taken to imply that (1) behavior is determined by "motives" (for in no other way can "purpose" enter into behavior); and (2) the "common good" is a definite state of affairs (otherwise it cannot be the aim of the purpose). Even so, the application of the method remains uncomfortably hazy.

Without further explicit definition that would indicate which elements of the common good can be related to which individual motives, the rule of reason would appear to result in no recognizable pattern at all.

(3) The distribution of the *elements* supplies the answer. Let us take examples from the field of nature and society. A man has an interest in audition.[d] Most of it is, of course, practical: in conversation, or in listening to music, we indulge in this interest. But much of it is cognitive; it appeals to an intellectual curiosity that yearns for explanations and predictions. But even this cognitive strength of the interest turns toward a specious "corner" of the universe, where a variety of elements are hiding. "Hearing" may link sound with human anatomy and produce the discipline of physiology of the senses; it may deal with "sound" and the measurable space and time, which physics has so successfully explored; it may refer to "music" and the laws of harmony; it may turn toward the history of musical instruments, or toward the technique of operatic singing. Each time, a different set of elements appears on the scene.[e] Live sounds, together with parts of the human anatomy in the physiology of the senses; masse, space, and tone in acoustics; musical notes in the theory of

---

[d]Editors' note: Polanyi uses here *audition* in the archaic sense of "power of hearing."
[e]Editors' note: Typo here in the original (*screne*) but his meaning is clear.

harmony; artifact, manufacture in the history of musical instruments; orchestra and the organs of the body in vocal training. Sound hearing, song, music, and human speech are all huddled together in that corner of the universe to which our interest faces; and yet, as the searchlight of one method after another is turned on this region, different elements come into view. The strands of interest also intermingle in the most varied ways. While each separate discipline satisfies some of it, none satisfies it completely, nor perhaps do they do so together. Indeed our original interest does not only direct the beams of the searchlight, but also combines the results of this operation. As long as that interest has not been impaired, it can perform the vital function of putting to use the results of the various disciplines. Without this it would not be possible to apply theoretical knowledge to empirical reality.

The social sciences turn toward the human work, which occupies an altogether different place in our consciousness from that of nature. Much has been made of the fact that the elements of nature and society are largely identical; our physical body, our sensations and appetites, indeed even our mental faculties are such as may connect our world with that of the minerals, plants, and animals. It has been overlooked that, although this may be true and indeed explains why some parts of the human world could be satisfactorily explored with the help of methods rightly described as those of natural science, the character of the interest is utterly different. The job of living arises here with an immediacy unknown in the field of the natural sciences, and even if cases of similar urgency can be found there, the meaning of living is itself different. However, the formal analogy of nature and society holds insofar as in both cases there is a distribution of variegated elements, susceptible to a number of disciplines.

What are these disciplines and what is their relation to political theory?[f]

Human society is, of course, primarily of practical, not merely of theoretical interest to man.

The various scientific disciplines concerned with human society are mainly the different branches of sociology, anthropology, political science, economics, and statistics. Although they are all concerned with the human community, with interpersonal relations, with group history and group life, with regularities observable in man's behavior in society, yet the actual elements made visible in them are different,

[f]Editors' note: This question is followed by a subheading which has been entirely deleted in the original typescript.

or at least they are related in a different fashion. Even the distribution of the same elements varies enormously, if sociometry is compared to law or ecology to the theory of sovereignty. But one of the most peculiar of all disciplines is political theory.

Interest is here narrowed down to that which the rule of reason can pattern out of the body politic. Only that, in the individual, shows up that is volition directed toward the common good – the latter being a state of affairs such as can be an object of human purpose. The individual is here a mere idealized shadow of himself – a citizen whose volition is determined by civic virtue. Conversely, service of the common good is legitimate, since it is rooted in the will of the citizens. Sovereignty appears as a function of individual freedom. Civic rights and public duties, as well as the hierarchy of legitimate power, form part of a pattern that has gained clarity and finiteness at the price of shading all other elements of social reality except those encompassed by the rule of reason. It is a gaunt structure, as empty as mathematics.

And yet no discipline is perhaps more vital – as we will see – to the survival of organized society than political theory, without which no progressive human community is indeed possible. For, the more general its proposition, the wider is applicability. However, it remains to be shown how such an application of theoretical propositions to empirical reality is possible at all.[g]

The answer, again, lies in the "third dimension" of science: the interests that give rise to it. Human interest is not simple but complex. Strands of interest intermingle in the most varied ways. Numberless interests of various character, tone, and intensity combine in the apparently simple "interest" with which we turn toward our "corner" of the universe. Now, the elements of reality existing in that region are dispersed in a manner that is utterly unpredictable. The pattern produced by the methods applied to those elements is also unpredictable.

Now this comprehensive interest has the quality of persistence. It does not disappear after having given birth to a scientific discipline. It continues to be active, its main function being to make use of the results obtained in the various disciplines. Although each method separates out a distinct pattern in "the region of interest," the interest, by virtue of the strands contained in it, is capable of relating the patterns to one another and thus of putting together again that which was separated through the methods employed.

[g]Editors' note: The top of this page is torn, so that the words "to be" and the best part of "empirical" are lost; their reconstruction is, however, unproblematic.

13

Public Opinion and Statesmanship*

The problem of the politician-statesman, which is touched upon in the following remarks, is brought in to illustrate the manner in which public opinion research may be employed very usefully, even if indirectly, in the service of the historian; indirectly, since the assistance would be rendered primarily not so much to the historian as to his collaborator, the sociologist of history.

Of all adventure stories, one of the most exciting and – assuredly – one of the most stirring is that of the victory of the great statesman over a narrow and recalcitrant public opinion. Historiography knows of no nobler subject. At the same time there are but few contemporary events concerning which the pollster can more readily draw on otherwise unprocurable facts. For the *peripeteiai*[a] of public opinion connected with the triumph of true statesmanship over common-run politics play precisely on that area of opinion formation where his research technique can claim precedence over all others. And so, in all seriousness, the question may arise as to whether public opinion surveying should not shoulder the task of attempting to provide the future historian with a clue to some of those unexpected changes of opinion that have made history. Or, to dramatize the subject as it is

* File 36–4, Karl Polanyi Archive: address delivered before the American Association for Public Opinion Research Princeton, NJ, on June 22, 1951.
[a] Editors' note: Polanyi uses here (ironically) a term of art from Aristotle's poetics: *peripeteia* (plural *peripeteiai*). *Peripeteia* was the reversal of fortune that marks the turning point in a literary plot – and, by extension, it can designate spectacular or adventurous reversals in real life too.

the historian's privilege to do, what can the pollster contribute to the unveiling of the secret of heroic statesmanship?

Now, the historian deals with history as a definite event that occurred at a definite time and place. His statesman is a singular, concrete figure; and what he wishes to ascertain is how this man solved his problem. Theories about the nature of statesmanship – whether produced by others, or even by himself – are, for him, no more than accessories. For the hub of his interest remains the singular case. In sharp contrast to this, the typical figure of the statesman belongs in the realm of the sociologist of history. For him, the task[b] is to investigate the conditions in a society that make great statesmanship possible – and to inquire into the objective criteria of the success stories of those statesmen-politicians whom posterity ranked in this special class of eminence. Yet the sociologist's generalizations are not restricted to drawing from the historian's data. His field encompasses the liveborn and the stillborn events, those that lived in the consciousness of contemporaries and those that never achieved the dignity of historicalness, no less factual though they were than those rescued from limbo by Klio's pen. The sociology of statesmanship, similarly to the sociology of war and peace, of revolution and evolution, deals essentially with the laws of society. Eventually the sociology of history never loses touch with past actuality, and thus with the human interest that attaches to history; nevertheless it is not, by itself, an historical but a sociological discipline.

Before we define more closely the sociological problem of statesmanship as we understand it here, let us briefly recall the illuminated plates of the chronicle in which the statesman's picture is drawn by the sympathetic historian. It is this flamboyant portrait that inspires the imagination of the young, sustains the endeavor of the mature, and ultimately sets a meaning upon the featureless account of the ages. It is against this background of life and meaning that the bare skeleton of the sociological problem will eventually be viewed here.

The historian's figure of the statesman stands out, drawn in almost superhuman proportions. Here is the man who, towering above the crowd of run-of-the-mill politicians, serves his country's true and permanent interests at a crucial moment. His reward is the gratitude of a nation, maybe a tragic prize that he hardly lives to grasp. His means of achieving the grand purpose are superior courage and superior insight. Nations, great and small, have their Solons,

---

[b]Editors' note: The original reads here *it*; this, we gather, must be its referent.

Themistocles, and Aristeides; their Churchills, Lenins, and Weitzmans; their Smuts, Gandhis, and Abraham Lincolns. Each of these was a politician – and remained a politician – yet eventually, owing to his moral courage and political wisdom, each one managed to be a statesman whose name, resplendent of victory, is enshrined in the hearts of a whole people. And the formula for victory, too, is familiar: long, arduous, and seemingly hopeless struggle against public opinion, until unexpectedly the miracle of success intervenes.

The bare bones of the problem are here displayed. The statesman started as a politician. He rose to power through the favor of public opinion. This fact limited his effectiveness to conditions set by the climate of opinion that made his rise possible. Yet eventually we see him achieving a political feat that presupposes an entirely different climate, in which public opinion seems to have veered round by hundred and eighty degrees. However, the one thing that, on our assumption, a politician could not attain was to change the climate of opinion itself to which he owed his success. We are left with the question: What made the politically impossible historically possible? And what was the sociological mechanism of this piece of white magic? Clearly, we are facing here a scientific problem of public opinion research.

The answer is to be sought in the total structure of opinion: public opinion in the narrower sense, together with that much less changeable underlying phenomenon, the climate of opinion. Public opinion proper, by which we usually mean the surface pattern of beliefs and emotions in which the mass is organized, is always ambivalent: its reaction to any stimulus may be either positive or negative. By positive we mean here the direction in which the statesman himself happens to seek the ultimate solution; by negative we mean the opposite direction. A psychological stimulus such as a sensational warning, a passionate exhortation, an immediate threat, a sudden easing of the outlook or its aggravation – practically everything within the range of a politician's activities – may have, in principle, two different and contrary effects on opinion. Even deliberate propaganda has sometimes an effect opposite to the one intended. Which of the opposites will occur must ultimately depend on objective circumstances, which structure the situation. As long as the circumstances are what they are, the superficial field of opinion will continue to react by going in one and the same direction. In one instance, almost any stimulus will have a more or less positive effect; in the other, a negative effect.

The element by which the superficial pattern of public opinion is related to the objective circumstances that structure the situation is that deeper layer that has been called the climate of opinion. The sociology of the climate of opinion must provide us with the postulated link between the ambivalent surface opinion and the objectively structured situation.

What distinguishes the statesman from the mere politician is his superior understanding of the objective situation, and thereby also of the climate of opinion. While both he and the politician are limited, in their fight, to the sphere of surface opinion, the statesman consciously acts on surface opinion for the purpose of changing the situation – not only to maintain himself in power (as every politician must), but for aims that transcend the political sense. Briefly, he attempts to use his power partly to organize the public for the interim period until conditions change, partly (if at all possible) to bring about himself some favourable change in the conditions. Small though the change may be, it may just suffice to shift the climate of opinion and thus to give the political stimuli opposite effects, eventually releasing the pent-up flood of *positive reactions*.

As for examples, I will take them from Greek antiquity. Solon, Themistocles, and Aristeides rank among the greatest politician-statesmen of Athenian democracy. You will readily see how little[c] the basic laws of social action are affected by the lapse of time. Franklin Roosevelt at his height bears a close resemblance to Solon in his memorable archonship.

Solon, a man of aristocratic extraction but of middle-class ways, was elected to the position of chief executive, as an arbitrator vested with dictatorial powers, at the height of an unprecedented total crisis of the political and economic life of the Athenian city-state. A free population was literally sinking into debt bondage and enslavement. Bloody strife was on the move, threating to engulf the community: on the one hand, the threat of mob rule and of the expropriation of all landed classes; on the other, the immediate threat of a massacre of the common people under a regime of white terror. In either case, the ruin of the state. Solon, with his genius for publicity, put his political program in verse and introduced it by the following words, as reported by Demosthenes:[d]

> Lo, even now there cometh upon the whole city a plague which none may escape. The people have come quickly into degrading bondage; bondage rouseth from their sleep war and civil strife; and war destroyed many in the beauty of their youth. As if she were the prey of foreign

[c]Editors' note: Polanyi wrote here, arguably by mistake, *how like.*
[d]Editors' note: Demosthenes 19 ("On the False Embassy"), 254 ff.

foes, our beloved city is rapidly wasted and consumed . . . Thus public calamity cometh to the house of every individual, and a man is no longer safe within the gates of his own court . . .

Aristotle's account of the events makes it clear that the chief trouble was psychological and moral: the mass of the people, sunken into shameful debt bondage, were afraid to stand up for their constitutional rights. Solon first stopped famine conditions through an embargo on the export of corn; secondly, he proclaimed a disburdening of private and public debts, which were anyway hardly enforceable. With these measures, he restored the popular forces physically and morally. Eventually it was these *relief* measures that made it possible for him to steer a middle course of *reform* and to change the constitution only to an extent that was still tolerable to the propertied classes, so that they resigned themselves to their loss of privilege while they retained their property. Then only, in a less partisan atmosphere created by the great political compromise, did Solon proceed to those *reconstruction* policies in relation to the currency – a change in weights and measures that objectively improved the long-term balance of the country and – after a generation of transition – put Athens on a new foundation.

A hundred years later, Themistocles, foreseeing a Persian revanche in spite of the brilliant victory won by the Greeks over the Persians at Marathon in 490 BC, was full of apprehension for the military safety of the country. Plutarch relates:[e]

Now the rest of his countrymen thought that the defeat of the Barbarians at Marathon was the end of the war; but Themistocles thought it to be only the beginning of greater contests, and for these he anointed himself, as it were, to be the champion of all Hellas, and put his city into training, because, while it was yet far off, he expected the evil that was to come.

And so, in the first place, whereas the Athenians were wont to *divide up among themselves* the revenue coming form the silver mines at Laureion, he, and he alone, *dared to come before the people with a motion that this division be given up*, and that with these moneys triremes be constructed for the war against (the neighbouring island of) Aegina. This was the fiercest war then troubling Hellas, and the islanders controlled the sea, owing to the number of their ships. Where all the more easily did Themistocles carry his point, not by trying to terrify the citizens with dreadful pictures of Darius or

[e]Editors' note: Plutarch, *Life of Themistocles*, 4.3–4.3.

the Persians – these were too far away and inspired no very serious fear of their coming, but by making opportune use of the bitter jealously which they cherished toward Aegina in order to secure the armament he desired. The result was that with those moneys they built a hundred triremes, with which they actually fought at Salamis against Xerxes.

According to one version, Themistocles tried to sell his plans in still another way. He suggested that the windfall silver be entrusted to the "wealthiest" citizens – dollar-a-year men[f] – who would safety return it to the people unless they had used it within a year for a satisfactory public purpose. Meanwhile the international situation became more and more acute, the climate of opinion changed; and the fleet was built that saved Athens at Salamis only one year later.

Lastly: only one year after Salamis Aristeides, Themistocles' great rival in statesmanship and a conservative politician, came out with a no less far-sighted, but intrinsically even more unpopular plan: namely that a large part of the people should quit the country districts and settle in the city. His purpose was to guard against a second Persian attempt at revenge, which would sooner or later overwhelm Athens by force of arms or starvation; and, as a means to this end, to set up, organize, and administer a defensive naval empire, which would provide the ships and the money contributions required to secure the importation of corn and to deny the sea to the Persians and their large Phoenician fleet. At Marathon and at Salamis, Athens had got away by the skin of her teeth. How often could the performance be repeated? But the idea of a voluntary synoecism – a moving into town – was naturally most unpopular with the farmers. The whole plan was therefore presented by him to the poor as a scheme of public maintenance at the government's expense, while the wealthy were induced to agree by the tempting prospect of booty and command. Yet the substance of the matter was that the minute city-state of Athens,[g] with its 30,000 to 40,000 families, could not undertake the dominance of the seas unless every free citizen personally participated in the organization of administration and defence. The plan was immensely daring. Perhaps the most surprising thing about it was that this supreme bid for a defensive empire was

---

[f] Editors' note: "Dollar-a-year" men were managers who offered their services to help the US government during the two world wars and during the Korean War, for a symbolic salary.

[g] Editors' note: The original here has "Attica" – obviously a slip: Polanyi refers to the city-state by the name of the entire region in which it was situated.

actually put into effect. Aristotle describes the details of the scheme as follows:[h]

> He [Aristeides] pointed out to them that all would be able to gain a living there [in Athens], some by service in the army, others in the garrisons, others by taking a part in public affairs; and in this way they would secure the leadership. *This advice was taken.* [. . .] They also secured an ample maintenance for the mass of the population in the way which Aristeides had pointed out to them. Out of the proceeds of the tributes and the taxes and the contributions of the allies more than 20,000 persons were maintained. There were 6,000 jurymen, 1,600 bowmen, 1,200 knights, 500 members of the Council, 500 guards of the dockyards, besides 50 guards in the city. There were some 700 magistrates at home, and some 700 abroad. Further, when they subsequently went to war, there were in addition 2,500 heavily armed troops, 20 guards' ships [each carrying 200 marines], and other ships which collected the tributes, with crews amounting to 2,000 men selected by lot; and besides these there were the persons maintained at the Prytaneion, and orphans, and gaolers, since all these were supported by the state.

If Themistocles "trapped" the Athenian people into an armament effort that very soon proved to be its salvation, Aristeides laid the foundations for an empire that, under his guidance, was a genuine federation of Hellene states for defense. It was not his fault that, under his successors, the grand alliance turned almost into a rule of Athens over her allies, thus eventually causing her downfall in the Peloponnesian War.

I suppose I need not add many words in order to bring my account of the politician-statesman of 2,500 years ago up to date. How – on American soil, in the early 1930s – to stem the general panic caused by economic disorganization and avoid a social catastrophe? How – again in the late 1930s – to prepare an isolationist public for internationalist tasks through clever maneuvering and wise judgment? That much discounted miracle happened: the transfiguration of the party politician into Franklin Roosevelt the statesman.

Yet the mechanism is at all times the same. In some deeper layer of public opinion there is an essentially correct appraisal of the objective situation: of the present danger and the oncoming dangers of the future. The statesman senses the coming change; or, if the calamity

---

[h] Editors' note: Pseudo-Aristotle, *Constitution of the Athenians*, 24. (The Aristotelian *Constitutions* are not by Aristotle himself, but they are indeed Aristotelian in the sense that they were produced in his school.)

is on, he discerns the possibilities of overcoming the crisis. His super-lative achievement is to employ the weak forces of politics as a lever in shifting the objective situation, until the danger is met.

When all is said, in his day's work he remains a politician whose profession is to handle public opinion, though in the depth of opinion slumber the forces of history. There is, as we have seen, a weighty content to the question of what enables the statesman to transcend the mere politician.

I believe that, with regard to problems of this type, the historian will draw on the work of the sociologically minded pollster.

14

General Economic History*

The subject we are proposing to study – general economic history – is on the threshold of an advance as important as that which has revolutionized in the past generation the disciplines of physics or biology, psychology, or economics. No true science ever stands still.

I am going to deal in this introductory lecture with (1) the broad scope of this advance, (2) the reasons for this comprehensive change, and (3) the definite direction in which it points.

1   The Scope of the Advance

Economic history cannot be confined anymore to the study of the economic data of the past together with their changing background, but must comprise *the place occupied by the economy in society as a whole*, in other words the changing relation of the economic to the noneconomic institutions in society. Among the latter we should primarily mention (a) the political or governmental sphere and (b) that of man's culture, including religion, technology, and so on.

Several disciplines may serve this purpose in the future.

1   *Sociology* may offer a study of the manner in which the structure and the functioning of society as a whole is related to the economy

---

*File 31–6, Karl Polanyi Archive: introductory lecture for a course on "General Economic History" at Columbia University, New York, 1950–2.

and its various institutions. Such a study might *roughly* follow the lines on which Spencer, Marx, Durkheim, Veblen, Pareto, or Max Weber approached the question of the sociology of the human economy.

2   *Comparative economics* focuses on contemporary economy and its main institutions, analyzing their similarities and differences as observed under varying circumstances. (I mention only Colin Clark, the statistician, J. B. Condliffe of the League of Nations Surveys, or Professor A. R. Burns of Columbia.)

3   *Anthropology* allows a different approach again. By inquiring into the economies of primitive societies, it tries to discover the manner in which the livelihood of man is bound up with the totality of his motivations and valuations as organized in his culture (Malinowski, Thurnwald, Ruth Benedict).

4   Finally, I come to the *institutional* and *historical* approach, the one to which my present course is dedicated. Through an analysis of economic institutions as they present themselves in the societies of the past, we should be able to gain worthwhile indications concerning the general nature of the mechanism and the structure of economic institutions, as well as of the conditions of their *shifting place in the society as a whole*. Among the economic historians who came nearest to such an approach in the past we would have to mention Cunningham in England, Pirenne in Belgium, Rostovtzeff in Russia, Gustav Schmoller, Carl Buecher, and Max Weber in Germany. Of these authors, it is Max Weber whose *General Economic History* comes nearest to my own starting point, and I regard the work done here as a continuation of the line inaugurated by him.

Let me now briefly point out the main difference between the present period and that during which Max Weber made his memorable attempt at a recasting of economic history.

1   Weber nourished an unshaken belief in the viability and vitality of the market economy. He attached no special significance to Bolshevism and fascism, which had just made their appearance. The Russian Revolution seemed at that time to most observers as a mere continuation of the march of the French Revolution toward the East, overthrowing absolute monarchy, emancipating the peasant from semi-feudal landlordism, and liberating racial minorities oppressed by a dominant nationalism. Fascism was still restricted to Italy. Max Weber's own life experience was thus limited to the nineteenth-century type of civilization. He never

lived to see the Great Depression of 1929, the breakdown of the gold standard in 1931, and the worldwide transformation of the economic system that followed.

2　This explains Weber's firm adherence to the tenets of the neoclassical school of economic theory, which had achieved its greatest triumphs in his lifetime. In monetary theory, for example, he was a follower of the terms and methods of Mises and Knapp, who, in spite of their antagonism, were stolid adherents of the gold standard.

3　Weber refused to concede any topical interest to the study of economic history. In 1895 he asserted in so many words that the study of the decline of the Roman Empire had no aspects that could be regarded as illuminating for our own time. And he never altered his view.

On all three points the position has changed radically. This indicates the *scope of the advance*. In discussing these points of charge, we are entering on the reasons of the advance of our discipline.

2　The Reasons for the Change in Subject and Method

The collapse of the institutional set-up of the world economy

In the 30 years that have elapsed since Weber's death, the economic organization of the world as inherited from the nineteenth century has undergone a *transformation*. The cataclysmic events of the world wars were certainly not solely responsible for this fact. They would not have had this effect, were it not for the fact that the utopian character of the market economy established in the wake of the Industrial Revolution began to assert itself.

a　The market organization of the economy involves that all economic activities are organized through the market: consumption goods are bought in the market on incomes derived from sales on the market. Everyone buys everything in the market, with the help of incomes derived from selling other things in the market.

b　Such a *market system* involves that the factors of production, labor, and land also have markets and are available in the market. For all have something to sell. The propertyless laborer "sells" his labor power.

c　The self-regulating system of markets emerges from the fact that the factors of production, too, have markets (market economy).

Consequently, capital can move from one field of investment to another according to profitability, by selling the factors and – in principle – recombining them so as to achieve a higher profit. *This* makes the system self-regulating.

d The inclusion of man and nature into a self-regulating system is, of course, utopian. No such system is possible in practice. They would be both destroyed. But, together with the self-protective measures taken by society, it worked (double movement). (1) Factory laws plus unions; (2) agrarian tariffs and land laws; (3) management of currency – these were the three most important measures of self-protection. *But* precisely this made self-regulation unworkable. It[a] involved *nationalism*, which was merely the inevitable reaction of political bodies to the social dislocation caused by the international trade system (everywhere except in the strongest country – England).

e In the market economy, trade and money are organized into and through the market. *Trade* is the movement of goods through the market, and money is the means of exchange that facilitates this. But trade and money are market-function – the catallactic triad.

In consequence of these accompaniments of a market economy, its breakdown caused *a transformation of the institutional set-up connected with the world economy. Trade, money and markets* hardly resemble their former selves any more.

The result is a most dangerous crisis in our *economic politics* and *theory.*[b]

We are leaving in an age of unprecedented transition and need all the orientation that history can provide if we are to find our bearings.

1 A change in the *institutional reality*. Exchange – the dominant form of integration – is receding, and reciprocity and redistribution are coming to the fore.

2 Our economic *policies* are antiquated.

3 Out *theory* of international trade and international monetary phenomena needs reforming. Its equilibrium basis has been impaired by the breakdown of the gold standard.

---

[a]Editors' note: I.e. self-regulation.
[b]Editors' note: In relation to this statement Polanyi intended to develop two points, which he marked in handwriting (A) and (B); but the ink has faded almost completely. Point (B) seems to have been about "econom . . ."

3 Definite Direction of Advance

We need therefore:

1 to give clarity and precision to our concepts, so that we may be enabled to formulate the problems of livelihood in terms fitted as closely as possible to the actual features of the situation in which we operate;
2 to widen the range of principles and policies at our disposal through a study of the shifting place of the economy in human society and of the methods by which civilizations of the past successfully engineered their great transitions;
3 to safeguard the institutions of freedom and the changing organization of the economy.

Accordingly, the theoretical task consists in establishing the study of man's livelihood on broad institutional and historical foundations.

The method to be used is given by the interdependence of thought and experience. Terms and definitions constructed without reference to factual data are hollow; a mere collection of facts without a readjustment of our perspectives is barren. To break this vicious circle, conceptual and empirical research must be carried on *pari passu*.

We will begin tomorrow with the conceptual clarification.
•••

4 Introduction

The subject we are proposing to study – general economic history – is on the threshold of an advance as important as that which has, in the past generation, revolutionized the discipline of physics or biology, of psychology or economics. No true science ever stands still.

I am going to deal in the introductory lecture

(a) with the reasons for this advance; and
(b) with the directions in which it points.

The advance points toward the fact that economic history cannot be confined to the history of economic institutions themselves (and even less to that of business enterprise) but must comprise the study of the place of the economic system in human society, in other words the study of the relationship between the economic and the noneconomic institutions in it.

(A)   Theoretical sources of the change

First come the discoveries made in the contiguous fields of anthropology – discoveries connected with the names of Franz Boas and Bronisław Malinowski, to which Richard Thurnwald's should be added. Their insights implied a critique of a so-called "economic man" of classical ancestry and led to the establishment of the discipline of primitive economics as a branch of cultural anthropology.

Second, while the history of the eighteenth and nineteenth centuries seemed to bear out the economic interpretation of history as formulated by Hahn,ᶜ investigations into earlier periods did not yield the same positive results. Descriptions of the rise of modern industrial society by A. Toynbee, H. Cunningham, Ashley, the Webbs, the Hammonds, Mantoux, or even Eli Lipsen, not to mention American writers like Brooks Adams and Charles Beard, successfully employed the methods of economic interpretation. The earlier work of Werner Sombart as well as that of Henri Pirenne used a similar approach fruitfully. But to mention only two examples: E. D. Mayer's and Rostovtzeff's works on ancient history – the latter was himself an economic historian – pointed in new directions. The limitations of the economic interpretation were becoming apparent.

These two factors – the impact of cultural anthropology and the considerable broadening of our knowledge of ancient history – put a different meaning on the discussion started by Max Weber and R. H. Tawney in the first quarter of the century. It now appeared that their essays on the influence of religious morality on the rise of capitalism raised the even bigger issue of the relation of economy and society. In this wider field, Max Weber's posthumous *Economy and Society* remained a significant fragment, if only a fragment. As its title suggested, it pointed to the necessity of relating economy institutions to human society as a whole.

(B)   Practical sources

Our own time has added a dramatic chapter to the vicissitudes of man. The collective experience of a generation cannot fail to have a

---

ᶜEditors' note: The typescript here is now unreadable, but this was presumably a reference to the famous economist L. Albert Hahn, whose theory of credit provoked hot controversy in economics from the 1920s on.

deep influence on outlook, especially if events are shaped in so obvious a way as happened here. The collapse, after World War I, of a large part of the institutional system of the nineteenth century coincided with economic experiments carried on a vast scale; suffice it to mention only fascism in Germany and state socialism in Russia. Yet it could hardly be denied that the manifest forces determining the venture were in both cases political and ideological rather than economic.

Thus, again, change in *economic* institution was not explained by so-called *economic* development. The answer had to be sought in other fields.

This had the accumulative effect of:

1   making us aware of the eminently *economic* character of the nineteenth-century episode, in contrast with earlier periods in history – and indeed in contrast with our time, in which much greater weight is attached to noneconomic factors;
2   indicating that economic history could not be studied in isolation from, but only in the wider framework of, human society.

Let us consider these factors separately, with and an eye on the manner in which they make influence our approach to general economic history.

5   Primitive "Economics"

By a freak of history, during World War I a trained anthropologist was marooned in his own "field." Bronisław Malinowski was an Austrian subject, and thus – technically – an enemy alien among the savages off the southeastern tip of New Guinea. For two years the British authorities did not give him permission to leave, and Malinowsky returned from the Trobriand Islands with the material for "The Primitive Economics of the Trobriand Islanders" (1921), *Argonauts of the Western Pacific* (1922), *Crime and Custom in Savage Society* (1926), *Sex and Repression in Savage Society* (1927), and *Coral Gardens and Their Magic* (1935). He died in the United States in 1942. But his words are already affecting not the study of anthropology alone, but also the viewpoints and methods of economic history. Richard Thurnwald of Berlin, very nearly 80 years of age, whose field was New Guinea, published his account of the Banaro in 1916, in the *American Anthropologist*. His influence was felt in the Anglo-Saxon world chiefly through its impact upon

Malinowski. (Thurnwald himself, though praised as an anthropologist, had been a pupil of Max Weber.)

Malinowski's account left the reader with the conviction that members of pre-literate communities behaved on the whole in a manner that was understandable to us. The explanation of their often exotic behavior hinged on *institutions* that stimulated sets of motives different from those we usually set upon – while in other ways not foreign to us. With regard to subsistence, there was a widespread practice of *reciprocity*, that is, members of a group, in their capacity as members,[d] behaved to members of another group as the members of that (or of a third) group were expected to behave toward them. Males of a village subclan, for instance, provided their sister's husband and children with garden produce, though the sister would be usually dwelling in or near her husband's village, at quite a distance from her brothers' habitation – an arrangement that resulted in a great deal of uneconomical hiking on the part of the diligent brothers. (Of course, if a brother happened to be married, a similar service would be rendered to his family by his wife's brothers.) Apart from this substantial contribution to the matrilineal relatives' household, a system of reciprocal *gifts and countergifts* was generated. Economic self-interest was only indirectly appealed to, the controlling motive being noneconomic, for instance pride in the public recognition of civic virtues as a brother or as a gardener. The mechanism of reciprocity was effective in the comparatively simple matter of food supplies; it also accounted for the highly complex institution of the "kula," an aesthetic variant of international trade. Kula transactions between inhabitants of the archipelago covered a number of years, dozens of miles of unsafe seas, and thousands of individual objects exchanged as gifts between individual partners living on distant islands. The whole institution was such as to minimize rivalry and conflict and maximize the joy of giving and receiving gifts.

None of these facts recorded by Malinowski was essentially new. Similar ones had been observed time and again in other spots. Although contrasting in tone and coloring with the *potlatch* of the Kwakiutl Indians, the kula was not more peculiar than that hypersnobistic display of willful destruction discovered and exhaustively described by the great American anthropologist Franz Boas (*The Social Organization of the Secret Societies of the Kwakiutl Indians*, 1895).

Yet Malinowski's brilliant attack on the concept of the "economic man" unconsciously underlying the traditional approach of

[d]Editors' note: The text says here, rather cryptically, "members of a group as such."

ethnographers and anthropologists created, in primitive economics, a new branch of social anthropology, of the greatest interest to the economic historian.

The mythical "individualistic savage" was now dead and buried, as was his antipode, the "communistic savage." It appeared that not so much the mind as the institutions of the savage differed from our own. Under the sociologist's microscope, even widespread communal ownership turned out to be different from what it was supposed to be. True, land belonged to the tribe or sib, but a network was found to exist of *individual rights* that deprived the term "communal property" of most of its content. Margaret Mead has described this as the man "belonging" to the piece of land rather than the land to the man. Behavior is not so much ruled by rights of disposal vested in individuals as by commitments from individuals to cultivate a definite plot of land. To speak of property in land, either individual or communal, where the very notion of property is inapplicable appears therefore hardly as meaningful. With the Trobrianders themselves, distribution happened largely through gifts and countergifts – of which Malinowski distinguished eight different kinds, according to the sociological situation in which they occurred.

As a general conclusion it can be stated that *the production and distribution of material goods was embedded in social relations of a noneconomic kind*. No institutionally separate economic system – no network of economic institutions – could be said to exist. Neither labor, nor the disposal of objects, nor their distribution was carried on for economic motives – that is, for the sake of gain or payment, or for fear of otherwise going hungry as an individual. If by economic system we should mean the aggregate of behavior traits inspired by the individual motives of hunger and gain, there was an economic system in existence at all.[e] If, however, as we should, we mean by that phrase the behavior traits relating to the production and distribution of material goods and services – the only meaning relevant to economic history – then we find that, while there was, *of course*, an economic system in place, it was not institutionally distinct and separate. In effect, it was simply a byproduct of the working of other noneconomic institutions.

Such a state of affairs might be easily understood if we concentrate on the role of basic social organizations in channeling individual

[e]Editors' note: Much of this sentence is insecure (the ink has faded away), but the desired meaning of this irreal hypothetic conditional must have been something like "if that's what we mean by 'economic system,' then *there was an economic system alright*; but of course *that's not he case*, as I'm stating clearly next."

motives. In studying the kinship system of Banaro of New Guinea, Thurnwald struck a complicated system of exchange marriage. No less than four different couples had to be united in marriage at one and the same occasion – each partner standing in a definite relationship to some other person of the reciprocating group. In order to work such a system, grouping had to be already in existence, splitting the sib artificially into sub-sibs. To this purpose the goblin hall (or men's house) was habitually divided; those squatting on the right (Bone), and those squatting on the left (Tan) formed subsections for the purpose of the exchange marriage system. Thurnwald wrote (1916):[f]

> The symmetry in the arrangement of the ghost-hall is the expression of the principle of reciprocity – the principle of giving "like for like" – *retaliation* or *requital*. This seems to be the result of what is psychologically known as "adequate reaction," which is deeply rooted in man. In fact, this principle pervades the thinking of primitive peoples and often finds its expression in social organization.

This remark was taken up by Malinowski in *Crime and Custom in Savage Society* (1926). He suggested that *symmetrical* subdivision in society, such as Thurnwald had found at Goblin Hall, would be discovered to exist everywhere as the basis of reciprocity among savage people. *Reciprocity* – as form of integration – and *symmetrical* organization went together. This may be the true explanation of the famous *duality in social organization*. Indeed we may ask, in relation to a pre-literate society ignorant of book-keeping: How could reciprocity be practiced here over long stretches of time by large numbers of peoples in the most varied positions, unless social organizations met the need halfway by providing ready-made symmetrical groups, the members of which could behave toward one another similarly? The suggestion carries important implications for the study of *social organization*. It explains, among other things, the role of the intricate kinship relations often found in savage societies, which are here the *bearers* of social organization.

Since there is no separate economic organization in being, but instead the economics of the society system is "embedded" in social relations, there has to be an elaborate social organization in existence, in order to take care of the articulations of the economic life in the

---

[f]Editors' note: Richard Thurnwald, "Bánaro Society: Social Organization and Kinship System of a Tribe in the Interior of New Guinea," *Memoirs of the American Anthropological Association*, 3.4 (1916), 251–391, at p. 258.

way of division of labor, disposal of land, work practice inheritance and so on. Kinship relations tend to be complicated, since they have to provide the groundwork for a social organization that is designed to *substitute* for a separate economic organization. (Incidentally, Thurnwald remarked that kinship relations tend to become simple as soon as *separate* political–economic organizations develop, since "there is," as he said, "no need for complicated kinship relations any more.")

This embeddedness of the economic system in social relations, which we encounter in primitive society, raises some points of great interest to the economic historian:

1　If an economic system based on distinctively economic motives should prove identical with the market system, then the much greater part of human history did without any separate economic system at all. (This may be, of course, a matter of degree, since isolated markets, market system, and market economy form a gradation.)
2　Economic institutions should be studied *in the framework of society as a whole*; not merely on the background of political and social history, but as *part of social organization*.

6　Limitations of the Economic Interpretation of History

The other factor, we said, was the recognition that the economic interpretation of history is bound to be less fruitful in respect of history in general, then in respect of the eighteenth and nineteenth centuries.

The influence exerted by economic interpretations of history writing was greater and deeper than is commonly realized. Economic historians either were influenced by the Marxian analysis or had come to similar conclusions independently. I mention only Sombart and Max Weber in Germany, Mantoux in France, Pirenne in Belgium, A. Toynbee, the Webbs, the Hammonds in England, Beard in the United States. Non-Marxian writers like Lambert in Germany or H. Cunningham in England were equally impressed by the importance of the economic factor in history. Indeed subsequent warnings about the *limitations* of the economic interpretation did not come so much from writers of the opposite school as from scholars like Werner Sombart, Max Weber, and Henri Pirenne, who were broadly favorable to an economic interpretation of history.

Nevertheless, the analysis of Max Weber in his *The Protestant Ethic and the Spirit of Capitalism* led to the acceptance of the fact that the actual development of capitalism could not be accounted for apart from a simultaneous significant development of religious ethic and its influence on everyday behavior.

Subsequent strictures on Weber's position did not shake his thesis of the importance of Protestantism for the development of capitalism in the West. Later he developed this thesis and put forward propositions on the origins of western civilization, which he regarded as a specifically urban product, that is, as originating in the cities. Now the western city, he asserted, had no parallel in history. Here alone urban citizenship transcended tribe and caste – a result that M. Weber credited to the influence of Jewish–Christian religion. Jewry transcended magic, made it evil instead of good; Christianity transcended blood and race, thus creating the universal citizen of the western town. I record these views *without necessarily endorsing them*.

W. Cunningham, another eminent historian sympathetic to the economic interpretation of history, came to the conclusion that medieval Christian ethic, by asserting the dignity of manual labor, created in the *monastic movements* a powerful economic pioneering factor, civilizing Western Europe.

Henri Pirenne, an outstanding historian appreciative of historical materialism, concluded that the crusades, in spite of their vast economic consequences, had to be regarded as primarily religious movements. According to him, Islam also was a specifically religious movement, though its economic consequences were undoubtedly enormous.

Yet all these writers, of so divergent background, would have been unanimous in accepting the economic determination *of the eighteenth and nineteenth centuries in western history*. Economic determinism, in effect, seems to be only another name for the *market system*, under which economics is not embedded in the society but, on the contrary, society is embedded in the market system. The simple reason for this development is the creation of competitive markets for *labor* and *land*. Since labor is only another name[g] for man and land for nature, the very substance of human society is involved in the market system. No wonder there is "economic determinism." Marxism mirrored the recognition that the nineteenth-century society was essentially an economic society. Just as there had been religiously or politically

[g]Editors' note: Mistake here in Polanyi's typescript: *another man for man*.

determined societies in the past, this society of ours was characterized by the determinative position of an economic institution in it, namely the market system. Where Marxism went wrong was the notion that economic determinism was a *general* law of human history. The opposite is true. With regard to the past, economic determinism is a mere anachronism. With regard to the future, it is no more than a prejudice. This throws a sidelight on such forecasts as are being made by Hayek, Burnham, and others as to the inevitable disappearance of freedom with the eventual introduction of *planning* into industrial society. They can point to the fact that our present justly cherished personal "freedoms" were a result of a development that led to capitalistic market organization. This I believe to be largely true. But then, they proceed to argue, this "freedom *must disappear*" – and, together with it, the "unregulated market." This seems to me to assume the validity of the economic interpretation of history *outside* market economy, for which there is no warrant. It is hardly logical to try to infer the effects of the absence of a market economy on the strength of a law that is limited to the presence of a market economy, namely economic determinism.

In truth, we will have just as much freedom in the future as we desire to create and to safeguard. Institutional guarantees of personal freedom are in principle compatible with any economic system. In market society alone will the ‡. . .ᵗʰ economic mechanism lay down the law for us. Such a state of affairs is not characteristic of human society in general, but only of an unregulated market economy.

This is borne out by experience. Neither the freezing of labor nor selective service abrogated the essential freedoms of the American people. Great Britain, during the war, introduced an all-around planned economy, yet never were public liberties safer in Britain than at the height of the war. Argumentations from economic determinism with regard to future developments have no scientific foundation, as soon as the matter passes beyond the scope of the market mechanism. For economic determinism, we repeat, is only another name for that mechanism.

The effect of these recognitions on the history of other periods than our own, and on other systems than the present, will obviously tend to be in the direction we have indicated:

1 the inclusion of noneconomic factors shaping economic institutions, such as military and political factors;

ʰEditors' note: Unreadable.

2   the study of the relations of the two in the broad setting of *society as a whole*;
3   the experience of our generation.

The experience of our generation, of our time – the Russian and German upheavals. While the New Deal experience, on the whole, took place *within* the setting of the market mechanism and was therefore – largely – economically determined, the Soviet and the Nazi experience – though otherwise very different in character and tendency – were essentially noneconomically determined and the process they started transcended the mechanism of the market economy.

The Russian Revolution was the most complete refutation conceivable of economic determinism, as a general law of history. Stalin enjoined members of the Russian Communist Party that economic determinism has ceased to operate in Russia. As he put it: "There are no objective economic conditions determining policy in a socialist country."[i] What he referred to was the absence of economic determinism outside of market economy. On other points of economics, thought in communist Russia is deplorably backward.

We conclude:
[First:]

1   the discoveries of primitive economics;
2   the realization of the limits of the economic interpretation of history; and
3   the impact of the historical experiences of our own time –

are so many factors influencing the study of economic history in the same *general direction*.
[Next:]

1   The relation of *economic and noneconomic* factors should be studied in the framework of society as a whole.
2   We should recognize the nineteenth-century interpretation of the place of the economic system in society as strictly time-bound. The existence of an institutionally *separate* economic system such as the nineteenth century created cannot be taken for granted in all types of society.

---

[i] Editors' note: Unidentified source.

3   As a rule, the *economic system* is fused with *noneconomic institutions*, and one of the main tasks of economic history – as already
Max Weber recognized – is to determine the *place occupied by
economic life in different human societies.*

The study of the history of economic institutions, in general, involves
today a new approach, similar to that of Max Weber, yet differing
from it essentially.

(A)   It resembles Max Weber's in insisting on
    (i)   thorough *conceptual* analysis:
        (1)   definition of terms,
        (2)   clarity with regard to method;
    (ii) broadening of the survey to that of the place of the economy
          in society.
(B)   But it differs
    (i)   in extending the survey to *cultural anthropology*; and
    (ii) in avoiding that economic or marketing approach that
          identifies "economic" with rationality.

Accordingly, our task will be:

1   to define the meaning of "economic";
2   to classify economic systems in a manner that does not prejudge
    the issues;
3   to illustrate the changing place of the economy in human society
    through *historical examples*.

Eventually this should do two things for us – give us (1) a grasp of
economic systems; (2) a clearer understanding of *economic history.*

Here you have a significant change in the meaning of the word
"general" as applied to economic history. Traditionally it meant all
civilized peoples of the West and ancient civilizations that preceded
it.

In the future, general economic history may mean *the general
characteristics of economic systems*, whether of civilized or noncivi-
lized peoples, using concrete descriptions as illustrations. *Factual
history* has in no way lost its importance. Indeed it alone can provide
evidence for the place of economic systems in human society.

It is in this direction that economic history is shifting its emphasis.
It may become one of the leading social sciences in this period of
institutional change through which we are passing.

In this course we are going to devote ourselves to its study.

15

Market Elements and Economic Planning in Antiquity*

I will endeavor to give you, in the briefest outline, a picture of the present state of research into the economic history of antiquity. As you may (by now) be aware, this is not a subject as far removed from topical interest as it would have appeared even a short time ago. Whether this fact should be credited more to our rapidly advancing knowledge of antiquity or rather to our even more rapidly changing appreciation of "price curbs" is a matter that, in fairness, should be left to the headlines of the newspapers.

Let me choose the following as the starting point for my report. Eighty-five years ago, Rodbertus-Jagetzow, the Prussian Junker socialist from whom Karl Marx learnt so much, published a series of essays on taxation in the Roman Empire. It is still the most suitable peg on which to hang a discussion of the economic problems of antiquity. For the clash of opinions to which that essay[a] gave rise introduced a *long-drawn effort* to see antiquity in its true character, undistorted by preconceptions that had made the high points of antiquity appear almost as a replica of the modern world. Eventually this seemingly

* File 42–14, Karl Polanyi Archive: undelivered lecture for Yale University, probably dating from the 1950s.
[a] Editors' note: This must be a reference to J. K. Rodbertus, "Zur Geschichte der römischen Tributsteuern seit Augustus," *Jahrbücher für Nationalökonomie und Statistik* 4 (1865), 341–427. The singular used here (*that essay*) contrasts with the plural "essays" used before (*a series of essays*); but "essays" replaces another word that was completely crossed out, most plausibly "lectures." So Polanyi seems to imply that the published article was the outcome of a series of lectures or public speeches of some sort.

simple and obvious requirement of critical thinking – not to interpret the past in terms of the present – involved no less than a revolution in our institutional concepts.

Accordingly I will *firstly* deal with the so-called *oikos controversy* – in which Carl Bücher on the one hand, Eduard Meyer on the other were prominent. What was the result of this prolonged clash of views, which Rostovtzeff still regarded as a live issue in 1941? *Secondly*, I will try to formulate the *new and even broader* issues, which are replacing the dissolving ones and range far back before the time of Greece and Rome, to the irrigational empires of the Nile Valley and Mesopotamia. *Thirdly*, I will endeavor to evaluate the overall results of recent research for an understanding of the past and, if possible, for a firmer grasp of the problems of the present.[b]

1   The *oikos* Controversy

In fairness to the modernizers, it must be conceded that, on the fact of the *oikos* – the strictly self-sufficient household – both Rodbertus and Bücher were wrong, or at least they were guilty of crass exaggeration. The ancients, Rodbertus wrote, had no taxation system of the modern kind, because antiquity did not know different types of revenue such as are formed in markets differentiated into land, labor, and capital markets. Domestic and plantation slavery formed the foundation of a large, completely self-sufficient household, which he called the *oikos*. Land and labor power (the slave) were property of the owner, and raw materials were produced and productively consumed *within the precincts of the household*. This was the birth of the *oikos* theorem. Thirty years later Bücher took up the point of the allegedly self-sufficient *oikos* and generalized from it to the primitive character of the whole economic life of antiquity, which he likened more to that of savage society than to that of the modern world.

Now, as I indicated, the households of Roman plantation slavery were *not* self-sufficient; they carried on, as a rule, some kind of trade or other. Similarly mistaken was Bücher's picture of pre-literate communities. His primeval savage, allegedly engaged in a "lone search for food," was a mere construction, which ignored all of the more recent finding of primitive economics.

[b] Editors' note: This remained an unfulfilled intention: the topic of the present is not covered here, and Polanyi crossed out this sentence.

This is, however, hardly to the point. In spite of inaccuracies, Rodbertus' *oikos theorem* implied a significant warning not to assume that economic activity and market activity were coterminous. And Bücher's call to consult social anthropology as a guide to classical antiquity has proved exceedingly fruitful. Though neither Rodbertus nor Bücher realized fully the implications of their position, it was *their* initiative that eventually led, in Max Weber's work, to a radical reformulation of the *problem of capitalism in antiquity*, and may lead us eventually to the solution of some of the riddles of Babylonian economy.

This brings us to the subject matter of the controversy. As early as 1893, Carl Bücher rejected the modernizing views implicit in the presentations of those great historians – Niebuhr, Grote, and Mommsen. With regard to political history, these scholars had taken a long step in the right direction, but they failed to do justice to the economic realities of antiquity. They broke with an age-long tradition of legendary historiography and at last presented Greek and Roman history as the story, not of gods or half-gods, but of human beings like ourselves, using terms of everyday life. But, inevitably, their own everyday surroundings were (as ours are) very different from those of ancient Rome – including in the description of our surroundings, factory town, stock exchange, colonial expansion, class struggles of employers and employees, conflict of capitalist and socialist ideologies. No wonder that the figure of Pasion the banker made them feel at home in fourth-century Athens and that Brutus' usurious loans (advanced to colonial governments) or the speculative boom worked up by equestrian corporation promoters reminded them of Law and the "Bubble,"[c] just as they still remind us of closer events. Similarly, the rise to power of a merchant and trader class at Athens and Rome, the revolt of plebeians, and other allegedly socialist and communist movements – all this appeared familiar in their eyes (as it still largely appears to us) and gave a modern tinge to ancient life.

This *fin de siècle* portrait of antiquity was in hopeless contradiction to Rodbertus' marketless and exchangeless *oikos* of slave barracks, and even more so to Bücher's primitivism, which tended to strip the ancient Mediterranean of its alluring modernity and to reduce it to the level of an African *kraal*, as Julius Beloch complained. While Eduard Meyer, in 1895, still reveled in the description of the teeming trade and commerce of the ancients, Bücher, starting from Babylonian

---

[c] Editors' note: This is a reference to the "Mississippi Bubble," a disastrous financial scheme devised in 1718 in France by the Scottish adventurer John Law.

banks and manufactures, insisted that at no time before the establishment of the modern western state was there anything in existence
that deserved as much as the name of a national economy – the
German *Volkswirtschaft* – in other words a complex territorial
economy of any considerable extent.

This, indeed, was a head-on collision. The clash between modernizers and primitivists seemed at first to involve the whole realm of
facts, as well as that of interpretation. True, on close analysis it
emerged that it was more on the interpretation of the facts than on
the facts themselves that they disagreed. But it was a long time before
this was recognized, and an even longer time before the obstacles to
some clarification were removed. This last step, I should perhaps say,
has not yet been generally taken, and it will be one of my objects
tonight to show how it can be successfully undertaken. Indeed, unless
we are able to avoid inappropriate modernization with regard to
ancient Greece and Rome, it appears hopeless to expect any real
understanding of the much more remote problems of Babylonia,
Sumer, Akkad, or Assyria.

Now, as to the *facts* of the controversy. Naturally, discussion at
first centered around the numerical dimension of economic life, pri-
marily in ancient Greece. What was the actual range and volume of
Greek trade? How much of it consisted in manufactured articles
produced for export? On what scale were Athenian factories run?
How many slaves, how many free wage earners did they employ?
What was the state of affairs with regard to credit, freight, and insurance facilities? What were the activities and business methods of an
Athenian banking house? What was the state of commercial law?
How intensive was the trade carried on between founding state and
colony? What ideas underlay monetary policy and currency reform?
What were the trade policies of Athens, and to what extent were her
wars trade wars? How influential was the trading and commercial
interest in shaping domestic and foreign policy? What was the precise
socioeconomic content of the Solonian and Cleisthenian revolutions?
And so on.

Much detailed knowledge was gained, yet the total result of the
research was singularly inclusive. Roughly, the more was known
about the facts, the more drastically were modernizing exaggerations
reduced with regard to the scale of manufactures, the level of trading
organization, the refinements of banking, the scope of private business enterprise, and so on. Eventually not only the facts, but also
their interpretations were deflated. The enormous colonizing activity
of the Greeks in the eighth and seventh centuries turned out *not* to
have been inspired by trade interests, as Meyer and Beloch taught.

The tyrants of the seventh and sixth centuries had *not* been pluto-cratic – super-employers, as Professor Ure argued. The *stasis* that rent Athens during the sixth century did *not* primarily arise from urban manufacturing sources, as Glotz and Toutain, Ferguson and Rostovtzeff held. The Solonian reforms and, for that matter, the Cleisthenian revolution were *not* gained by the pressure of a rising urban middle class allied to a nascent proletariat, as Pöhlmann believed. The foreign policy of Attica was *not* shaped to any noticeable extent by trade interests, as was almost generally thought by historians. Indeed, Attica through the whole course of her history continued to impose a flat 2 percent import and export duty on all wares, thus providing conclusive evidence of the absence of any industrial protectionism whatsoever. Incidentally, Rome did the same, and she made it 5 percent.

Yet, on the other hand, some hard facts made it impossible to accept the primitivists' victory and to grant them the trophy. There was the fact of Minoan world trade in the Mediterranean down to the middle of the second millennium; and, after a gap of a few centuries, that of Phoenician world trade, which some time about the eighth century was gradually replaced by Greek trade from the Azovian Lake to the Atlantic and from the Danube to the Nile. Also there was the equally undeniable fact of Athenian banking facilities, which were destined to exert a deep and lasting influence on the forms of economic life under Hellenism. There was thus certain proof not only of the existence of world trade, but also of Greek initiative in providing it with financial facilities. And could it be reasonably doubted that the world trade and banking of the seventh and fourth centuries, respectively, had been preceded by less advanced forms of trade and credit, thus attacking primitivism at its very foundation?

All in all, the outcome was disconcerting. While ancient society – its colonies, its wars, its classes – appeared anything but "modern," trade and the use of money undeniably existed on a scale comparable to the beginnings of modern times.

The explanation was fairly simple. Both primitivists and their opponents failed to realize that to contrast "modernity" with "primitivism" in relation to human society meant to contrast the *presence* or *absence* not of trade or money, but of the market mechanism.

What makes a society "modern" in our eyes is nothing but the pervasive influence of *market* institutions – a supply–demand–price mechanism – on the total culture, and especially on the economic life of a community. Market institutions are inseparable from definite motivations and situations, techniques and culture traits of a marketing character. The distinctively modern traits of contemporary life such as speculation and advertisement, cut-throat competition and business lobbies are precisely the features that are connected with the effects and accessories of the market system. Thus the term "modern," when applied to economic life, is not as vague and superficial as it might appear; it comprises a variety of traits that have their common root in the market organization of society.

This is, of course, wholly in accordance with what we should expect. For, in the last resort, the modern organization of production *is* a market organization; modern social classes *are* classes formed through incomes determined in specific markets; the modern social struggle is a struggle between economic classes – that is, groups the status of which is defined in market terms and the conflicts of which are conflicts about those terms. All this was, of course, *implicit* in Bücher's reference to the self-sufficient *oikos*, since absence of exchange and markets was precisely the criterion that Rodbertus had claimed for his *oikos*. Yet neither Rodbertus nor Bücher made their conclusion *explicit* – that, in arguing for the primitive character of ancient society, they argued for the absence of a market system and a *market system only*. Consequently they made the mistake of *lumping trade, money and markets* together under the total heading of *exchange institutions*, thus precluding all profitable institutional analysis. Instead of distinguishing trade – that is, the acquisition of goods from a distance – and the non-exchange uses of money, on the one hand, from markets on the other, they fused them in an institutional trinity. Consequently, where there was division of labor, there were trade, money, and markets. Incidentally, this semantic weakness made it almost impossible to ascertain the facts, especially the crucial presence or absence of organized markets, since it led to the delusion that, where money was met, trade could be *assumed*, and where trade was met, markets could be *assumed*.

Actually these assumptions were hangovers from modern conditions, reinforced by traditional concepts of exchange economics. It is remarkable that, in spite of their intellectual courage and methodological radicalism, Rodbertus and Bücher missed the decisive formulation that alone could ensure clarification. They failed to *isolate* the market as the source of modernity, and consequently failed to *contrast* market institutions with trade and money, which are relatively independent of the market mechanism. The trinity of trade–money–market is indeed a distinctive feature of *our modern market system*, where all trade is carried through markets, in other words by way of a supply–demand–price mechanism. With us, trade is carried through markets; and, with us, insofar as it is used in trade, money does *function* as a means of exchange. But in the ancient world the opposite was true. Trade was not carried primarily through markets, and money did not necessarily functions as a means of exchange.

Since clarity on this point is crucial for the understanding of antiquity, and indeed to a large extent of all economic history short of the last few centuries, I should like to add this. Trade may take – and largely took in the past – *nonmarket* forms such as gift trade, expeditionary trade, ceremonial trade, chartered trade, and other forms that are more a matter for the collectivity than for the individual as such. Similarly, the most widely spread *uses of money objects*, in other words of quantifiable objects, were those of (1) *means of payment* and (2) *standard of value*, the two functions not being necessarily performed by the same kind of object. Use of money (3) *as a means of exchange* is exceptional outside of institutionalized markets, which, as I said, should themselves be regarded as a specific development, the presence of which should not be taken for granted merely on account of the presence of *trade* or of the presence of *nonexchange uses of money*. In principle, therefore, an absence of markets is compatible with a relatively high degree of trading activities and various non-exchange uses of money, such as means of payment or standard of value. In brief, trade and money on the one hand, markets on the other, must be sharply distinguished.

In these terms the factual results of the *oikos* controversy no longer appear contradictory. There is no evidence that the *world trade* of the ancient Mediterranean or the *banking* that accompanied that trade was carried through a supply–demand–price mechanism. Under these conditions, it is not surprising that ancient Greek society and economic life do not strike us as "modern."

At this point it will be noted that the very terms *world trade* and *banking* are singularly misleading. Not as if they were not appropriate – since there was banking, and the ends of the known world were involved in trade – but on account of the *evolutionist fallacy*, which goes with our modernizing perspectives. World trade in antiquity was not the culmination (as with us), but rather the *starting point* of foreign trade, and probably the only form of trade in neolithic times, just as ancient colonization has been shown to start, as a rule, with the colony that was farthest away, not with the nearest one – the intervening sites being occupied later on. Eduard Meyer gave, a long time ago, a list of analogies from the history of explorations, starting with those of pharaonic Egypt; circumnavigators of Africa, Vasco da Gama and Columbus in more modern times. In fairness to Columbus, he should not be blamed for never having reached his aim, the Indies, being unexpectedly held up halfway. Obviously, had he known before, he would have thought America much too close to his home port to be worthwhile.

With regard to banking, again, we tend to think of it as an advanced form of dealing with money and credit. Actually coins could not be used at all during that period – the fourth century BC – without the manual (and menial) occupation of testing and changing, which made the trapezoid. But not even Pasion the freedman ever got beyond safe keeping of deposits, payment on direct order to definite persons present on the spot, pawnbroking, and loans on noncommercial security. The crucial point, of course, is – again – that the economic life of antiquity was not worked through markets and therefore did not produce the *credit instruments* that are the raw material of modern banking. Roman banking was rather on a lower than on a higher level than Greek, and Ptolemaic banking developed in the direction of transactions in "kind" and not in money. Banking is therefore as misleading a criterion of "modernity" as world trade, when judging of the economy of the ancients. Here again, as in the trinity trade–money–markets, it was the modernizing remnant in the primitivists' own thinking, with its rigid evolutionism, that permitted modernizers to adduce ancient world trade and ancient banking as alleged proofs of the "modern" character of the ancient world.

We may conclude by saying that the debate started by Rodbertus and Buecher has – broadly – led to a vindication of their essential position, though only with the help of institutional insights that were still hidden from them. At the same time, it should be added, they entirely overlooked the fact that the *highly significant beginnings* of a market system in civilized society actually started during the *later* part of classical antiquity, approximately from the fourth century onwards. True, this market system developed within a primitive framework of a warrior-type society that fatally limited its capacity of expansion.

This takes us to the second part of this address, to the *broader issues* that seem to be taking the place of the controversy on "modernism."

2   New Issues

These results are, of course, in complete harmony with Max Weber's diagnosis of the sociological character of the Greek and Roman *poleis* as settlements of partially detribalized populations, the leading strata of which never ceased to be organized as a warriors' gild, and the democratization of which involved therefore the inclusion of *all* strata of the population, primarily the peasantry, in such a gild. Essentially it[d] was a predatory community, a group organized for war and conquest, raid and piracy, forcible colonization, naval power, exaction of tribute, exploitation of subjects, barbarian or otherwise. Both *aristocratic leadership* and *equalitarian* claims to the maintenance of citizens by the community formed part of that tribal heritage. We possess a document of the highest authority, which gives realistic details of the manner in which such a group can be organized for common maintenance through a common effort at domination. Aristotle's *Constitution of Athens*, the manuscript of which was recovered in 1891, gives an account of the procedure: after the victory over the Persians, he says – the date is 479 BC – the aristocracy was in high repute on account of its services at Salamis. Aristeides and Themistocles were leaders of the people and directors of policy. Aristeides founded the Delian League, of which Athens was the chief beneficiary. This was in 478 BC. Aristotle continues:[e]

> After this, seeing the state growing in confidence and much wealth accumulated, he – Aristeides – advised the people to lay hold of the leadership of the league and to quit the country districts and settle in the city. He pointed out to them that all would be able to gain a living there, some by service in the army, others in the garrisons, others by taking part in public affairs; and in this way they would secure the leadership. *This advice was taken,* and when the people had assumed the supreme control they proceeded to treat their allies in a more imperious fashion, with the exception of the Chians, Lesbians and Samians. These they maintained to protect their empire, leaving their constitutions untouched, and allowing them to retain whatever dominion they then possessed. They also secured an ample maintenance for the mass of the population in the way which Aristeides had pointed out to them. Out of the proceeds of the tributes and the taxes and contribution of the allies, more than 20,000 persons were maintained [the total number of citizens of Attica is estimated at less than 50,000]. There were 6,000 jurymen, 1,600 bowmen, 1,200 knights, 500 members of the Council, 500 guards of the dockyards, besides 50 guards in the city. There were some 700 magistrates at home, and some 700 abroad. Further, when they subsequently went to war, there were in addition 2,500 heavily armed troops, 20 guards' ships [representing

---

[d] Editors' note: I.e. a *polis*.
[e] Editors' note: See note to p. 131 in Chapter 13, where Polanyi quotes this same passage from the Aristotelian *Constitution*. Here he gives the entire chapter (24) and the starting sentence of the next.

another 4,000 men], and other ships which collected the tributes, with crews amounting to 2,000 men selected by lot; and besides these there were the persons maintained at the Prytaneion, and orphans, and gaolers, since all these were supported by the state. This is how the population earned its livelihood.

A few decades later, the value of citizenship had reached a record height. Under Pericles, no one who could not boast of all his grand-parents – male and female – having been born Athenian citizens could maintain his citizenship (and this in a minute city-state, the aristoc-racy of which was wont to intermarry with the princes and rulers of all Hellas). The genteel poverty that went with such a state of affairs is given away by the following passage from Plutarch's *Cimon* – Cimon was the son of Miltiades and himself a famous Athenian general, who was a most popular conservative leader in Pericles' time. Plutarch writes:

> And since he [Cimon] was already wealthy, Cimon lavished the reve-nues from his campaign, which he was thought to have won with honor from the enemy, to his still greater honor, on his fellow-citizens. He took away the fences from his fields, that strangers and needy citizens might have in their power to take fearlessly of the fruits of the land; and every day he gave a dinner at his house – simple, it is true, but sufficient for many, to which any poor man who wished came in, and so received a maintenance which *cost him no effort* and left him *free to devote himself solely to public affairs*. (Plutarch, *Cimon*, 10)

Not exchange, but reciprocity and redistribution were the forms of integration that originally dominated the economic life of Attica. True, the *reciprocity* elements were greatly weakened with the loosen-ing of the clan tie in the eighth/seventh century (with its blood feud, family rights in landed estate, inalienable property). Gift trade and the other, highly developed, gift and countergift systems common in the times of the epics were now fading out. But the *redistributive* forms of tribal life did not disappear in the same manner as reciproc-ating ones. The *polis* took over much of the redistributive inherit-ance of the tribe. The distribution of land (*klēroi*), of booty, of a lucky strike in the Laurion mines – similarly, of the gold mined on the isle of Syphnos; the claim to maintenance or to corn distribution in an emergency; the claim to participation in public displays or to payment for the performance of citizens' duties – all this is a very real tribute to the strength of the *redistributive factor in classical communities*. The basic economic organization of the *polis* was redistribution of the proceeds of common activity, share in booty and tribute, share in conquered land and in colonial ventures, in the advantages to be gained from third-party trade.

I wished to remind you of all this through reflection of Aristotle. Yet scholars of rank – such as, for example, Ulrich von Wilamowitz-Moellendorff – refused as much as to consider Aristotle's account of the organization of Athens, which he regarded as a skit on Aristeides and mob rule. I think that the time has come when authentic evidence should be given its due and even the most venerable grounds of prejudice should be discounted when they are contrary to plain fact.

And yet, with the fourth century BC, we part company with the primitivists. The great contribution of the Greeks to the economic life of antiquity consisted in the development of the market habit and private trading, although the relationship of the warriors' gild of Athens to the new world trade remained more parasitic than positively participant. The *polis* – and this is a dominating fact in the sociology of antiquity – *had not only a free constitution but also a city market*. The two together made the *polis* way of life. I'll go first to the market. The new development of the city market cannot be dated with any precision, but it is fair to assume that Solonan Attica was already familiar with the market, but that it was only after the fall of the tyranny[f] (560 BC) that it fully developed.

One of the chief factors, I believe, was the rise, rule, and fall of tyranny itself. In support of this it might be said that the tyranny episode was almost as characteristic of the *polis* as the acceptance of the market habit itself.

1   The *rise* of tyranny was usually the result of the burning need for the development of public services, which were mostly supplied by private persons (though, as a rule, of noble birth). Such services included the police, night watch, land-surveying, tax collecting, public works such as temple building, repair, and reconstruction, irrigation, other waterworks, port facilities, the supplying of mercenaries, the minting of money, the collecting of other revenues such as market dues or customs tariffs, and so on. All this involved hosts of employees: skilled workers and laborers recruited from the thetes and metics, strangers, farmed prisoners, slaves.

---

[f] Editors' note: Polanyi uses throughout the term "tyrannis": this is an Anglicized transliteration of the ancient Greek *turannis* (τυραννίς), an abstract noun designating both sovereignty in general and the specific institution of tyranny in the Greek world of the archaic and classical period.

Polyaenus, who is a good source for culture traits, reports the rise to power of Deinias, Phalaris, and Theron in almost identical terms: how they contracted for public services, for temple building, night watch land surveying, and tax collecting (any or all of these) and how they seized power with the help of the people they had engaged to perform the jobs.

2   After the *rise* comes *rule*. With the new king ‡. . .‡ᵍ the public services are nationalized. His employers become civil servants – a new bureaucracy. Peisistratus is the great example. Under him the government itself undertook public works – they were no longer given in contract – including temples and waterworks. His private mint becomes the public mint, his "owls" the device of Attica's trade for centuries to come. And how did he provide for the *feeding* of this Scythian slave police, his mercenaries, the skilled workers and laborers in the public works, the host of land surveyors and magistrates? Obviously from the tithes (in kind) that Athens had under him – never before and never afterwards. A passage in Aristotle points in this direction.

3   After *rule* (and very soon) comes *fall*. And what do we see happening, but the reprivatization of the nationalized services? State revenues, public works are again contracted out. True, Athens retains the ownership of the mines, also the mint, and the Scythian police. But all other public services are again farmed out, given out to contractors, handed to private persons to run under public control. Some services are discounted altogether, or rather put on an emergency basis, among them two rather important ones: army and taxation. Hence Attica raises armies or entrusts generals to do so (partly from public funds), and collects the *eisphora*ʰ in case of need – an emergency capital levy, we would say. But the mass of recently nationalized, and now denationalized, laborers, workers, and bureaucracy is again is again on private hands.ⁱ

It was, we believe, at this point that the market habit gained great public importance. The old primitive methods of organizing labor with the help of treasure and its political influence on tribal chieftains and manorial lords – these archaic methods of aspirants to tyranny – were no longer practicable. The public utility

---

ᵍEditors' note: Unreadable.
ʰEditors' note: *Eisphora* was a direct system of taxation. It was imposed at Athens after the Persian invasion in the fifth century BC, as an emergency tax in cases of war.
ⁱEditors' note: Unreadable sentence.

employers – and there were many – now had to procure their provisions from the *agora*, with their pay. In one field we have proof of this development: that of the army. In the second half of the Peloponnesian War, and even more definitely under Agesilaos in Asia Minor, the provisioning of the army is done from markets that the general has "provided," "stocked," "prepared" on his prospective route. The Greek soldier buys his own food and keeps himself on his own pay.

Only if no market is available is the commanding general expected to provide in some other way for supplies (through raiding parties or requisitioning, or through the provision of camp markets frequented by sutlers). This use of markets on the part of armies seems significant and indicative of the manner in which the whole question of feeding the personnel of the public services was henceforth met, namely the market way.

But, while the *agora* became part and parcel of the *polis* way of life, the rapidly developing private trade in foreign parts was never absorbed into the *polis*, at least not so far as Athens was concerned. (The earlier story of Corinth and the later one of Rhodes carry different features. Not these *poleis* – these two just as little as Sparta – not they but Athens became the prototype of the *polis*, which in its contrast with the oriental countryside, the *chōra*, became the nuclear problem of Hellenism.) For the warrior gild never gave in. Of the two types of traders known to men's early history, Athens knew only one. The man who belongs to the community, the merchant by status, the *damkar* of Sumeria and Babylonia, had not developed in early Athens, and in post-Peisistratidian Athens there was no room for him any more. The other type of merchant is the person who doesn't "belong": the foreigner and stranger, the member of a trading people such as the Phoenicians or the Beduin (they are rare), or maybe a detached person, a DP, of which the world was full, the floating population of the time, someone who settled as a *ger* in Palestine, as a metic in Greece. This trader could gain honor and status by following his despised occupation. Mediterranean trade became Greek when it ceased to be Phoenician, but "Greek" in this sense did not mean Athenian or Spartan: it did not mean that it[j] had become a civic occupation, an acceptable profession for a *politēs*.

From the intimately civic and internalized position of the *agora* on the one hand and the utterly external relationship of the *polis* to foreign trade on the other, the essential structure of the *polis* can be deduced. Athens never became the home of proud merchant

[j]Editors' note: I.e. being a trader.

burgesses, and the hundred of *agorai* that came to birth in imitation of the one in Athens never penetrated an inch into the *chōra*. The politico-sociological framework of the *agora* precluded that. It was an organization of citizens. The *polis* never overcame this constitutional limitation. If eventually the market system of the Hellenistic world failed and the Roman Empire, in its sudden expansion, could not adapt that system so as to cope with the tasks of integrating a world empire, this was in the last resort due to that limitation. (Something faintly analogous might have already happened once before, to take up an idea of Heichelheim's: neolithic markets, which definitely existed, did not continue to develop in the irrigational empires of the bronze age city-states, or certainly not at anything like a rate comparable to that of the growth of economic activity in this amazing outburst of civilizing forces.)

Here lies the new, decisive problem of ancient history. The recognition that not Babylonia but Greece was the birthplace of market methods shifts the problem of market and nonmarket forms of integration of economic activities in more than one way. These nonmarket methods are based on *reciprocity* and *redistribution* – together we will briefly call them planning. The relation of market elements and economic planning appears in a new light. Our ability to give an adequate description of the economies of Babylonia will be the test. Not so much Egypt is in the foreground as Mesopotamia; for it was in Mesopotamia that the eclipse of the market took place while economic activity increased enormously – an activity that included trade and the use of money, as well as – widely – business transactions. It is here that the new conceptual tools will be tested. To keep to the instance of money: How is money as a standard of value possible, and also as a means of payment, while in the absence of markets it is hardly used in the domestic economy as a means of exchange? These and similar questions require an answer . . .

In early Babylonia, that is, under the first Babylonian dynasty, silver functioned as a standard of value, while in the decisive sector of the economy the temple accounts were carried in the units of the means of payment, which was barley. Barley was, in effect, the only means of payment with regard to taxes, rent, wages, and so on.

What did the equations mean, by which the laws proclaimed definite amounts of goods to be equal to one shekel of silver? What was the purpose of the striking stability of the equation level over long periods of time? And what was the purpose of formal stability in those cases – not rare – when the actual standard of measurement was altered in order to keep the equation stable? (Incidentally, what was the operational device used to achieve this without disrupting the metrological system?)[k]

Such and similar questions will need more knowledge than we possess as yet for a satisfactory answer. But so much may be already said without prejudging the limits of our ignorance: the traditional picture of a world gradually moving toward the consummation of a market economy is inadequate for a grasp of the past. Market elements have been with us again and again, and, when a sudden expansion of the territory to be integrated made the market organization fail, nonmarket elements came to the fore. The study of the manner in which market and nonmarket elements are jig-sawed in the various periods of history is of the greatest interest and importance – importance also for the present and the immediate future, in which roughly similar problems are again set to us. The study of ancient history may prove to be one of the most urgently needed toolboxes for the conceptual mastery of the problems of everyday life.

[k]Editors' note: Sentence crossed by the author.

Part IV

Crisis and Transformation

16

The Crucial Issue Today
A Response*

In an article entitled "Machinery of Commonality"[a] published in issue 25/26 of the *NE*,[b] Professor F. W. Förster contrasted the Christian–Tolstoyan viewpoint with that of Bolshevism. This prompted a response from Adele Jellinek in issue 29/30 ("The Ethical Value of Socialism").[c] In issue 31/32, the author of the present remarks put pen to paper to present a critical contribution on the issue of the Marxist worldview that was based on the positive spirit of Förster's standpoint. This article appeared under the title "Crisis of Ideology: On F. W. Förster's 'Machinery of Commonality.'"[d] The starting point is the following: "The amalgamation of Marxism and socialism prevailing today remains the bugbear of all modern thought. Every intellectual attempt to address the most urgent social problems of our time becomes bogged down in this intellectual · swamp" (p. 458). The result: "Utilitarian ethics, materialistic conception of history, positivist epistemology, deterministic philosophy: These are no longer viable in the new conjuncture. But Marxism, as an ideology, is built upon this basis. Its time is over" (p. 461).

---

*File 2–9, Karl Polanyi Archive: German typescript from 1919, entitled "Worauf es heute ankommt: Eine Erwiderung."
[a] Translator's note: The original title is "Maschinerie der Gemeinsamkeit."
[b] Editors' note: This is most likely a reference to the Austrian journal *Neue Erde*.
[c] Translator's note: The original title is "Der sittliche Wert des Sozialismus."
[d] Translator's note: The original title is "Weltanschauungskrise": Zur 'Maschinerie der Gemeinsamkeit' von F. W. Förster."

I have *only now* received Fritz Müller's rejoinder in issue 36 of the *NE*, in which he discusses both Förster and me. It bears the title "On Christian Anarchists and Prophets of Crisis: On the Discussion Förster, Polanyi, etc."[e] Toward Förster, Müller is deferential in form and downright condescending in substance; toward me, he is downright condescending in form and utterly heedless in substance. However, the result is the same in both cases. Förster is deemed to be a nobleman; his views are therefore true – though, like any views of a noble spirit, they must remain inconsequential. Polanyi, by contrast, is for unknown reasons branded as the "former Hungarian communist," hence as a subhuman, as it were; his views, even if they were true, evidently must be inconsequential for this very reason. In this way Müller does not take a coherent position on the content of my article set forth above but merely engages in a literary exercise that has precious little to do with the matter itself. Since I have never been a communist, whether of the old or of the new persuasion, but have long been regarded in Hungary as an adherent of an anti-Marxist ideology, I will address F. W. Förster's observations once again here, in an attempt to defend our common concern in an objective manner.[f]

Since the dawn of the capitalist era, all social philosophy has split into two camps: an *apologetic* camp and a *socialist* camp. The latter calls for the abolition of all exploitation and sets itself the goal of creating a society of free and equal persons.

The socialist schools of the nineteenth century take in turn two directions: the Marxist socialists – who, as a reformist party, would call themselves social democrats, and as a revolutionary party now call themselves Bolshevists (communists); and the liberal socialists – who, as reformists, are known as radicals and land reformers, and as a revolutionary party dissolve into the different anarchist groups.

In contrast to the uniform edifice of Marxist socialism put forward and bequeathed as a closed legacy by Marx and Engels, liberal socialism stands as a free intellectual community of independent nineteenth-century thinkers. This series leads from Turgot and Adam Smith, through Carey, Proudhon, Dühring, and Bastiat, to H. George, H. Spencer, Krapotkin, Hertzka, and Oppenheimer. *Transcending all of their differences and divisions, the unifying central theme of their work emerges all the more clearly and significantly.* This central theme is the following:

Freedom is the foundation of all true harmony. The condition to which freedom gives rise is the natural condition, whose harmony is grounded in itself and is solid and unshakable. It is not "requirements of natural law" that lead to this ideal image of all human life; on the contrary, this necessary ideal is what leads to the notion of natural laws in the first place. This specific and excellent image is far removed from any despotism [*Willkür*]. It is the necessary and clear image of that condition to which the absence of all violence, hence true and genuine freedom, inevitably leads.

1 The Economic Ideal

The goal of the great English–French Revolution was to realize this economic freedom; but the revolution left its work unfinished. The feudal institution of monopoly on land survived the revolution and, as a result, turned the new forces of the free economy on their head. *Only free ownership of land in addition to freedom of movement could have brought work and natural forces into a free relation.* This is what led to capitalism: a hybrid of violence and freedom, a vile product of the raw forces of the past coupled with the new forces of a free future. Far from being a "necessary developmental phase," capitalism is instead a product of the retardation of this development at the very point where its creative power would have found full expression for the first time. The capitalist's profit is not the result of pure ground rent (of Ricardo's differential rent, which plays a subordinate role), but of the rent that marginal land also generates. The coercive monopoly on land [*Bodensperre*][g] means that there will always be landless workers who are disposed to hire themselves out as dependent workers at a lower wage than the yield their labor would generate on their own land. The surplus value that the landless class delivers to the landowning class is distributed among the individual members of the latter according to their shares in "capital." As long as this monopoly on land continues to exist, not only land, but all capital must "yield a profit." No wage can rise above the wage of the agricultural "marginal worker," since it is always the latter's

[g]Translator's note: This was the term used by Franz Oppenheimer for the monopoly on land enjoyed by the Junkers, the German landed gentry. (My thanks to Gareth Dale for this reference.)

starvation wage that determines the base of the wage pyramid. Thus capital profit is founded on pure ground rent – and not on ground rent on capital profit, as the Marxists assume. Exploitation does not derive from the economic law of free competition that supposedly prevails, but from the *political* law of coercive property in land that actually prevails and nullifies free competition.

Submissive forms of labor have been the political result of violence from time immemorial. Slavery and bondage, the products of political conquest, are the foundation of economic exploitation. Capitalism as an instrument for extracting surplus value is founded on the submissive form of labor whose real name is monopoly on land [*Bodensperre*]. The army of cheap workers driven by hunger from the country into the cities is everywhere the root cause of capitalist industry, which is itself merely the fruit of the prevailing submissive form of labor, of the monopoly on land.

Today not freedom but monopoly prevails in the economy. This monopoly on land is not a "result of the free economy," as the Marxists claim, but it is precisely what prevents a free market economy from arising. It is the "extra-economic force" (Marx) that precludes an economy among free and equal human beings and turns the so-called competition of the present day into its opposite: the exploitation of the propertyless class by the class of property owners. Surplus value does not arise *in accordance with* the law of value of free market economy but *in contradiction* to it, because a free economy is restricted by coercive property.

This line of thought was first encapsulated by Eugen Dühring as follows:

> Institutions such as slavery and wage bondage, along with which is associated their twin-brother, property based on force, must be regarded as social-economic constitutional forms of a purely political nature, and have hitherto constituted the frame within which the consequences of the natural economic laws could alone manifest themselves.[h]

Friedrich Engels described these ideas as the "basic theme" of Dühring's entire work and tried to refute them, in our opinion in vain.

---

[h] Translator's note: E. Dühring, *Cursus der National- und Socialökonomie*, originally published in 1876 and quoted here from a quotation in Friedrich Engels, *Anti-Dühring*, at http://www.marxists.org/archive/marx/works/1877/anti-duhring/ch13.htm (accessed April 7, 2014).

For liberal socialism, the *fundamental problem* of capitalism, its unjust economic constitution and the exploitation underlying it, are consequences of restrictions on the true freedom of labor.

The *secondary* problems of capitalism also spring from the same source.

In an economy completely liberated from surplus value, supply and demand function as harmonious regulators of production and distribution. Here there is no "entrepreneurial profit" other than the eligible wages. There are no crises, because prices no longer realize concealed surplus value but only equal labor values. The perversities of the "profit economy," which can bring production into conflict with social need, are transformed into an eminent guarantee of the interest of society.

Under this social constitution, free cooperation becomes the general form of collaboration. The organization of consumption and production in an organic structure of autonomous cooperatives is *organized* by the market itself, extending to the complete exclusion of all intermediate trade, speculation, and other parasitic practices. However, *this* is an organic form of organization – no longer a mechanical one. Every member is able to *survey* his position in relation to his environment within the narrow scope of the consumption, production, or other cooperative enterprise to which he belongs. He is able to derive the impulses of both economic self-interest and cooperative altruism from vivid intuition, to re-examine these impulses continually, and to preserve and nourish them with his entire personality. The second source of crises, the lack of market organization, is thus rectified in an organic way, without in the process destroying the active individual, the invisible driving cell of the whole organism.

The image of social life that, as liberal socialism conceives of it, measures up to reality is an image of an *organic entity*. The economy is a living process that can by no means be replaced by a mechanical apparatus, however subtly and ingeniously conceived. Hoping to determine the needs, capabilities, and interests "of society" by using statistical methods in order to build a corresponding system based on these determinations – a system whose operation does not appeal to the needs of the individual, the capabilities of the individual, and the interests of the individual – this is a completely unfounded and vain hope as far as liberal socialism is concerned.

The method of "statistical determination" is beset by a fundamental fallacy. What can be counted here is not things that should be determined in accordance with their magnitude. One can "count" human beings, commodities, working hours, parcels of land, crop yields, and horsepower; but one cannot count the needs and capabilities of these human beings, the intensity and quality of their work, the fertility of the land, the technical possibilities of an invention – and these are the only factors that count in the life process of the economy. Identifying the portion of the vascular tissue of the economy that is illuminated by the numerically analyzable market with the actual economy that has to be brought under control would be like identifying the illuminated portion of our mind that appears in consciousness with the latent and hidden content of our unconscious mental organism whose function this consciousness itself is. The market is a peculiar sense organ in the literal sense, and without it the circulatory system of the economy would collapse. The operation of the market that accomplishes this perceptual function, however, is *free price formation*.

There are two conceivable methods for distributing the product of social labor, namely *by means of the market* as the center of a web of prices that delivers good to needs, or *without a market*, through direct allocation. The former is reality; the latter, in the national and world economy, an impossibility. Nothing could replace price formation here, for prices do not express a distribution quotient of existing goods to existing needs, for instance, even though a human price is at least theoretically conceivable. On the contrary, the price is a floating indicator that does not show the manifest needs and the manifest work effort, but instead the *moments of change* of the needs and means of work hidden behind these manifestations; not real magnitudes as such, but differentials of the organic life process of the economy. It is the regularity and relative consistency of the price manifestations that belied their purely functional character. Prices are certainly not characteristics of the commodities, but relations among the producers. However, the modality of these relationships is concealed from us by the dense web of myriads of economic cells, and all that we know is the result of their integration. This result is the prices. Expecting prices to regulate themselves according to the statistics would be as futile as expecting one's manometer to operate in accordance with the factory settings. But there is no middle ground between market economy and marketless economy. This would be like presupposing a collection of limbs with an active circulatory system, or a living human being with an artificial heart mechanism.

This is why cooperative socialism is synonymous with market economy: not the anarchic market of the capitalist profit economy as a field in which the plunder of the surplus value concealed in the prices is realized, but the organically structured market of equivalent products of free labor.

This organic intuition means that liberal socialism is in principle a *physiocratic* doctrine (Turgot, Carey, Oppenheimer, A. Dániel). The dependence of production as a whole on agricultural yields is a fundamental principle of liberal socialism. Therefore the forms of organization of industry must always remain a secondary matter for liberal socialism, one that can never determine the constitutional forms of land unilaterally. The meaning and content of all urban movements is decided in the countryside. Although the technical productivity of machinery raised the *average* standard for workers in the early capitalist era, the ocean of misery in the countryside that benefited from this simultaneously pushed the level of the urban worker far below the wage of medieval journeymen and craftsmen (Franz Oppenheimer). Moreover, the effect of all industrial socialization, insofar as this is supposed to raise production, would still have to be absorbed in the long run by the rising standard of living of the *agricultural* laborers, which is a result of political revolutions.

Therefore, for liberal socialism as a liberal and physiocratic economic conception, the question of the *agricultural cooperative* has priority. Of course, this must be a voluntary enterprise, for otherwise it would not be a cooperative enterprise at all. There is no middle ground between enforced cooperation and free cooperation either. On paper they may be indistinguishable; *in reality* they are as different as a living human being is from the panopticon mannequin. Their construction, their efficient cause, their metabolism, and hence their durability and vital function are fundamentally different. Apart from K. Kautsky's exemplary lack of appreciation of agricultural issues, it is his fatally offhand treatment of the cooperative question in particular that constitutes his historical omission. This led to the serious error of treating the cooperative as a decorative subsidiary form, as it were, alongside the communist state economy as the principal form, as though a cooperative were conceivable under conditions of a marketless economy. The omissions of Marxist theory and practice of the past decades have nowhere been as grave as in respect of the cooperatives, and nowhere else have they avenged themselves as much as in this very point.

A *state-created cooperative* is nothing but a large-scale public enterprise where the relations in which the participants stand can be generated only by coercion, no matter how just or how reasonable this coercion may be felt to be. The cause of the existence of such a cooperative is not the insight, purposes, and interests of the individual but the will of others, which gives rise to a shared fate. The hidden sources of strength of the individual are not at its disposal. The relationship in which the ultimate, inconspicuously small but still expended effort stands to the likewise inconspicuously small but still expected increase in value of the joint product is the quotient that determines the productivity of cooperative labor. Without this infinitesimal moment, the cooperative is in no way superior to wage labor. On the contrary. For in the case of wage labor it is the profit mania of the capitalist wielding the scourge of hunger that squeezes this final expenditure of effort – albeit not to such a high degree [*Potens*] – out of the worker *for the capitalist's benefit*.

But feudal estates are the last thing that can be transformed into communist "large-scale cooperative enterprises" by decree. This is a *twofold impossibility*: first, the impossibility just outlined, of decreeing cooperatives at all – that is, of forcing agricultural laborers, farmhands, tenants, and so on to cooperate freely and voluntarily; and, second, the impossibility of simultaneously forcing them to regard the product of their labor as public property that is supposed to be exchanged for industrial products. This amounts to forcing the semi-enslaved people of the countryside to engage in free cooperation and at the same time, in a single breath, to engage in the marketless state economy. Such attempts are completely futile. For liberal socialism, only voluntary cooperatives can exist; it knows no others. The red-painted large-scale feudal enterprises of the Soviet era in Hungary are the prototype of revolutionary Potemkin villages. Civil war may necessitate such undertakings; far from refuting, this actually demonstrates their untenability in the context of national economies.

Liberal socialism is fundamentally *hostile to force*. For liberal socialism, not only the state as an organism exercising domination over persons, but also the state as an administrator of things is, practically speaking, a necessary evil and, theoretically speaking, a superfluous and harmful construct. Any attempt to use state power to replace what can only arise through the life and activity of the individual inevitably has devastating consequences.

"Communist state economy" is viable only in the domain in which *its idea arose*, which is the domain of the urban enterprise. These industries are great in number and importance and their socialization is urgent and necessary. But the reorganization of industry must not abolish the market economy, because otherwise the economy itself would come to an end. On the other hand, it must not extend to agriculture, for this is the true home of the cooperative large-scale concern. Socialization should not be synonymous with state economy either. The state should not be the agency of socialization, or at least it should not be the ultimate owner of the enterprise; the agency should instead be the economic autonomy of all – as represented by their organs, the workers' councils and the other representatives of autonomous consumption and agricultural production. More on this later. Here suffice it to show that liberal socialism considers the socialization of the principal mechanical means of production – without violating the principle of a free and cooperating market economy – to be an urgent measure and calls for it.

Thus "communism" is a twofold necessity for liberal socialism – though this in no way leads to a marketless economy, to communism proper. The one necessity is permanent, the other temporary. The first is the socialization of large-scale industrial concerns. The second is the communism entailed by every war and every revolution, which is a result of the provisioning of warring armies or of the strategy of civil war. *This is merely an accompaniment of the proletarian uprising, not its historical meaning.* This will be explained in greater detail in the political–historical section of this presentation.

Before we turn to that part, I would like to list briefly the practical means available for the positive construction of the liberal–socialist society:

1 Complete liberation of land through the free allocation of arable land to anyone who is willing and able to cultivate it.
2 The assurance of complete security of property to all agricultural workers – to productive cooperatives and other cooperatives of whatever kind that constitute themselves as large-scale enterprises.
3 The transfer of the corresponding large-scale industrial enterprises to the economic autonomy of all, as represented by the organs of the organized economy. The complete separation of organic economic autonomy (council and curia system) from the democratic representation of all. The latter has no right to interfere in the economy.
4 Complete organic equalization of mental and physical work. Only a form of representation in which mental and physical work are represented equally counts as just. Free wage agreement with the productive workforce.
5 The complete cessation, as soon as possible, of all price and wage regulation, requisitioning and land division [*Requisitien und Rayonierung*], all duties and quotas, and all other interferences in the free market.

2 Political–Historical Perspective

The history of Bolshevism is brief, but conclusive in its results:

Fourteen months ago the author of these lines described the doctrines of the Russian Revolution as follows:

The political triumph of Bolshevism in Russia means the complete defeat of the communist economic program. Every success of the Soviet government is purchased at the cost of relinquishing the demands of the centralized state economy. What is to be found in Russia is not marketless exchange, not production through and for society, not the nationalization of land, but instead market, private property in land, voluntary free cooperatives as the dominant force in the market of food products, piecework with monetary wages, and all of this in the necessarily depraved forms brought about by the civil war – specifically black marketeering, speculation, state-guaranteed company profits, wages for skilled labor first artificially lowered and then artificially raised, underproduction, and overexploitation. What was not understood at the time – or was, at best, misunderstood – is, today, an acknowledged historical reality: the complete political triumph of the Soviet government, coupled with the complete collapse of the centralized state economy in Russia. What reigns in Russia today is Lenin's political power and the economic power of the new, free Russian agricultural cooperatives producing on their own land, which have come together to form a voluntary, mighty colossus. The negative proof of the same truth was provided by Hungary: there the political power of the Soviet is inferior, solely as a result of the seriousness and energy with which it exerted itself to the utmost to realize its economic program. Without the generous but completely failed attempt of the communist economy, Hungarian Soviet power would still be in control today. Both Russia and Hungary teach us the same thing: the political success of the dictatorship of the proletariat and the economic success of the dictatorship of the proletariat are mutually exclusive. By political success here is meant the attempt to concentrate state power in the hands of the working class; by economic success, by contrast, the attempt to restructure the economy in accordance with communism (marketless, centralized state economy). *But every other socialist economy, except the communist, is compatible with the political power of the working class.* This is the fact that will determine the future of Europe.

The historical meaning of the Bolshevik movement is not communism. Its true meaning, which is realized in the dictatorship of the proletariat, is a twofold one: (1) it will permanently efface the stifling boundaries of historical states; (2) it will tear the power of large agricultural estates and of monopoly capitalism out of the soil of the economy by the roots. This effect – theoretically intrinsically destructive – will leave behind a scene of complete economic anarchy and political despotism in a Europe laid waste for decades to come, if the liberated forces of the land do not devote themselves to the task of reconstruction in a timely fashion and in the form of cooperative socialism, which is the only possible one.

The elevation of the bourgeoisie created the nation-states; the elevation of the workers will create the world state. However, the bourgeois revolutions were sustained by the material interest of the revolutionary class, the bourgeoisie; the more complete its victory, the higher the standard achieved by that class. No political reaction could economically undo its triumph. For the industrial proletariat, the communist path means, on the contrary, hardship in the struggle, hardship as a result of the struggle, and hardship in the case of a political defeat. But, as indicated above, every economic advantage must in the long run benefit the ocean of misery that the proletarians of the countryside still represent today. All of these are indicators of a political, not an economic revolution. The final political, legal, and monopolistic privileges of the former "higher estates" are what will be destroyed here, and the forces of free labor on free land are what will be rendered all-powerful. That is not a revolution in the most profound economic sense, however, because it does not represent the inversion, but instead the completion of the movement that began with the great English–French revolutions. But it is the most important economic advance that human society is capable of far into the future, *provided that it survives the convulsion.*

Human society will be able to make this advance only if the communism of necessity that is intrinsic to all wars and revolutions is not confused by the great world revolution with its true meaning, which is not communism but the final creation of free cooperation among free workers, on the liberated land of the world. For this world will either perish or survive, in the words of F. W. Förster, "as the final result of a richly articulated, cooperative interaction among maximally free individual actions."[i]

---

[i]Translator's note: Possibly a quotation from "Maschinerie der Gemeinsamkeit," mentioned at start; otherwise unidentified.

3   The Crucial Issue Today

The crucial issue today, however, is to understand that liberalism is not the policy of the past and anarchism the policy of the future, but that their shared ideological content constitutes the reality of the present.

The crucial issue today is to grasp that what is currently being satisfied is the demands that the liberal and anarchistic socialists have been making for the past century – not in their utopian form, but in accordance with their real political substance. The world revolution will not bring about communism, but liberal socialism instead.

The crucial issue today is to understand, finally, that the cooperative economy is incompatible with communism, for the former can only survive where free cooperation and free exchange interact freely.

Today every militant must feel profoundly that he is not called to coerce humanity to its salvation but to restore humanity to its freedom, and he must have the inner conviction that what will save the world is freedom – and nothing else.

That is the crucial issue.

Translated by Ciaran Cronin

Acknowledgments

I would like to thank Gareth Dale for kindly making available to me his photographs of the 8-page typescript of Karl Polanyi's unpublished 1919 essay "Worauf es heute ankommt: Eine Erwiderung" from the Karl Polanyi Archive at Concordia University and for his help with a number of points of translation. The typescript contains numerous typos and errors, most of which were corrected by hand, in pencil (presumably by the author); moreover, a couple of passages were barely legible, and one passage was illegible. However, the associated difficulties of interpretation could be resolved with a high level of confidence – in the case of the illegible passage, with the kind assistance of Giorgio Resta – and hence have not been commented upon in the translation.

17

Conflicting Philosophies
in Modern Society*

LECTURE 1

This subject is commonly understood as the challenge of fascism and communism to democracy.

The aim of this lecture course will be to discover the true nature of that challenge. Incidentally, we will discover whether or not the above is an accurate description of the issues involved.

I English and Continental Ideals of Democracy

We are used to describing political philosophy as *democratic*. But is it justified to apply one and the *same* term to two as widely differing sets of ideals as are embodied in English and continental democracies, respectively?

---

*File 15–2, Karl Polanyi Archive: series of lectures entitled *Conflicting Philosophies in Modern Society*, University of London, Eltham London County Council Literary Institute, 1937–8. The typescript contains six lectures, and each lecture is identified at the top right-hand corner of each page with a running head: "Lecture 1," "Lecture 2," "Lecture 3," "Lecture 4," "Lecture 5," and "Lecture 6." The lectures bear individual titles from the second one on – but not the first. Clearly all six formed a close unit. At the start of the third lecture Polanyi refers to the previous two as "the first lecture" and "the second lecture," by way of summarizing them (and there are two other cross-references of a similar sort).

It is generally assumed that English and continental democracy are but different variants of the same species. The parliament of Westminster is often referred to as the mother of parliaments. Continental parliaments are supposed to have been fashioned on the English model.

The differences between the English and the continental specimens are simply attributed to the inadequacy of the imitation. Accordingly, the *crisis of democratic institutions on the continent* is attributed not to their adherence to the philosophy of democracy but rather to their failure to adhere to it adequately. Is this appreciation correct?

1　Ideals

(a)　English democracy　English democracy centers upon the idea of *liberty*. It is a method of getting the affairs of a community done according to the greatest measure of common consent and with a minimum of coercion. The revealing figure of English democracy is the chairman. He has no parallel on the continent. The functions of a continental president are indeed almost the opposite of those of an English chairman. The task of the chairman is to ensure that discussions and deliberations are carried in such a manner as to allow *articulate expression to all relevant trends of opinion* (preferably with some indications of the volume of opinion that is supporting the various trends). The ascertaining of the "sense of the meeting" should involve unnecessary prejudging of the issue. No other but unavoidable coercion shall be used in the enforcement of these decisions. Especially, no greater degree of coercion against the minority shall be used than the overwhelming majority of the meeting deems on general grounds, that is, whether or not they themselves happen to belong to the majority or the minority with respect to the question at issue. It is by methods such as these that the greatest measure of liberty in the community is achieved.

If the meeting be that of a *representative body* periodically elected by a permanent constituency, a further safeguard against the abuse of the right of the majority to use coercion against the dissenting minority is found in the *two-party system*. The majority that would abuse its function of representing the greatest measure of common consent by coercing the minority beyond the limits of the unavoidable would almost automatically see itself put into a minority at the next elections.

The two-party system thus embodies the main features of English democracy. It *gets things done*, and gets them done by using *a minimum of coercion*. For without a stable majority parliament would be unable to provide a backing for an efficient government; and without an alternation of parties in power[a] the majority system would amount to a dictatorship over the minority.

At this juncture it may be appropriate to point to the inherent limitations of democracy as a form of government designed to ensure liberty. Obviously, it is impossible to translate any abstract principle, whatever it may be, into practice altogether. But what we are referring to are the inherent limitations of the principle itself. The need for getting things done is itself an essential part of liberty. It is not merely a practical aspect of life in the community, which bears no reference to the main problem of achieving liberty in the community, but, on the contrary, it is a matter of principle that things should get done. Imagine, for example, a community that would be unable to achieve its purpose for lack of an adequate machinery of government and you will realize at once that stable majorities are a condition of democracy as a form of government designed to achieve liberty. Yet the establishment of a stable majority implies the subordination of individuals and groups to the convictions and interests that dominate in the majority. The same holds true, of course, of stable minorities. Thus both individuals and permanent minorities represent an inherent limitation to the application of the democratic method. They must be dealt with, as the phrase goes, by common sense (which is only another way of saying that the principle upon which we were working has broken down).

It is an essential feature of democracy as a method that it will, eventually, attempt to overcome its own limitations, as far as possible in the spirit of liberty. The permanent minority of race, language, and nationality, of geographical reasons, of religious convictions, and of special economic or vocational interest will be to some degree protected by the self-denying ordinance according to which the powers of the democratic state must, in their very nature, be limited. It is this limitation that is expressed in the principle of local and vocational self-government, of tolerance, of cultural and religious autonomy, of noninterference into industrial and economic matters.

The method of liberty demands that its spirit should be applied even beyond the boundaries of the two-party system.

(b) Continental democracy Democracy is centered around the principle of equality (the opposite of an aristocracy or an oligarchy). Democracy, accordingly, is an aim: it is the achievement of such a condition of affairs, in which common human equality is significantly

---

[a] Editors' note: The words "in power" are deleted by the author.

expressed in actual social conditions. In practice this means that distinctions of birth and wealth are less stressed, while the difference in individual natural abilities has a wider scope. The state becomes the safeguard of equality; it is designed to prevent the domination of individuals by other individuals, of one by another group. The result is a *strong state*, but scant consideration accorded to dissenting minorities; a wide jurisdiction and a strong executive.

A great measure of social democracy is achieved. The overwhelming majority of the dignitaries of the Roman church, of the imperial army, and of the Austrian higher civil service is recruited from the sons of the lower middle class and peasants.

2   Institutions

(a)   England   A constitution based on the principle of popular sovereignty, together with that of feudal prerogative. Franchise restricted to a few hundred thousand voters. Popular education a new feature; actually elementary education obligatory since 1891, and secondary education since 1903.[b] In Austria, since 1867, public elementary schools are not only obligatory, but practically no other schools are allowed. The upper class [families] sending their children to public elementary schools. Incidentally, this being one of the reasons why schools reached such a high level. Secondary schools of two types: the lower type up to 14, the higher type up to the university – but only one kind of higher secondary schools in existence. Thus education a lever of national unity rather than an expression of class distinction.

Thus two sharply contrasting types of democracy must be distinguished: the English *libertarian* form of government, based on the democratic method, with limited powers of the state and hierarchic social stratification; as opposed to the continental *egalitarian* form of government, designed to ensure social equality, powerful central government, universal suffrage, and educational equality as its main institutional features.

Can it be that liberty and equality are mutually exclusive principles of social organization?

II   Liberty and Equality

Far from being mutually exclusive, freedom and equality are actually correlatives, that is, they are corollaries of the Christian concept of personality.

[b]Editors' note: We should have here a new subheading "(b) The continent."

Freedom is the essence of the spiritual nature of man. Indeed it is only another name for spirit. The Christian discovery of personality is the discovery of the truth that every human being has a soul to save, and in this decisive respect all human beings are equal.

But must anything follow from this assertion? There are some who would say that it applies only to an ideal society, such as the society of those who are in communion with the church. But those who assert this would be at a loss to explain why they continue to work for the perfection of society. But, however this may be, we usually think of both freedom and equality as principles that ought to be applied to actual institutional life in society.

It is at this point that our problem arises. For the institutional achievement of a principle is necessarily a *partial* achievement of the principle and, as such – or to that extent – a falsification of it. No wonder that it must clash with the equally partial realization of another principle. In fact equality is never achieved by law but at the cost of liberty, nor was liberty secured in an unequal society but at the price of maintaining inequality.

It is in the field of institutional achievement that we must look for the causes of the divergent development. To this purpose we must go back as far as the common origins of English and continental democracies require, namely for more than a thousand years.

III   The Two Sources of Liberty

When the Germanic village community and its tribal society came in touch with Roman civilization, the blood bond gave way to land as the new basis of economics and politics. The freeman's community was doomed. No organization of national sovereignty was possible on the basis of the blood bond. The manorial system emerged as the new local unit of economic and political life.

But there are only two ways in which national territorial sovereignty can be established on the basis of the manorial system:

(a)   either trough a national federation of the lords of the manor, namely a republic of barons, with the king as a mere *primus inter pares*; this is the case in pure feudalism, for example in France;

(b)   or through absolute monarchy, the divine right of kings, the establishment of direct and effective sovereignty over all the king's subjects – whether they be barons, freemen, villains or slaves.

Western European history – continental and English – roughly from 800 to 1800 is the history of the alternation of the two.

Both methods of setting up national sovereignty became a source of liberty:

(a) the barons limiting the power of the king;
(b) the king limiting the power of the barons.

The first type of liberty, usually called constitutional liberty, was often at the same time synonymous with the regained[c] liberty of the barons to enslave his subjects; the second leads to social liberties.

In England the slave, the lower tenant, the villain, the journeyman were indebted for their liberty to the king. From William the Conqueror, who tried to stop slave trade, to Henry II and the Inquest of Sheriffs[d] to the Statute of Merton,[e] which limited enclosures, this holds true almost all the way. Politically the king was allied, as on the continent, with the nonfeudal classes against the barony (except at times of general economic emergency, like the Black Death period).

On the other hand, the barons were responsible for the increasing safeguards against the arbitrary power of the king.

Thus liberty was being nourished from two sides: the constitutional and the social.

The process on the continent was essentially similar. There, too, the king was trying to curb the barony, and the barons were asserting their constitutional rights. And here as there king and baron allied themselves with the other social classes to achieve their end. The difference lay in the classes they allied themselves with. And this, again, was dependent on the stage of economic development at which the struggle was decided.

Now, English development was ahead of development on the continent. The manorial system, which in Germany for instance continued up to the first quarter of the nineteenth century, declined in England by the end of the fourteenth century. This was the result of the wool trade. By the end of the fourteenth century services were mainly commuted in the manor and the villainage had disappeared. A new rural middle class made its appearance in the leaseholder, and – this is essential – the new wool industry remained an agricultural industry, without the use of machines. England became an

---

[c]Editors' note: Our conjecture; the original reads *re-rained*, which is obviously a typo, most probably for *re-gained*.
[d]Editors' note: Issued in 1170 by King Stephen II.
[e]Editors' note: The first English statute, agreed upon in 1235.

industrial country centuries before the industrial revolution. No industrial proletariat accompanied this development. When the decisive stage of the constitutional battle was reached, the new middle class, which by this time had been mainly assimilated to the country gentry, fought its battles itself. No working class was present with which it needed to compromise in order to win it over to its side.

On the continent the decisive struggle came at the beginning of, or well into, the period of the Industrial Revolution. Both the king and the middle classes had to try to gain its support. In the French Revolution the working class was an effective ally of the middle classes in the battles in which feudalism was abolished. In 1830, and later on in 1848 all over Central Europe, a similar happening took place on a minor scale. Eventually, in 1917 and 1918, the same process spread to Eastern Europe, the Balkans, and Russia.

This explains, incidentally, the kind of class consciousness that is characteristic of the continental working-class movement when compared with the Anglo-Saxon, whether English or American. The historical role that fell to it in the past became a constitutive element of the consciousness of the continental working class. Social equality and more or less socialist ideals thus became an inherent part of democracy on the continent.[f]

LECTURE 2

Laissez-Faire and Popular Government

In the course of our inquiry into the nature of the challenge offered to democracy in our time we have proceeded to distinguish between the English and the continental type of democracy. We found that the one was centered around liberty, the other around equality. The one may be called *libertarian*, the other *egalitarian*. We had to go far back in order to discover the source of the divergent development. We found that, in England, the democratic form of government was finally established at a time when the industrial working class had not yet come into existence – that is, a full century before the industrial revolution. In England the middle classes established the

---

[f]Editors' note: At this point, at the end of the first lecture or between pages 10 and 11, Polanyi inserted in his lecture notes a page "10a," which contains a kind of chronological table summarizing the situation in England and on the continent. Unfortunately the organization of this table is too unclear to permit reproduction.

democratic form of government themselves; they based it on the idea of liberty. On the continent the democratic form of government was the result of a struggle in which the working class played a historic role alongside of the middle class, as in France, Prussia, and later on in the Austrian and the Russian Empires. Apart from these countries, democracy is of an egalitarian type only in these countries where, although established early, its establishment was the result of a *national* revolution against foreign feudalism – as in Switzerland in the thirteenth century, in the Low Countries in the sixteenth century, or in America in the eighteenth century.

1

Thus we are able to formulate our problem somewhat more precisely: the challenge to democracy is, primarily, a challenge to he continental type of democracy. However, only *primarily*; for the crisis of parliamentarism is embedded in a much broader crisis. The majority of the people belonging to our type of civilization have undergone in the last five or ten years (at the most) a change in their political or their economic system. The number of people engaged in this process can be put at 500–600 millions. If you add up Russia and America, Italy and Germany, you get some 400 millions; if you add up countries like Austria, Poland, Portugal, Greece, Yougoslavia, and half a dozen other small states – and perhaps Japan, where also a very radical change in the system is going on – you may reach a figure nearer 600 than 500 millions. In all these countries either the political system of constitutional government (as in Germany and Italy) or the economic system (as in Russia) has disappeared, or rather the relationship between the two has been radically altered.

This is the *historical background of the conflicting philosophies* in modern society, with which we are dealing here.

2

In order to discover the origin of this crisis we must go back to an earlier period in the history of modern society. We must investigate the relationship between *economic liberalism* and *political democracy*.

The characteristic feature of our civilization is the existence of a separate distinctive *economic sphere* within society. Both under the manorial system and later, under mercantilism, the political and the economic system were but different aspects of the social organization.

It is generally characteristic of human society that its legal, moral, and economic organization is *one* – that it is artificial to insist upon these differences. Thus the present state of affairs is unique in that a distinct economic sphere has developed which is *separate from the political*. To introduce terms that are less open to misapprehension, we will call economic liberalism by the name *laissez-faire* and political democracy by the name *popular government*. This makes it clearer what type of economic liberalism and what type of political democracy we have in mind.

3

The principle on which our present economic system rests is that the production and distribution of goods in society goes on without conscious interference or planning. The economic sphere is *autonomous*, in other words it stands under laws of its own, which regulate its processes. The processes are *automatic*, that is, no outside intervention is needed to set them going and to keep them going; they are self-regulating. The economic sphere reacts unfavorably to the infringement of its autonomy, that is, to interference to its automatism. The sum total of material goods produced within a specified period of time tends to diminish as a result of interference.

In what manner is the system regulated? It stands under the command of prices. Useful articles have commodity prices; the use of capital is called interest; the use of land is called rent; the price of labor is called wages. These prices come into existence on different markets: capital, land, labor, and commodity markets.

It hardly needs to be stressed how much such a system tends to be artificial. It is enough to remind you of the commodity character of land and labor. Obviously, no society could exist in which land and labor were merely a commodity bought and sold, produced and reproduced according to laws of the market. Land, to begin with, cannot be strictly produced at all. Also, in more than one way, the quality of life in society depends on the use that society as such makes of land. Labor as a commodity has a human being attached to it as an appendage. This makes it almost a satanic joke to regard labor actually as a commodity. Except in economic theory, it has, of course, never been regarded so. The reaction to economic liberalism is as old as economic liberalism itself.

To put this in more general terms: economic liberalism, if it were to take hold of the whole of the material life of a society, would almost instantly destroy society. Society does only partly consist of material production and material goods. Life consists of many other values that would be destroyed in the process of producing the goods. Society would disintegrate.

This, in fact, was threatening during the earlier period of the Industrial Revolution. Long before laissez-faire could extend its sway over the whole of industrial life, the destruction of the essential values became too obvious to be overlooked. Under the conditions of the Industrial Revolution, the relation of man to nature, his craft, his family, his tradition was utterly destroyed.

The reaction to this process came from two sides: partly, from those who cherished the traditional values – the enlightened conservatives, led by Christian reformers of the type of Wilberforce; on the other hand, from radicals of the type of Bentham, who based their social criticism on the strength of human reason. It is in these two that we must see the ancestors of the later Christian socialists of the Kingsley–Maurice type, as well as the socialist criticism of the Morris type. The same grouping is present in other countries, for instance Bismarck's "alliance" with Lassalle. Everywhere both the traditional feudalist classes and the new industrial classes reacted sharply to the extension of *laissez aller*.

The history of the nineteenth century is dominated by the reaction of society as a whole to the new growth in its midst. The vast extension of government functions was its main consequence. In countries where, as in England, the powers of the state were limited other factors emerged – voluntary associations as trade unions, cooperatives, the churches – and restricted the principle of unchecked competition in various respects.

The actual condition of affairs was a mutual limitation and interpenetration of industry and government: a coexistence of laissez-faire and popular government.

4

Obviously the egalitarian type of democracy would have to contend with a special difficulty. The more popular government developed, the more parliaments would tend to become the instruments of the economic self-defense of the working classes, especially in case of a crisis.

It is here that the class structure of society reacted to the situation. The feudal class system was leveled out partly in the great revolutions; but the distinction between the owners of the apparatus of production and those who worked under direction took largely the place of the former classes of the manorial system. Under the industrial system it was essential that nobody but the owners should have (and in fact *could* have) an influence on the provision of employment and so on. But, if the system ceased to function or functioned badly, it was inevitable that the workers should make use of their political influence to protect themselves against the insufficient working of the industrial system. Incidentally, the gain in human values was bought at the price of increasing difficulties in the industrial sphere. The cruel automatism of the economic system would have perhaps shortened the trade cycle at the cost of the lives of some hundred thousand, who would have to be allowed to starve. But could our civilization accept the principle of human sacrifice as an integral part of its methods of producing material goods? Not if it wished to continue as a Christian society.

By this analysis it is becoming clear that, in case of a breakdown of the industrial system, laissez-faire and popular government would become mutually incompatible. The one or the other would have to go.

But that major crisis *was in itself inevitable*. For the delicate balance between laissez-faire and government intervention described above made the price system more and more rigid and less adaptable. Taxation, social insurance, municipal activities, tariffs, wage regulations, and the like tended to fix items of costs and thus to make the system as a whole less elastic.

The need for elasticity was especially great in the *international sphere*. The gold standard, free trade, capital exports could function only if the price system within the country would adapt itself to the international situation. In other words these great features of the international economic system were conditioned by an elastic adaptation within the national system. But it was precisely the capacity for adaptation that was diminishing. The closely knit national units of our time were preformed in the prewar period.

All over the world, after the war, *major adaptations needed*. Vast efforts at adaptation broke down. The haphazard interventionism of the prewar period had to make place to a full-blown national unity of the industrial and economic system. This is the background of the present crisis.

5

The sources of the conflict are thus in the sphere of industrial and political organization respectively – but with very important modifications as to their philosophy. The nature of the critical situation out of which fascism springs offers a key to the transformation.

A point is reached where neither the political nor the economic system functions satisfactorily. A feeling of general insecurity takes hold of society as a whole. There is fascist short cut to safeguard production at the price of sacrificing democracy. Democracy can continue only with a change in the property system. Therefore the destruction of democratic institutions is a safeguard for the continuation of the industrial system.

Democratic philosophy tends to be socialist. Laissez-faire philosophy tends to be antidemocratic.

Lecture 3

Self-Sufficiency and International Trade

Introduction

In the first lecture a distinction was drawn between English and continental ideals of democracy. Libertarian and egalitarian types were contrasted, and it was found that mainly the latter were involved in the "crisis of democracy."

In the second lecture the philosophy of laissez-faire and that of popular government were regarded in their mutual interaction. It was found that liberal economics and popular government reached a delicate balance in the nineteenth century, at the expense of the elasticity of the economic system. The interpenetration of state and industry resulting in more closely knit national units emerged. These comparatively rigid systems were put to the test when, under postwar conditions, sudden major adjustments in all countries became imperative. It is in the course of these efforts of the various countries to adjust themselves to the new conditions that the two main features of the present epoch emerged:

1   in the *national* field, the rise of dictatorships;
2   in the *international* field, a move toward *self-sufficiency* (autarky).

It is with this latter development that we are concerned tonight. The development toward autarky was no less startling than the rise of the dictatorships.

The Origins of Self-Sufficiency

The decisive factor in the development of self-sufficiency was the pressing need for sudden major adjustments in an increasingly rigid economic system. Let us first consider the effects of diminishing elasticity.

The international gold standard is rightly regarded as the axis of the international economic system in prewar times. Long-term loans are dependent upon the gold standard; and so is that freedom of the flow of trade that is needed to keep the balance of payment even (tariffs do not necessarily impede this flow).

But the gold standard implies the unimpeded rise and fall of the price level within a country. This, under our present system, may mean a difference between boom or depression and unemployment. When prices are falling, production is carried on at a loss and is therefore discouraged, if not altogether brought to a standstill. Anyhow, the determination to uphold the gold standard implies the will to suffer the consequences, if necessary. As long as the consequences are not disastrous, the proposition is reasonable.

The war and the treaties upset the traditional economic balance between the different countries. The adjustments that would have been needed to maintain it without a break would have meant a complete stoppage of industrial activity and, in many cases, actual starvation for the masses.

All the more impressive were the efforts made in the various countries to restore the gold standard by the traditional methods. It is in this first half of the postwar period that the seeds of the ulterior developments were sown.

Let us distinguish between three groups of countries:

(a)   the "defeated" countries of Central and Eastern Europe, including Russia;
(b)   the "victorious" powers of Western Europe;
(c)   the United States of America.

Currencies were restored first in group (a) – Russia, Germany, Austria, Hungary, and half a dozen other small countries – between 1922 and 1925; secondly in the victorious countries, as in France, Belgium, England (1925 and 1926).

Thirdly, the USA since 1927 was helping Great Britain to keep on the gold standard, and in order to do so it kept interest rates low, thereby causing a secret – or rather latent – inflation within the country that, in 1929, led to the most terrific business crisis in its history.

On the whole, what happened was this. Group (b), which had persuaded the governments of group (a) to return to the gold standard (prematurely, as we now know), shouldered the inevitable costs of this process through a continuous stream of long-term loans, which they granted to group (a) in order to help them cover the deficit of their balance of payments. The United States of America from 1927 onwards was behaving in a similar fashion toward group (b). Ultimately she was burdened with the accumulated deficits of both group (a) and group (b). For all her wealth, she hardly managed to cover it by inflation.

The reason for this apparently purely humanitarian action lay in the reluctance of the people of the United States to accept the fact that the world as a whole, including themselves, was not the richer but the poorer for the war. They attempted to keep European impoverishment from their shores by putting an embargo both on the import of men and on that of goods originating from this impoverished territory. Had they not done so, the masses of poor immigrants or, alternatively, the cheap goods produced by them would have necessarily depressed the excessive American wage and income level, thereby leveling out the American and European standards. Only in this way could a free movement of men and goods have been restored after the war. But America preferred to keep European immigrants and European goods from its shores, even though this meant a continuous flow[g] of American long-term loans to European countries.

During this whole period of attempted adjustments *by traditional methods*, practically from the Armistice to the end of December 1929, when the storm broke in Wall Street, a heavy strain was put on national economies. In Europe, a drastic balancing of budgets that cut social services and benefits to the bone, increasing exports by pressing on wages, was inevitable. The sufferings of the Central and Eastern European peoples in this period were appalling.

In England trade depression continued and unemployment was rampant. The balance of payments was becoming more and more passive.

---

[g]Editors' note: Originally Polanyi wrote "the continuously increasing flow," then deleted to "the continuous flow."

Autarky

In the first major depression the precarious balance broke down again.

America dropped its unofficial monetary agreement with the Bank of England, and ultimately, in 1933, went off gold herself, without the slightest consideration for the needs of England – which, by that time, was keen on stabilization.

England went off gold to the amazement of the whole world, put an embargo on foreign loans, and left Central and Eastern Europe to its fate.

Central and Eastern European countries were back in the melting pot.

But the countries concerned, although they were forced off gold, did not throw up the sponge. New vast efforts were made to restore the gold standard. But this time serious restrictions on trade (quotas, embargos, preferential tariffs, clearing systems, restrictions of currency) had to be introduced in order to protest the national currencies. However, this happened, as we see, not in order to achieve self-sufficiency but, on the contrary, to *overcome the isolation* forced upon the countries concerned by the battle for the stability of the currency. The tragedy is that this isolation was never overcome.

In spite of their efforts, all countries ultimately failed. The unelastic system refused to be further pressed and deformed. In order to stabilize their currencies, the various countries, mainly unconsciously, proceeded to the establishment of semi-controlled, semi-autarkic economies. They intended these measures to be provisional. Actually this meant the end of the gold standard – of an international capital market and an international commodity market. Incidentally, it was in the effort to adapt their now isolated economy to the disappearance of the traditional economic international systems that the dictatorships emerged. This explains why the tendency toward autarky is worldwide. All countries in the world today have managed currencies, control foreign lending, and restrict in various ways the inflow of foreign goods.

We can now proceed to clear the question on the have and havenots. The legend will have it that autarky is forced upon some nations by the lack of raw materials and colonies. Obviously, this is putting the cart before the horse. As long as an international economic system of interchangeable currencies, capital movements, and unrestricted flow of commodities lasts, the lack of raw materials and colonies means no drawback to national economy. Confer Belgium, or Switzerland, or in fact the brilliant industrial success of Germany herself. It is under conditional autarky that national sovereignty gains special economic importance. For the advantages of using one's internal currency for the purchase of raw materials may be an asset *under a managed currency*.

The true importance of the haves and have-nots business is this: under the conditions of self-sufficiency our economic system cannot last without general impoverishment. On the other hand, no changeover in colonial possessions could remedy the evil. The haves have not all they need. The have-nots could never have all they need. An internal international division of labor must again be achieved.

In the light of these facts, it is important to realize:

a   that the nineteenth-century philosophy of international trade has had its day: the identification of internationalism with the international gold standard, with free trade, with free capital movements is anachronistic. The international economic system of the prewar period will not and cannot return;
b   that the meaning of self-sufficiency must be judged in the light of the need for the establishment of a *new* system of international economic cooperation.

Managed currencies, equalization funds, control of foreign land lending, and foreign trade have come to stay. They are the embryo of the new organs of the semi-controlled or fully controlled society in its economic relationships. Both as an instrument of economic warfare and as one of economic cooperation, they are infinitely more effective than the methods of bygone times. The real alternative is presented by the *two ways* in which they can be made use of.

It is here that the real significance of the haves and have-nots business can be gauged. The so-called have-nots are the powerful states that appear to nourish the idea that the empire is the adequate solution of the new international organization. In order to achieve it, they are prepared to make use in the most drastic fashion of the fighting value of the new organs of self-sufficiency. The so-called haves are that group of states that are inclined to make the rule of law in world affairs the basis of the new international economic order. The political phrase that expresses this line of thought most adequately is *collective security*. Whether a country wishes to fit in with this pattern of life or not can most readily be judged *by the manner in which it interprets the need for self-sufficiency*. Some think of it not only as an instrument of economic warfare, but as the precondition of launching the most deadly forms of modern mass warfare upon their neighbors. Others see in it a warning of the pressing need for the re-establishment of an international community; and, over and above that, also *the instrument by which this aim can be achieved*. This difference in the various national philosophies of self-sufficiency represents what is probably the truest dividing line among nations today.

LECTURE 4

Socialist Russia

In our enquiry into the nature of the challenge that is offered to democracy in our time we have now reached the stage at which a discussion of the actual institutional developments in Europe today – notably in Soviet Russia, in fascist Italy, and in national socialist Germany – becomes possible.

In our first lecture a distinction was drawn between the English and the continental ideals of democracy. The difference between the two was traced to their historical origins, that is, to the period at which institutional democracy was established. In England this occurred well before the Industrial Revolution, while on the continent this event took place after the inception of the Industrial Revolution. Accordingly, the role of the working classes was different here and there. English democracy was established mainly by the rural and urban middle class. On the continent the industrial working class acted as an ally to the middle class. It was to its influence that the egalitarian features of continental democracy were due.

Turning to socialist Russia, we must keep in mind that:

(1) The Russian was the most recent of the revolutions that followed in the wake of the French Revolution and spread its ideas eastwards across Europe. These revolutions resulted in the abolition of semi-feudal absolutism based on an aristocratic society and feudal forms of land tenure. Moreover, the rise of national consciousness that began with the French Revolution continued. First in Germany and Italy, then in the Balkans, later still in the Danubian basin and in the middle of Eastern Europe, lastly among of the numerous nations of western Russia and the peoples inhabiting central, eastern, and Siberian Russia, freedom for the national language and culture was won. The fall of czarism, the abolishment of semi-feudal land tenure, and the liberation of more than a hundred

smaller nations within the Russian Empire are to be regarded as the last stage of the process that had its origins in the French Revolution of 1789.

(2) The later the downfall of feudalism happens in the course of *industrial development*, the greater the influence of the working class and the more democracy tends to be egalitarian. In Russia, where feudalism lasted longest, the egalitarian idea appears in its socialist form. No other development could be expected.

For the working class naturally played a leading role in the abolition of absolutism and semi-feudal land tenure in Russia. Accordingly, the institutional system that replaces czarism and semi-feudalism tended to be a socialist democracy.

But in what sense is Russia socialist? And how far was Russian development determined by democratic ideals? These two questions can be fairly said to sum up the important conflict of philosophy that is being waged around Soviet Russia today.

1

The leaders of the Russian Revolution were inspired in their political action by their (*Marxian*) *philosophy*.

Three points bear a special reference to our subject:

1 The road from a feudal to a socialist society leads through capital-ism. In socialism the apparatus of production that has been devel-oped in and by capitalism is taken over and managed by the community.
2 While history is made by men, it is not made at the whim of so-called great men. (The "great men" are those individuals who recognize the necessities of their age and put their abilities at the service of those necessities.) *Necessary stages of industrial devel-opment cannot be skipped.*
3 In this process the true nature of man expresses and fulfills itself. Under modern conditions a society that is free both of exploita-tion and of compulsion and coercion is the ultimate ideal.

In the light of these principles – Leninist principles – it was asserted by Leninist groups:

1 The Great War has been caused by imperialist rivalries and was bound to lead to world revolution.

2   Russia could not take the lead in the establishment of socialism. Such a lead could come out from the working classes of capitalist states of the West.
3   Socialism could be established only intentionally, that is, in the course of a successful world revolution.

Accordingly, the main outlines of their *policy* can be summed up as follows:

1   to end the war at all costs and to turn the world war into world revolution;
2   to secure the victory of the *middle class revolution* in Russia over czarist autocracy in the face of the expected counter-revolutionary attempts; to prevent the middle class from defrauding its working-class allies of the fruits of their common victory, as happened in other continental revolutions; to carry the revolutionary process as far as possible in order to achieve these aims;
3   never to lose sight of the *limitations* that are set to the Russian Revolution by the backward condition of the country: (a) its agricultural character; (b) its lack of literacy and lack of industrial discipline.

The term "socialist" is used here as a synonymous with "communist." A difference between these two terms must, of course, be made in two different respects.

a   In discussing the different stages through which society would have to pass in order to reach communism, the term socialist applies to the first, the term communist to the second and ultimate stage. The difference lies in the principle on which the distribution of goods or incomes (which are here interchangeable terms) would take place. Under socialism, remuneration according to service, achievement, or merit would be the rule; under communism, where abundance of goods is assumed to have been achieved, each according to his abilities and to each according to his needs should be the principle governing the distribution of labor and toil on the one hand, of goods and services on the other.
b   In discussing the different methods by which socialism and, ultimately, communism can be achieved, two main political parties exist within the working class movement: the Socialist and the Communist Party. Their main difference refers to the method by which they hope to achieve their aim, namely peaceful and gradual

transformation of capitalism into socialism in the one case, dictatorship of the proletariat in the other. The first is, of course, the method upheld by the Socialist Party, the second by the Communist Party.

2

It is in the light of those Marxist principles of Lenin and his followers that the main course of the revolution can be best understood.

The industrial and commercial middle class of Russia, which had backed the Kerensky Revolution of February 1917, was comparatively small in numbers and lacking in cohesion and discipline. The industrial working class with which it was allied was comparatively numerous and had reached a very high degree of cohesion and discipline.

Russian industries were mostly centralized, in modern establishments employing a comparatively great number of workers.

If France, in 1789, had a class of artisans and industrial workers of a comparatively primitive type, if Central Europe in 1848 had a somewhat more advanced type of industrial proletariat, Russia in 1917 possessed a far greater percentage of modern factory workers among its industrial proletariat than probably any other country in the world. The weakness of the middle classes and the comparative strength of the factory workers determined the course of the Russian revolution.

1 It very soon became apparent that Kerensky's middle class government could not hope to maintain itself against the determined assault of the counter-revolutionary czarist generals unless Kerensky could rely on the whole-hearted support of the working class. On the other hand, working-class support, under the circumstances, inevitably involved the socialist character of the new democracy.

2 But the "socialist character" of the new democracy and socialism were two very different things to Lenin and followers. Even well after the taking over of power in November 1917, the Bolsheviks refused to establish socialism in Russia. Indeed this refusal was one of the cornerstones of their policy. Not until the sabotage of the employers and industrialists forced the government to take over the ownership of the factories did the Soviet government proceed beyond the introduction of workers' control in the factories.

3   The so-called *war communism* was partly an ulterior rationaliza-
    tion of military necessities due to foreign intervention and the civil
    wars. True, a fraction of the Bolsheviks was definitely pressing
    for the immediate establishment of a communist society. Trotsky
    was the most important in that group of leaders that stood for
    the militarization of labor through general conscription of labor
    and for a ruthless war against the whole mass of the peasantry,
    except the poorest. Lenin himself is known *not* to have favored
    war communism, and he certainly refused to justify it on grounds
    of socialist theory. It was contrary to one of his main political
    doctrines, namely that the working class must, in a agricultural
    country, take full account of the peasantry, which it must regard
    as its ally in the revolution. This alliance should be based above
    all on the village poor but should exclude only the well-to-do
    peasants while trying to neutralize or preferably win over the bulk
    of the peasantry.

4   The complete collapse of war communism in the great famine of
    1921 led to a strategic retreat in the NEP (New Economic Policy).
    Lenin suggested that a partial return to capitalist methods in
    agriculture should provide the revolution with a breathing space
    in which it could collect its strength to pursue its main task, the
    promotion of the world revolution. Without the advent of such,
    the Russian socialist regime could not hope to maintain itself in
    the face of the inevitable coalition of capitalist governments.

5   Long after the death of Lenin, the party continued on the lines of
    the NEP. But the world revolution failed to materialize, and
    instead a stabilization of capitalism was the order of the day. But,
    as Lenin had foreseen, the NEP inevitably tended to increase the
    political influence of the peasant proprietor; and, as Lenin had
    equally foreseen, this influence tended toward the restoration of
    capitalism in Russia. On the other hand, the administrative meas-
    ures of the Bolshevik government, directed toward the feeding of
    the urban population and the development of industry, necessarily
    led to punitive measures against and continuous interference with
    the peasants. What was true in Western Europe proved also true
    in Russia. Liberal economies and popular government were mutu-
    ally incompatible, especially if the latter was inspired in its actions
    by the interest of an industrial working class. The NEP became
    unworkable, because the peasants increasingly resisted the gov-
    ernment interference and refused to carry on [working on] their
    farms on anything but a profit basis. The great decrease in the
    agricultural raw materials of industry was the result. After 1926 a
    rapid deterioration of the heavy industrial plant became apparent.

6   The five-year plan in industry and the collectivization of agricultural land were a definite move toward socialism. Russia could
not afford to wait any longer. The NEP, conceived by Lenin as a
strategic retreat, could not be turned from a transitory into a
permanent position. Industry had to be made politically independent of the peasantry if the revolution should be safe against
a reactionary upheaval. The NEP, which was essentially a state
of suspension between capitalism and socialism, could not last.
While in several Central European countries a similar state of
suspension resulted in the return to capitalism under a fascist
dictatorship, in Russia alone the outcome was the establishment
of socialism under the dictatorship of a working-class party. Still,
the theoretical implications of Stalin's departure were very important. His program – it is true – implied that socialism could be
established in one country, which in this case was nothing less
than a continent. The means of production in Russia are, over-
whelmingly, under the administration of the community. Those
that are not are worked personally by their owners or by cooperatives of such. The exploitation of labor under the title of the
ownership of a productive plant has been successfully abolished.
On all accounts Russia is a socialist country.

7   But what about democracy? Only very few social convulsions, as
we have seen, have proved in such a measure subject to the social
philosophy of the leading figures as the Russian revolution up to
now. If ever a process of social transformation was therefore
appropriately judged by the philosophy of its originators, it is the
Russian. On this account, the philosophy of Marxist socialism is
of primary importance for the correct answer to our question. But
this philosophy in every relevant aspect is nothing but the consistent continuation of individualism under the conditions of a
complex industrial society. Its one basic principle of political
philosophy is freedom. The profession of revolutionary must be
taken literally, if he wants to go safe. And these are ultimately
directed toward the establishment of new forms of democracy . . .

LECTURE 5

The Corporative State in Italy and Austria

In my second lecture I have endeavored to show in what manner
the "fascist situation" arises as a result of the incompatibility of

laissez-faire economics and popular government of an *egalitarian* type.

The Italian so-called corporative state is the best example of the fascist solution, which mainly consists in suppressing the institutions of representative democracy, in which the working class could express itself either in the political or in the economic field. Parliaments and trade unions are abolished. What remains is the capitalistic structure of society. This, organized according to branches of industry, *is* the corporative state *in practice*.

In theory, the corporative state professes to be much more: the whole of economic life being subjected to the discipline of the state. Here at once a major problem arises. We have described the difficulty experienced by the popular government when interfering with the industry. Interference with the price system and the markets leads to a paralysis of the liberal competitive system. Has the fascist state succeeded in solving this problem of how to interfere with privately owned enterprises without shouldering the losses incurred? (No capitalist enterprise can permanently incur losses. This is axiomatic. If the state incurs the loss, there must be some permanent separate fund whence to finance it. This is *economically* impossible.) Has the Italian corporative state found the solution?

1 What is the Truth about the Corporative State?

The syndical phase of Italian fascist revolution lasted from 1922 to 1926.

The syndicates are unions of the employers and the employed, organized according to branches and geographic regions, so as to constitute a parallel organization. The two together are the syndical organization of industry. The jurisdiction of the syndicate concerns labor questions: wages, hours, and general labor conditions. In cases of non-agreement, labor courts decide. (This organization amounts to no more than a compulsory organization of employers and employed in national federations and confederations of syndicates.)

The fascist syndicate has no formal monopoly but has factual–legal monopoly, as only the fascist unions (a) can represent the branch in question; (b) can sign legally binding agreements; (c) can collect dues from all those belonging to the branch.

The Charter of Labor is not a legally binding document but a declaration of principles.

The corporative period starts in 1926.

A corporation is a syndicate bracketed together by a steel-ribbed framework of state, party, and expert representatives.

In this form the syndicates are supposed to be *state organs* in actual control of industry – that is, these organs are supposed to be able to allow state administration of the industry. How far has this organization proceeded?

1928   corporative ministry
1930   corporative chamber – nomination out of 800
1932   National Council of Corporations
1934   corporations (by the end of the year)
1936   emergency principle accepted (the war industry principle).

LECTURE 6

Party, State, and Industry in Nazi Germany

We very nearly reached the end of our course and it is time to sum up the results. Today's talk on Germany should be restricted to the question of how far German developments tend to confirm our propositions. In our course on *Europe today* we have been approaching our subject mainly from the angle of *conflicting philosophies*. This conflict is commonly summed up through the formula of the challenge of fascism and communism to democracy. We proposed to inquire into the validity of this formula by trying to discover the fundamental nature of the challenge to democracy in our times.

Our main results are the following:

The term "democracy," as a designation of traditional forms of government in Western European countries, is *not unambiguous*. It designates a different set of institutions when the reference is the libertarian or the egalitarian type of democracy. Historically, this depends on the stage of industrial development at which these institutions were established, and accordingly on what *social classes* were most immediately concerned with the abolition of monarchic despotism. In England the middle classes themselves fought their battle against the royal prerogative (monarchic absolutism), and in the course of the struggle they fused with the landed gentry into one social upper class. In consequence no element of social equality entered the conception of democracy. The modern industrial working class was not yet born when English democracy was established; it could therefore have no part in it. On the continent, the working class participated in the struggle against despotism and set its imprint on the democracy that emerged. It became egalitarian democracy. The more modern the working class was, the more its democracy tended to be socialist, in other words to press for such a change in the property system as would allow *the conscious and responsible participation of the people in an industrial society*. Thus the Russian Revolution appears as the last in a complex series of upheavals that started with the French Revolution. It must be regarded as the outcome of a democratic philosophy under conditions in which (a) political democracy cannot maintain itself in the face of counter-revolution unless it takes on socialist forms; (b) socialist forms would lead to specific developments on account of the unique conditions under which socialism was established (lack of literacy, lack of industries and of democratic traditions).

Thus we are unable to eliminate two false alternatives to democracy that commonly obscure the issue: (a) the role of dictatorship; and (b) self-sufficiency (autarky). Neither is specific to fascism.

Dictatorship is a common feature of emergency periods and, in the wider sense of a *strong executive*, it is a universal feature of our time. There is no essential difference *in this respect* between the Russian government and the German, the Japanese and the Italian, the New Deal powers or the national government of 1931 in England with its practical 9/10 parliamentary majority. The great difference lies in the *democratic intent* or otherwise that inspires these governments.

The *self-sufficiency* tendency is also a feature of our time. It is the inevitable result of the breakdown of the international organization of economic life, which obtained under liberal capitalism. The difference lies in the *cooperative* or *antagonistic* way the new organs of self-sufficiency are being made to work by the various national units. The organs themselves are common to them all; managed currencies (with or without exchange equalization funds), control of capital exports, bilateral regulation of foreign trade. Democratic and non-democratic states differ merely in the manner in which these institutions should be used to restore international economic organization on a new basis. While fascist countries propose to do this on the basis of empire, that is, by political unification under *one* control (their own), democratic countries wish to perform this by peaceful cooperation between the nations. Whether this will prove possible without a more definite move in the direction of so-called socialist transformation of their own national economies is yet to be seen.

But what, in our view, is the nature of this emergency – of which both strong governments or dictatorships and autarkic tendencies are but incidental concomitants?

The Nature of the Emergency

The principles underlying our industrial and our political organization respectively have become mutually incompatible – this is the heart of the trouble. Laissez-faire economics and popular government cannot continue to exist side by side. The delicate balance achieved between the two in the prewar period could not be lasting, for it did not provide for the necessary adjustments, primarily in *the international sphere*. The existing international organization of economic life rested on the automatic readjustment of national industry and trade to changing world conditions, an adjustment that became more and more difficult to make as the national economy became more and more rigid as a result of the increasing interpenetration of state and industry, and also of the more massive changes needed. When, as an effect of the world war and treaties, suddenly big readjustments became inevitable, almost all nations were faced with an emergency. A worldwide effort to deal with this emergency on the old liberal lines of automatic adaptation was made during the twenties but failed entirely in 1930, when the Great Depression broke out, partly in consequence of that effort. The international organization of economic life, which seemed to have been restored, collapsed and the nations were involved in a life-and-death struggle, trying to save at least the internal stability of their various currencies. In this period *self-sufficiency* and *strong government* became practically universal. And it was at this stage that the fascist tendencies suddenly emerged into the limelight. In the countries in which the egalitarian type of democracy prevailed they were victorious.

What was the reason for these (fascist) tendencies?

The Fascist Challenge to Democracy

In the course of this emergency, popular governments were forced to interfere with the industrial system *on a large scale*. It soon became apparent that our economic system will not broker interference from the *outside*. Unsatisfactory as its working in many respects is, if interfered with, it becomes even more unsatisfactory in the long run. For, under the system of private ownership of the means of production, state interference in industry leads often to the opposite of the intended results. Measures intended to release unemployment may lead to the increase of unemployment. The continuation of liberal economics is, on the other hand, patently impossible on account of the emergency (see above). In such a situation the leaders of industry become hostile to popular government and try to undermine the authority of the democratic party system; as an alternative, big business offers *its own government*, the direct administration of social affairs by the captains of industry – that is, the owners of capital and their appointed managers. Democratic parliaments begin to be restive and tend toward socialist measures in order to enforce the emergency legislation. Neither the political nor the industrial machinery can function under these conditions. *Society as a whole* is threatened with a deadlock. Fear of a sudden collapse of *both* the political *and* the industrial system takes hold of the population. If (as happened in America) the leaders of finance and big business stand discredited, the movement is toward the dictatorship of the political powers (called New Deal); if popular government is under a shadow, the move is toward the dictatorship of the owners of the capital enterprise and industrial undertakings. *Fascism emerges*.

Democracy is challenged by fascism. The content of this challenge lies in the necessity of interfering with an economic system when democracy is proving unable to do so effectively. Fascism becomes inevitable.

The Fascist Solution

The characteristic of fascism is therefore the change to which it actually leads. Not the fascist movements, but fascist institutions are the key to the study of the fascism. They offer the picture of a modern society in which democratic institutions have been abolished or put out of action, in the sense that the working people have no possibility of exerting an influence either in the political or in the industrial field, both labor parties and trade union organizations having been abolished. In the industrial field there is no essential change. The system of ownership continues. Private ownership of the means of production is maintained. The essential claim of fascism is that under these conditions it is able to deal with the three main complaints that are commonly brought against capitalism – namely trade depressions and *lack* of *planning*, *lack of security of tenure* for the employee, and unjustified *differences of income* at both ends of the scale.

Fascism implies, as it were, the promise of a reform of capitalism on these accounts, at the price of the permanent elimination of freedom, equality, and peace. Once the influence of the working classes is eliminated, it does *not* seem impossible, on the face of it, that capitalist industry and state should be mutually compatible.

Liberal capitalism would then be replaced by so-called corporative capitalism and popular democracy by the fascist state. This is meant by the corporative state.

In Italy, as we have shown, the corporative system has *not* yet been put to the test. Whether the fascist state is able to interfere with industry as an independent force is doubtful. *War industry* is the actual situation – that is, a new emergence, not a system or final solution.

And Germany?

In 1933 the movement toward the *Ständestaat* stopped. Policy ‡. . .‡ᵗʰ the time of war industries.

Organizational principles are vaguely competitive, without a clear consciousness of the problem involved.

Thus the challenge of fascism is threefold:

(a) Technical or organizational: *Can fascism reform capitalism* in these three ways?
(b) *Political*: Can the problem of peace be solved by the empire solution?
(c) *Moral*: Can we pay the price?

ʰEditors' note: Illegible. These final notes, from "In Italy . . ." on, are in handwriting – obviously ideas only jotted down for development elsewhere.

18

The Eclipse of Panic and
the Outlook of Socialism*

The mechanism of a market economy had important bearings on the
political struggle of the working class in the nineteenth century. Its
deep influence on the forms and the chances of that struggle has been
often overlooked. In our days that mechanism is undergoing a vital
change. Accordingly, it will appear that the socialist movement has
reached a new and significant stage.

A market economy, as approximated by liberal capitalism, is in
principle self-regulating. Essentially, it is a market system comprising
markets for labor, land, and money. Three points must be firmly
established in relation to its mechanism. First, that its working
involves grave dangers to the fabric of human society, especially to
man and his natural environment, thus inevitably calling forth protective reactions. Secondly, that, insofar as these reactions involve
haphazard intervention into the working of the market mechanism,
they may be harmful from a strictly economic viewpoint. Thirdly,
that any suggestion of planned intervention, which would be economically advantageous, is met by a panic of the financial markets.
As long as such a threat is present, all socialist solutions must appear
as most risky measures and naturally call forth desperate political
resistance.

* File 19–17, Karl Polanyi Archive: undated typescript.

I

The dangers emanating from a market economy are the direct result
of the conditions necessary for the establishment of such an economy.
These conditions include the abolishment of all traditional safeguards
of social security. In precapitalist systems of society, custom and the
law provide such guarantees both in the sphere of industry and in
that of agriculture, by making a man secure in his job and in the
tenure of land, respectively.

Under liberal capitalism, the traditional organization of labor and
land is replaced by the device of free competitive markets. Familiarity
with this peculiar arrangement should not blind us to the obvious
mishandling of the elements of social existence – man and his natural
environment – involved in such a departure. A competitive labor
market or a similar estate market, if allowed to function unchecked,
is bound to destroy the human beings and their surroundings, which
are being dealt with here, by virtue of a peculiar fiction, as if they
were commodities, in other words objects produced for sale.

The threat of utter destruction that springs from the mechanism
of a labour market if permitted to work itself out is too obvious to
need elaboration. To organize human labor as a commodity means
to deal with it as if it were something produced for sale. In reality,
labor is a human activity that bears no resemblance to a commodity
proper. It is part of man's functions as a physiological, psychological
and moral being; its "supply" is not a matter of "production" for
sale, just as – incidentally – the human beings themselves whose labor
is in question are not "produced for sale," but for an entirely different set of motives. In order to be able to speak of the "sale of labor,"
a number of fictions must be employed. First, matters must be assumed
to be organized in such a manner as to make all useful human activity
take place by arrangement of pairs of individuals, the one directing
and paying, the other working; this situation must be then interpreted
as the passing of the commodity "labor" from the worker to the
buyer; and so on.

The point at issue here is, of course, not the fictitious nature of
these assumptions. Neither the legal fiction that defines labor as the
subject of a specific contract nor the economic fiction that defines
the scarce and useful thing sold as the commodity "labor" affects
the actual world. What matters to us here is the human situation
postulated in the organization described as labor market. It makes
the child of five act as a trader, using his free will to arrange, for a
contract the object of which is his "labor," as much of it as he deems

profitable to sell – say, 12 or 14 or 16 hours. It is inessential to him, as a trader, when and where and under what conditions the commodity is to be delivered. In actual fact, the trader has become a mere accessory to his own goods, the fate of which he must follow through, even though he may perish in the process. To a lesser extent, this applies to any man or woman. No wonder that within a generation or so the populations of the cities afflicted with this system were losing all resemblance to any human form.

The same is true of land. Once it is parceled out to individuals to dispose of at their discretion, for profit – including the right of indiscriminate use, nonuse, and abuse as well as that of unrestricted renting, letting, and sale – the land is doomed, with all that this implies: the ruin of the owner, the occupier, and the laborer and the destruction of the amenities and resources of the surroundings, including the "indestructible" forces of the soil itself, together with the climate, health, and security of the country. Land is produced for sale as little as man: it is a part of nature. The legal and economic fictions with the help of which the fate of land can be brought under the sway of an estate market are, on the whole, analogous to those we met in the case of labor. Actually land is the man's habitation, the site of all his activities, the source of his life, the place of safety, the seasons, and the grave. Not even the soil itself can withstand commercial treatment. Eroded, denuded, pulverized, all regions may revert to the primeval forest, swamp, or desert. Wastage of assets undermines the future of the people. Alienation of resources threatens national safety. Forms of tenure that do not allow stable settlements and sound family conditions or wholesome shapes of living sap the strength of the race, which dwindles away. The degradation of a free peasantry to the status of scrap holders or a shiftless proletariat may mean the end of the stock. And man lives his life so close to nature that, unless the economic fate of the produce of the soil is organized in such a manner as to create a normal life for those who work on the land, agriculture will be destroyed.

Here lie the roots of interventionism. Outside interference with the working of the market is a reaction of society as a whole, essential to the protection of the social fabric against the nefarious effects of the action of the market. Some of these interventions come from governmental or legislative bodies; others originate with voluntary associations like trade unions or cooperatives; still others spring from organs of moral life or public opinion such as churches, scientific organizations, or the press. With respect to labor, interventions were responsible for factory laws, social insurance, educational and cultural minima, municipal trading and the various forms of trade union activities, and so on. With regard to land, protectionist intervention took the form of land laws, agrarian laws, tenancy and homestead laws, including some forms of agrarian protectionism. Clearly the social usefulness of the rules, regulations, restrictions, and nonmarket activities involved in these interventions lay in the protecting of labor and land, man and nature, from irreparable harm.

II

The advantages of protective interventions are primarily social; the disadvantages are mostly economic. The former accrue to the fabric of society itself, preventing the destruction of human beings and their natural environment; the latter may detract from the social dividend. For, as a rule, isolated haphazard interventions in the mechanism of the market make the system work even less successfully than would have otherwise been the case. The opposite is, of course, true of comprehensive planned interventions, which combine social protection with economic advantages. However, the mere hint of such measures of a "socialist" character would cause a crisis of confidence and would bring the whole system down.

Such a situation unavoidably had a deep effect on the forms and chances of working-class politics. The market system served as a defense mechanism, protecting the ruling class against the growth of popular democracy and, even more effectively, against any use that democracy might make of its power to press for socialist solutions.

The ambiguous position in which popular democracy found itself under liberal capitalism was mainly the result of this situation. While the action of the market called forth widespread reactions and helped to create a strong popular demand for political influence of the masses, the use of the power so gained was greatly restricted by the nature of the market mechanism: isolated interventions, however urgent on social grounds, could often be shown to be economically harmful, while economically useful interventions of a planned type could not even be considered. In political terms, while piecemeal reform could be discredited as a damaging interference with the working of the market, outright socialist solutions, which would have been economically advantageous, had to be excluded altogether. Under conditions such as these, the striking power of the forces of popular democracy was necessarily limited.

19

Five Lectures on the Present Age of Transformation
*The Passing of the Nineteenth-Century Civilization**

Introduction: The Institutional Approach

The subject matter of these lectures is a vast and unique event: the passing of the nineteenth-century civilization in the short period that elapsed between the first and the second war of the twentieth century.

At the beginning of this period, nineteenth-century ideals were paramount, indeed their influence had never been greater: by its close, hardly anything was left of that system under which our type of society had risen to world leadership. Within national frontiers, *representative democracy* had been safeguarding a regime of liberty, and the national well-being of all civilized nations had been immeasurably increased under the sway of *liberal capitalism*; the balance of power had secured a comparative freedom from long and devastating wars, while the gold standard had become the solid foundation of a vast system of economic cooperation on an almost planetary scale. Although the world was far from perfect, it seemed well on the way toward perfection. Suddenly this unique edifice collapsed: the very conditions under which our society existed passed forever. The tasks that face us in the present cannot, we believe, be understood except in the light of this tremendous event. It is both national and international, political and economic: all our institutions are involved. The historian is at a loss where to start.

*File 31–10, "Conference 1," Karl Polanyi Archive: lecture delivered as part of a course of five lectures at Columbia University.

The Conservative Twenties and the Revolutionary Thirties

The Great War of 1914–18 had been on the whole true to the nineteenth-century type: one alignment of great powers against another; belligerents and neutrals; soldiers and civilians; business and warfare – all distinct and separate. Defeat resulted in a treaty that was intended to ensure that life should continue very much as before. The war was about nothing in particular and had settled nothing essential; yet it had been more terrible than all its predecessors.

The trend of the twenties was distinctly conservative. The spectacular revolutions and counter-revolutions of 1917–23, even when they were more than upheavals resulting from the shock of defeat, introduced no new element into eastern society. Not only Hindenburg and Wilson, but also Lenin and Trotsky were in the nineteenth-century tradition. The tendency of the times was simply to establish, or eventually to re-establish, the system commonly associated with the ideals of the English, the American, and the French revolutions of the seventeenth and eighteenth centuries. Radical policies served traditional aims. The Great War had been, in the main, an attempt to overcome by fruitless violence the difficulties that bogged the system since the beginning of the century; in the peaceful twenties this effort was intensified, but the effect of the war had merely enhanced those difficulties.

Suddenly, in the early thirties, with an awe-inspiring vehemence, change set in. Its landmarks were the abandonment of the gold standard by Great Britain and subsequently by all other countries; the five-year plans, especially the collectivization of the farms in Russia; the launching of the New Deal, the national socialist revolution; the collapse of the balance of power in favor of autarkic empires. By 1940 every vestige of the industrial system has disappeared, and, except for a few enclaves, the peoples were living in an entirely new institutional setting.

The Theory of External Causation

The bird's eye view of the quarter-century 1914–39 shows clearly that change was sudden and worldwide, including in its range countries of the most various social and political complexion. Only a cause external to them all could have had such an effect. It was natural that contemporaries should have seen this event in the storm of blood and anguish of the Great War of 1914–18. But even at this short distance it appears, as we have seen, that the Great War, as well as the postwar revolutions, were themselves only an extension of the nineteenth century and formed merely a phase in a process of much greater depth and amplitude. We are thus forced to the conclusion that some other international development had silently shaped the course of history, until, by the end of the "twenties," change surged forth in a vast transformation. We submit that this underlying comprehensive event was no other than the *dissolution of the international system upon which our civilization had unconsciously depended for its life and growth.*

The gradual changes leading up to this result were in progress long before the war of 1914–18, but remained unnoticed at the time. Actually the system had been working under an increasing strain even since the turn of the century. In *politics* the formation of opposing alliances marked the end of the balance of power, which presupposed the existence of a number of independent national policies and was therefore incompatible with a system of permanent power groups. In the *economic* field, this was accompanied by trade rivalries that disclosed an undue strain on the national systems. But the Great War of 1914–18 that resulted merely impoverished and brutalized the world, without alleviating its troubles: eventually the western treaties even aggregated them. For it is easy to see that the permanent disarmament of the defeated countries removed the very basis of the balance of power and thus made the political problem insoluble. This, again, reduced the chance of a refloating of the world economy, and, quite apart from its other weakness, the gold standard could not be expected to function except in conjunction with an international political system assuming some measure of peace. Now that this safeguard against devastating wars had disappeared, a fortiori all attempts to restore the gold standard were bound to fail. In its endeavor to ease the tension under which the political and economic mechanism of the nineteenth century was labouring, the Great War had weakened that order fatally. The strenuous restorative efforts of the twenties were doomed to failure and their climax proved the threshold of catastrophe. When the international system finally collapsed, no country could remain unaffected.

The Facts

The theory of the dissolution of the international system is strikingly borne out by the fact that everywhere the crisis was focused on foreign events, mostly on questions of currency and exchange. There was hardly an internal political crisis in Europe that did not have a monetary origin. Exchanges were the all-embracing factor during the twenties. From the melting away of the external values of the Central European currencies to the World Economic Conference more than a decade later, there was an almost universal endeavor to return to the prewar monetary systems. An unbroken sequence of currency crises linked the indigent Balkans to the affluent USA through the elastic band of an international credit system that transmitted the strain of the imperfectly restored currencies – first from Eastern to Western Europe, and then from Western Europe to the United States, until America herself was borne down by the weight of the accumulated deficits of the greater part of the countries of the world. The trade depression that broke over Wall Street in 1929 waxed into a hurricane owing to the tension that had been latent on the Danube and the Rhine since 1919. When, in the early thirties, the two Anglo-Saxon countries went off gold, the watershed between two periods of history was passed. While the twenties had still directed their efforts to the prevention of the final breakdown of the gold standard, the thirties reversed this trend and exerted their energies toward adapting themselves to the accomplished fact of such a breakdown. In some cases the foreign situation turned more on political than on economic questions. But we need not attempt at this stage to distinguish too finely between the economic and the political aspects of the international system. It suffices that no analysis of the crisis can be adequate that does not allow for the principle of external causation.

The International System

As a matter of fact, the international system was both political and economic. The gold standard had become the basis of a world economy that embraced capital markets, currency markets, and commodity markets on an international scale. This state of affairs was factual rather than legal; the people who benefited by it hardly realized its existence. In the political field there was nothing strictly comparable even to this informal organization. The balance of power that safeguarded the nation from major wars and apart from which a world currency system such as the gold standard would not have been possible had even less the character of a legal institution than the gold standard had. But social organization does not depend for its functioning on formal sanctions. As a rule, a society does not become conscious of the true nature of the institutions with which it lived until those institutions have already passed.

However, the prevalence of the economic factor within the international system cannot be overlooked. The effective organization of the world was economic, not political. It was the economic strain that caused the imperial rivalries and smoothed the path to the Great War. It was to the restoration of the economic system of prewar days that the statesmen of the twenties bent all their energies: reparations, stabilization of the exchanges, international debts, foreign loans, trade embargoes, and cost of living indices were the immediate concern of the politicians as well as of the masses. And economic autarky was the one universally dominant trend in the thirties.

But the breakdown of the international economic system stands itself in need of explanation. The attempt will take us far afield; for such an enterprise involves no less than defining the nature and origin of the present crisis. In other words, it involves a definition of our basic institutions, capitalism and democracy, in general human terms.

It is to this task that our next lecture will be primarily devoted.

20

Five Lectures on the Present Age of Transformation
*The Trend toward an Integrated Society**

---

1   The Separation of Politics and Economics

Nineteenth-century society was based upon the two pillars of liberal capitalism and representative democracy. The economic and the political sphere were separate. This is the clue to its rapid downfall. For the expectation that such a state of affairs could be anything but transitory was an illusion. A society containing within its orbit a separate, self-regulating, and autonomous economic sphere is a utopia.

On the face of it, this may seem a paradoxical statement. Nothing appears more obvious to us than that a society should contain these two institutional systems as distinct and different as the needs that they serve. For have not human beings economic wants, such as for food, and political wants, such as for safety and protection? However much a person may prefer butter to guns – or, for that matter, guns to butter – as long as he is in his senses, he will never *mistake* the guns for the butter. It seems to be in the very nature of things that there should be separate economic and political institutions in society.

On closer investigation, however, this turns out to be a gratuitous assumption, with no more to substantiate it than the conventions and habits of a few generations. Human beings must have food and safety,

---

* File 31–10, "Conference 2," Karl Polanyi Archive: undated lecture, delivered as part of a course of five lectures at Columbia University.

but they need not have a separate set of institutions to satisfy these wants – that is, institutions based on a distinctive motive and directed by a separate set of people acting on such a motive. On the contrary, apart from the limited experience of some nineteenth-century societies, all human societies of the past seem to have been based on the institutional unity of society, in other words one set of institutions was designed to serve both the economic and the political needs of society.

2   A Price or Market Economy

Liberal capitalism is, essentially, a price (or market) economy. This means that the production and distribution of goods is controlled by *prices* resulting from the functioning of *markets*.

There are *markets* for all types of goods: commodity markets for all sorts of commodities; capital markets for the use of capital; estate markets for the use of land; labor markets for the use of labor power. In this way every factor of production has its market.

Accordingly, there are *prices* for all types of goods: prices for commodities, called commodity prices; prices for the use of capital, called interest; prices for the use of land, called rent; prices for the use of labor, called wages. Thus every factor of production has its price.

The *result* of the action of the market is twofold:

The *production* of goods, according to their varying quantities and qualities, is determined, and the resources of the country, whether land or labor, capital or commodities, are automatically disposed of.

The *distribution* of the goods thus produced is determined by the same mechanism. For some of these prices form the *income* of those who sell certain goods. Thus there is interest for the sellers of the use of capital; rent for the sellers of the use of land; wages for the sellers of the use of labor power; and, lastly, there is profit for the sellers of all sorts of commodities, profit being the surplus of selling prices over costs (the latter being, of course, simply the prices of the goods necessary for the production of the goods in question). The total of these incomes buys the total of the goods produced within a definite period of time. The pricing system thus automatically distributes the goods produced under it.

So much for the bare mechanism of a market economy, presented in a schematic way. If one conceives for a moment that hundreds of thousands of elaborate goods are produced by many millions of people and then distributed among them by and through this mechanism, which regulates every detail of the technological, financial, and consumptive process, then you agree that this is an achievement of the human mind compared to which the pyramids of Egypt appear as trivial. No wonder that, when it first appeared on the horizon of our consciousness, it dazzled and bewildered man as if this eye had met the naked sun. The Industrial Revolution and the machine age, with which our European society was pregnant, thus became the sources of an inspiration sufficiently powerful to carry mankind through the Inferno of early industrialism until the tremendous material benefits of the system began actually to appear.

But there was also another reason for the dogmatism of the liberal economist. For the more developed a price or market economy is, the more extreme it must be in the application of its principles. If early free traders like Adam Smith seemed dogmatic, their dogmatism was nothing in comparison to that of the later Manchester School; and Manchester liberals themselves were wavering and compromising in comparison to the present-day protagonists of liberal capitalism. A Cobden and a Bright appear as mere opportunists when contrasted with the unbending fanaticism of a Lionel Robbins or a Ludwig von Mises.

The reasons for this fact are fairly simple. A market economy, if it works at all, works only as long as you do not interfere with prices – whether commodity prices, rent, wages, or interest. For a self-regulating system of prices is dependent for its working on there being a surplus of selling prices over costs; nothing can be produced unless such a surplus exists. Therefore, if selling prices fall, costs must be allowed to fall also. This is independent of human volition, of sentiments and ideals. Production at a permanent loss is automatically excluded by the rules of the game.

This is why there must be, under this system, a free market for all factors of production, not only for commodities but also for land, labor, and capital. Unless the price system is flexible and prices are allowed to move freely according to the intercommunication of the various markets, the system ceases to be self-regulating even in principle and the vast mechanism must fall, leaving mankind in immediate danger of mass unemployment, cessation of production, loss of incomes, and consequent social anarchy and chaos.

3   Society and the Market

But the apparently simple proposition that all factors of production must have free markets implies in practice that the whole of society must be subordinated to the needs of the market system. Among the factors of production there are *land* and *labor*, both of which can be treated as commodities only on a more or less fictitious basis. For labor means the human beings of whom society consists, and land is only another word for mother earth, on which they subsist. In the attempt to establish a separate market economy within society, the whole of society is thus subordinated to the needs of a market economy. Almost unwittingly, a thing unheard of is brought into existence: an *economic society* – that is, a human community based on the assumption that society depends for its existence on material goods alone.

Such an assumption is demonstrably false. The safety of life and limb is at least as vital as the daily food; nor is there any definite preference for bread and butter, if the alternative is to be killed outright. But, if a society should permanently exist, there are a number of other requirements for which it must provide, such as reasonably stable relationships to our environment – that is, to nature, to our neighbors, to our craft; military qualities of the members of society, including health and physique; a sufficiently stable outlook on the future, such as would allow laying the foundations of human character and raising a new generation. Clearly these requisites cannot be substituted by an abundance of material goods alone. The "Satanic mill" of the market would soon dispose of a society that would allow its land to be atomized or to be left unused; that would allow its labor power to be overstrained or to be left to rust; that would permit its credit system to run into an inflation or to throttle business according to the whims of a blind mechanism removed by its very nature from the needs of the living community embodied in every human society.

The real nature of the dangers that are inseparable from the market utopia thus becomes apparent. For the sake of society, the market mechanism must be restricted. But this cannot be done without grave peril to economic life, and therefore to society as a whole. We are caught on the horns of a dilemma: either to continue on the path of a utopia bound for destruction, or to halt on this path and risk the throwing out of gear of this marvellous but extremely artificial system.

4 The Original Unity of Society and the Present Trend toward Integration

The separation of the political and the economic sphere is the unique peculiarity of our type of society. Neither the tribal, nor the city-state, nor the feudal societies of the past knew this trait. In all these societies one set of institutions provided for the satisfaction of the various human needs – such as for safety and protection, justice and order, material goods, sexual life and reproduction. The religious, the ceremonial, the family, and the other institutions of tribal and feudal society do not provide for such a separation. Also mercantilism, the immediate predecessor of our present society, was a politico-economic doctrine based on the institutional unity of society.

The utopian character of a market economy explains why it never could be really put into practice. It was always more of an ideology than of an actual fact. Factory legislation and protectionism, trade unions and the church were the outstanding factors in the violent reaction against the assumptions of an unrestricted market for land and labor. In other words, the separation of economics and politics was never carried completely into effect. The integration of society began even before the movement for a market economy had reached its climax.

But this development merely increased the strain on the social system. For the mutual interference of industry and state, economics and politics, was not disciplined by any higher principle. The working class made use of the institutions of the democratic state in order to protect itself against the worst effects of the competitive system; the leaders of business, on their part, made use of industrial property and finance to weaken political democracy. This is the false integration of which late nineteenth-century society showed so many examples. The adherents of a market economy justly point out that tariff policies and monopolistic trade union practices were often directly responsible for the aggravation of slumps and the restriction of trade. What they do not see is that these protective measures of the state and of voluntary organizations were the only means to save society from destruction through the blind action of the market mechanism.

In postwar Europe the separation of economics and politics developed into a catastrophic internal situation. The captains of industry undermined the authority of democratic institutions, while democratic parliaments continuously interfered with the working of the market mechanism. A state of affairs was reached when a sudden paralysis of both the economic and the political institutions of society was well within the range of the possible. The need for a reintegration of society was apparent.

This was the critical state of affairs out of which the fascist revolutions sprang. The alternative was between an integration of society through political power, on a democratic basis, or, if democracy proved too weak, an integration on an authoritarian basis, in a totalitarian society, at the price of the sacrifice of democracy.

The American social system is, in my conviction, not faced with this tragic dilemma. But if loss of freedom should be avoided, it will have to take two steps at the same time: accept the need for integration *and* achieve it through democratic means.

Postface
Observations on Karl Polanyi's Juridical–Political Thought

Mariavittoria Catanzariti

The essays contained in this volume offer the results of a close exami-
nation carried over more than half a century of world history. The
broad range of topics, which were covered in a span of time that
stretches from the 1920s to the end of the 1950s, is characteristic of
the scientific output of Karl Polanyi. Thanks to a remarkable intersection of his personal trajectory with events of great political and historical importance,[1] Polanyi was witness to several of the major
historical moments of the twentieth century, from the *belle époque*
to the Great War – in which Polanyi took part on the Austro-
Hungarian side – to the Hungarian Revolutions of 1918 and 1919
to the radical transformations that occurred between the two wars
to the first phase of the Cold War.

This history of the West, interwoven with the story of his life, is
the great forge that shaped Polanyi's work. He was trained as a
lawyer, worked as a journalist, and became a wandering exile, an
"expatriate" from a bourgeois social order. He was always a careful
and rigorous thinker.[2]

Simplifying the complexity of Polanyi's work is no easy task, but
we can perhaps identify a singular and enduring focus in it: establishing the compatibility of democracy with human existence. This, for
Polanyi, represented the goal of social activism.[3] The story of his
intellectual development is one of "nonconformism" and devotion to
this ideal.

As already noted, Karl Polanyi completed his studies in law, though
he never considered that field to be the primary focus of his intellectual efforts. In fact, reflection on legal theory is relatively marginal

in Polanyi's work by comparison to reflection on economics. None-theless, the attitude to law that can at least be gleaned, in certain passages, from a trace of absence offers interesting food for thought on Polanyi's institutionalist perspective on law. The various writings in this volume highlight this dimension of his thought. His purposeful distancing from formalism led him to favor a normative model in which legal phenomena can act as a tool for understanding "embed-dedness"[4] and the "economistic fallacy."

This "muting effect" invites reflection on a type of anthropology that deconstructs many traditional categories, and in particular that of the autonomy of the normative system. There are too few examples to allow an easy identification of Polanyi's position on law, and so we are justified in adapting an interpretation of his work that mini-mizes its significance. Just the same, the normative paradigm is rele-vant insofar as the legal scholar attempts to observe the law with the eyes of a "non-jurist."

Polanyi always approaches the law in a factual manner: he pays heed to the social factors that determine the norms[5] and uses facts taken from real life as the test of sociological analysis. This last premise would be taken up in studies of primitive societies and is notably convergent with the views of Malinowski[6] and Mauss regard-ing the existence of total social facts, namely those facts that intersect with every type of institution: religious, judicial, moral, economic.[7] Law, then, would join the group of those noneconomic institutions that serve to incorporate economy into society.

Of particular relevance in this regard is a passage from "The Eclipse of Panic and the Outlook for Socialism" in which Polanyi asserts:

> Neither the legal fiction that defines labor as the subject of a specific contract nor the economic fiction that defines the scarce and useful thing sold as the commodity "labor" affects the actual world. What matters to us here is the human situation postulated in the organization described as labor market.[8]

The problem of social "cogency" seems, then, to absorb the problem of normative prescriptions.[9] Further along he writes, more directly: "But social organization does not depend for its functioning on formal sanctions"[10] but on the tangible relationship established between the individual and her own environmental and social context.[11]

For Polanyi, the legal narrative is, in and of itself, parallel with the social narrative. His sociological analysis, neither legal nor historical, of the Speenhamland Law of 1795 in *The Great Transformation* provides a good example.[12] Polanyi focuses his attention on the social effects as a means to understanding the human condition in a given environment.[13] For example, the legislation drafted in favor of the poor in England, from the Poor Law of 1601 to the abolition of the Speenhamland Law in 1834, did not improve the conditions of those who received the subsidies,[14] because those laws were not rooted in the culture of the age. Instead they led to a deregulation of labor.[15] If this aspect of the analysis – constant attention to the social effects of formal rules – is overlooked, then the apparently contradictory attitude toward the legal effects of the process of separation and reincorporation of the economy into social institutions remains unresolved. In Polanyi's reconstruction of the rise of the market economy, the law assumes a dual function: it operates both as a factor that dissociates the economy from society and as a societal self-defense mechanism, and therefore as a mechanism of economic re-embedding.[16] One of the key elements in Polanyi's analysis is the enclosure – land that had at one time been free and open to communal use being closed off by aristocrats and other wealthy landowners. An initially gradual phase of enclosure, which accompanied the transition from cultivation to pastoralism,[17] was followed by a period of agricultural industrialization that served only to worsen the quality of life of the peasantry.[18] This second transition gave rise to that social disintegration, so well described not only in *The Great Transformation* but also in the essay "Culture in a Democratic England of the Future."[19] In parallel, a radical change in the relations between social classes occurred, following which the industrialists succeeded in dismantling the support system established for the poor by the monarchy. The development of cotton manufacturing is the main example of this phenomenon, and one in which law played a major role: "Just as cotton manufactures – the leading free trade industry – were created by the help of protective tariffs, export bounties, and indirect wage subsidies, laissez-faire itself was enforced by the state."[20] The creation of a self-regulating market was also furthered by the repeal of the Elizabethan Poor Law in 1834 and of the Corn Laws in 1846 and by the approval of the Bank Act of 1844, which introduced the gold standard.[21] On this interpretation, law acts as a mechanism for the institutionalization of the market. It also works to insure that the system functions freely, insofar as "nothing must be allowed to inhibit the formation of markets."[22] At the same time, however, law can present numerous constraints and limitations to the operation of the market. Polanyi cites the example of medieval guilds and mercantilist policies, under which land and labor constituted the foundation of military, juridical, administrative, and political systems; and their use was regulated and protected by law and custom,[23] being thus withdrawn from the price mechanism. The paradoxical nature of law, as defined by Polanyi, is summarized in the saying "laissez-faire was planned; planning was not."[24] So, while laissez-faire was implemented by means of a variety of social systems and law played a particularly relevant role among them, the reaction to it was spontaneous. The conflict between the self-regulating market and the human instinct of self-preservation gave rise to a collective social reaction, aimed at neutralizing the destabilizing effects of a mechanism that was focused on reducing land and labor to the status of goods. However, the spontaneity of this reaction did not signify the absence of the law; on the contrary. This sentiment emerges clearly in the essay "The Eclipse of Panic and the Outlook of Socialism":

> Some of these interventions come from governmental or legislative bodies; others originate with voluntary associations like trade unions or cooperatives; still others spring from organs of moral life or public opinion such as churches, scientific organizations, or the press. With respect to labor, interventions were responsible for factory laws, social insurance, educational and cultural minima, municipal trading and the various forms of trade union activities, and so on. With regard to land, protectionist intervention took the form of land laws, agrarian laws, tenancy and homestead laws, including some forms of agrarian protectionism.[25]

In the spontaneous nature of this counter-movement, Polanyi identifies a legal space in which society can make an attempt at self-preservation and oppose the use of force by the state: "the market has been the outcome of a conscious and often violent intervention on the part of government which imposed the market organization on society for noneconomic ends."[26] This same passage contains an interesting observation about the separation of economics and politics: "Economic history reveals that the emergence of national markets was in no way the result of the gradual and spontaneous emancipation of the economic sphere from governmental control."[27] If one takes into consideration the rise and fall of liberal economy, the symmetric processes of disembedding and re-embedding – what Polanyi defines as the double movement – must be interpreted as related consequences of the same phenomenon. The role of law in this process appears, then, to be neutral, and its relevance changes in relation to a given conflict as a function of whether it is used in the assertion of power or in the settling of a claim. We can find a relevant example in the lecture "The Trend Toward an Integrated Society": "The working class made use of the institutions of the democratic state in order to protect itself against the worst effects of the competitive system; the leaders of business, on their part, made use of industrial property and finance to weaken political democracy."[28] It is worth noting, however, that Polanyi does not view these counter-movements as necessarily "positive" phenomena, as can be gathered from his analysis of the effects of self-protective measures like laws on factories and unions, agricultural tariffs, and monetary controls: "*But* precisely this made self-regulation unworkable. It involved *nationalism*, which was merely the inevitable reaction of political bodies to the social dislocation caused by the international trade system (everywhere except in the strongest country – England)."[29]

From observations like these we can deduce that law can play a significant, if not always obvious, role in the context of Polanyi's discourse on economics as an institutional process.[30]

Nevertheless, in order to have a clearer idea of the function of law in Polanyi's thought, it is helpful to consider his 1920s writings on socialist accounting, in which the relationship between law and economics, though applied to a purely abstract model, is observed from a markedly different perspective.[31]

It is in the context of this reflection that the idea of "social law" emerges – by which "we mean those principles that point the orientation of production in a direction that is useful for the community."[32] In other words, within the framework of an ideal socialist economy in transition (like that described by Polanyi), social law seeks to fix the mistakes produced by a capitalist economy, directing productivity to social ends and ensuring an equal distribution of goods. For the author, the main objectives of social law are maximization of productivity, equitable distribution of social production, and orientation of the process of production toward public utility.[33]

In particular, the essay "The Crucial Issue Today: A Response" can be reread in the light cast by Polanyi's writings on socialist accountability.[34] According to him, the associative legal form that distills the objectives of market socialism is the voluntary agricultural cooperative, wherein each member "is able to *survey* his position in relation to his environment."[35] This is a more personalized vision of the economy, which runs counter to the alienation produced by the market economy. Polanyi imagines a kind economy where management and organization are negotiated between associations of producers and consumer cooperatives. A method of industrial organization subject to the needs of agriculture would make a good example.[36] In

Polanyi's view, it follows that the legal framework – that is, the system of ownership and management – should be made subordinate to the interests of agriculture as defined by agricultural cooperatives. Conversely, an a priori legislative system for ownership and management that functions without taking into account those needs seems distant from Polanyi's point of view.[37]

The investigations reviewed above lead us to reflect on a type of social, economic, and political analysis that uses complexity as a metric of reality and prompts consideration of the relevance of scientific methods. In this regard it is worth citing two of the essays contained in this volume – "How to Make Use of the Social Sciences" and "On Political Theory" – in which Polanyi reflects on the methods and characteristics of the social sciences. As he writes in the former, "every science necessarily restricts its subject matter to such elements in the context of its environment as are susceptible to its method."[38] Therefore science, operating selectively in order to create an applicable abstract model, borrows only partially from – and occasionally excludes entirely from its purview – that natural or innate interest that gives rise to the problem of science itself. According to Polanyi, there is no continuum of knowledge,[39] but rather an array of diverse techniques. The "innate interest" of humans when faced with their surrounding environment[40] can never be exhausted by the methodology of the social sciences, including legal and political science.[41] This point is stated concisely in "On Political Theory," where Polanyi observes that the methodology of political science does not determine the knowledge of a political body but instead promotes the discovery of the potential rules of existence within it.[42] Furthermore, the impact of the social sciences may cause a shift in evaluation criteria, and thus it may involve processes of constant differentiation that progressively distance themselves from the innate interest.[43] Therefore Polanyi attempts to analyze the problem of consciousness in a non-self-referential manner: "The strands of interest also intermingle in the most varied ways. While each separate discipline satisfies some of it, none satisfies it completely, nor perhaps do they do so together."[44]

The reference to political theory invites further consideration of Polanyi's use of certain juridical–political categories of western modernity – including the political, democracy, war and peace, and the very idea of Europe.

Polanyi firmly believes that an economy must exist and develop within political institutions and that the phenomenon of the self-regulating market, which emerged in the golden age of liberalism, was a function of that age. The essential element of every social system is not economic but political. By "political" Polanyi means – unequivocally – the ability to make choices for a given territory. He fully embraces the theory of modern law and, displaying his European background, employs the terminology of the nation-state, sometimes even when referring to global phenomena. While in the 1919 essay "The Crucial Issue Today: A Response" he still expresses a belief in the possibility that the borders of the nation-state are cancelled by the socialist revolution, in his later writings he appears to take a different approach, wherein the passage from struggle between states to struggle within the state entails only a quantitative difference. In reference to the second kind of struggle, Polanyi uses the phrase "internal civil war." As Cangiani has pointed out, the allusion to Schmitt's friend–enemy pair, described in Schmitt's 1927 book *The Concept of the Political*,[45] is significant, even though the allusive phrase is used in a completely different manner and on a par with a descriptive element of events related to war, but not constitutive of the political. For Polanyi, war is characteristically impersonal and does not embody a specific negative value of enmity, so much so that he cites the example of an unwanted war.[46] Instead, as he argues in several chapters contained in Part II of this volume – "The Nature of International Understanding," "The Meaning of Peace," "The Roots of Pacifism" – war is an institution that serves to resolve conflicts. In order to do away with war, one would have to find new institutions that fulfill the same function.[47] Polanyi's position is markedly different from that of Benjamin Constant, as the latter stated it in *The Liberty of Ancients Compared with that of Moderns*: "War is all impulse, commerce, calculation. Hence it follows that an age must come in which commerce replaces war. We have reached this age."[48] Constant presumably uses the term "commerce" not in a technical sense, but more likely to refer to contractual activity more generally. On the contrary, for Polanyi war can only be replaced by a political institution. One such institution is the international treaty, which serves to prevent duplicating the problem of civil war at an international level. The alternative mechanisms for resolving a conflict between states are, then, international treaty or armed conflict.

Elaboration on the "political" highlights a perpetual conflict between government of the people and government of the law, and between governors and governed. The essay "Public Opinion and Statesmanship" focuses on the responsibilities of a good ruler. Such a figure, according to Polanyi, would be able to comprehend public opinion and to consider its deeper levels in cases where "there is an essentially correct appraisal of the objective situation: of the present danger and the oncoming dangers of the future."[49] Ruling power must always reckon with a people it recognizes as the true custodian of culture, a people therefore called upon to act with social responsibility. By culture Polanyi means the use of the products of civilization[50] in line with living conditions, and hence in correspondence with "the social realities of those who shape their way of life in conformity with it."[51] In the essay just mentioned, Polanyi identifies Roosevelt as a great statesman, capable of reviving America's fortunes after the crisis of 1929 through the political reforms of the New Deal. In fact he uses the example of this great statesman in order to analyze the characteristics of the statesman and his relationship with public opinion; and the latter is based on knowledge and understanding, both defining elements of a strong executive power.[52] Regarding executive prerogatives, Polanyi significantly draws a parallel between the centralization of powers during the New Deal and the economic crises that developed under the Russian and German dictatorships.[53] In a piece from 1935 Polanyi defends the possible adoption of emergency measures by the executive branch, demonstrating his skepticism toward the well-known Schechter ruling[54] – which deemed the delegation of significant powers to president Roosevelt by Congress unconstitutional, banned federal decisions on economic policy except for those regarding commercial exchange and interstate transport, and ruled that legal and administrative actions that violated that principle were similarly unconstitutional.[55] It is not, then, hard to imagine that, in the matter of the noted 1930–1 squabble between Kelsen[56] and Schmitt on the "guardianship of the constitution," Polanyi would prefer to assign that role to a constitutional court rather than to a president of the Reich [*Reichspräsident*], even though the concept of liberal constitutionalism had only been given as a hypothesis. What is, then, the role of the "political" in Karl Polanyi?

The concept of a statesman capable of monopolizing consensus and of translating the choice of the majority into his own decision, debatable though it may be, must be placed in a wider discussion of constitutional form. That discussion recalls the noted conflict between Polanyi and Mises in the early 1920s regarding the practicality of a socialist economy based on functionalist principles.[57] Mises claimed that a reconciliation between syndicalism and collectivism was not possible because the constitutional form was the product of a conflict that could only end in victory for the stronger force. Polanyi, moreover, considered the alternative between syndicalism and collectivism unfounded, mainly because in the constitutional form the power relationship could never be independent from the relationship of social recognition; both would necessarily have to find an equilibrium. According to Polanyi, the economic activity of the individual is determined by two fundamentally distinct motivations – that of the producer and that of the consumer – both of which converge in the act of decision making.

The question of political legitimacy and of its various forms emerges against this backdrop. Polanyi's conceptual point of reference is Rousseau and not Hobbes,[58] and his field of study is the institutional dimension.[59] By institution he means something that can exist independently of legal or rational power. Frequently, however, institutional forms coincide with legitimate power structures, as in the case of the courts, which serve the purpose of guaranteeing social peace:

> The advantages (or disadvantages) to the individual that derive from the existence of the court are of an entirely different character from the advantages (or disadvantages) deriving from the existence of the court to the community and, incidentally, to the individual as a member of the community. In this capacity the individual reaps the benefit of internal peace, while in his capacity as a litigant he may be securing for himself (or having to suffer) the various advantages (or eventual disadvantages) inherent in his personal contact with the law.[60]

Polanyi therefore recognizes that the goal of political obligation lies in the individual's pursuit of peaceful coexistence, which one realizes precisely with the help of those institutions in which one is at once free and "everywhere in chains."

Polanyi's reflections on law and politics also focus on the subject of territory. In addition to the three essays on war presented in this volume,[61] he addressed the topic in a 1937 essay entitled "Europe Today."[62] That work dealt mainly with Polanyi's disillusionment over the failure of the League of Nations of 1919 and focused on a critique of two articles in the Pact: Article 16, on the principle of collective action should any member of the League be the target of aggression; and Article 19, on the revision of treaties that have become inapplicable. His main accusation was that short-sighted international legislation was one of the factors that had led to the rise of totalitarianism among the democracies of continental Europe. Those opinions placed him in the company of his contemporaries Hans Kelsen and Carl Schmitt, both of whom had critiqued the Treaty of Versailles, although from different perspectives. Kelsen, in particular, criticized the shortcomings of the system of sanctions imposed by the Pact of the League of Nations, proposing instead the creation of an International Court of Law.[63] Schmitt, on the other hand, criticized the system of reparations as being out of proportion with the offense.[64] Polanyi meanwhile drew inspiration from a traditional idea of modern politics: that a state can exist solely within determined boundaries, and that disagreement relating to the definition of these boundaries can be resolved through one of two decision-making processes: through an international treaty or, *in extremis*, through war.[65] Polanyi's position was not one of exclusion – in fact he proposed a collective security policy enacted by the democratic and socialist nations within the League of Nations.

The border problem entails, according to Polanyi, a distinction between internal space and international space, which are not in reality heterogeneous. Where borders are undefined, no sort of political form can exist.[66] War is the inevitable outcome when "the states in conflict owe no common allegiance to a higher sovereignty."[67] What seems to emerge here is the idea of a Weberian bond of obedience that joins people together in the face of rational legal power. Polanyi defines it as "loyalty":[68] "communities are organized in states; and, without some loyalty to the state, the community cannot function satisfactorily."[69]

This problem is linked to the complex question of the West, and particularly to the international opportunities created by the Bretton Woods Agreement. If Polanyi's thoughts on the political at the end of the 1930s could be compared with the positions expressed by Carl Schmitt in *The Concept of the Political*,[70] his criticism of western universalism in the late 1950s can be readily compared to Schmitt's *The nomos of the Earth*.[71] Polanyi attributes the triumph of western universalism to the affirmation of political power. Even if the goal of *ius publicum europaeum* does not belong in Polanyi's mental landscape,[72] it is nonetheless interesting to explore certain ideas in this connection. Polanyi defines as "empty" only that space where there are no borders and attributes the success of England – the triumph of the logic of the sea, according to Carl Schmitt's postwar perspective[73] – to two factors: the internal cohesion of the state and its external alliances. Nonetheless, he draws a political distinction between the European nation-state and a political state with limited power like the United States.[74] In the essay on America contained in this volume, Polanyi offers a penetrating analysis of the institutional mechanism of the United States, emphasizing that, in contrast to European states, the US is much less invasive. According to Polanyi, "In the USA the *political state* is banished by the constitution to a remote corner in society. It exists only on sufferance and on condition that it will on no account try to gain powers and competences similar to those enjoyed by the European States."[75] Therefore society in the United States exists without the support of the political state. In fact the American system, alongside the continental model,[76] can be counted among the egalitarian democracies, provided that we understand its outcome to be "the result of a *national* revolution against foreign feudalism."[77] Social differences in America – as compared to England – are only the product of income, not of class. Furthermore, since everyone is potentially subject to drastic changes of fortune, integration can, for this very reason, be achieved by democratic means,[78] without running the risk of loss of freedom. Polanyi, then, does not have any bias toward Europe, in fact he considers Europe the source of the global crisis. His thoughts on the state are entirely oriented to the idea of freedoms, which Polanyi describes as

> concrete institutions, civic liberties – *freedoms* (in the plural) – the capacity to follow one's personal conviction in the light of one's conscience: the freedom to differ, to hold views of one's own, to be in a minority of one, and yet to be an honored member of the community in which one plays the vital part of the deviant.[79]

The freedom in question is clearly one born and defined within the confines of a state, since "no community of this character can produce law and order, safety and security, education and morality, civilization and culture unless its frontiers are settled and there is no reasonable danger of their becoming unsettled."[80] If it is true, then, that the state is the guarantor of constitutional freedom understood as a negative freedom, and also of social freedom in the form of equality, it is also true that such freedom is only fully realized when society manages "to transmit to the masses the sense of labor, life, and routine."[81]

Polanyi seems to endorse both the prospect of a European state as guarantor of equality in the form of social freedom and the prospect of an egalitarian society in which the role of the political state is marginalized to allow for the growth of personal freedoms. For Polanyi, the fundamental point is the impact of industrialization and of the development of class consciousness with regard to the dynamism of constitutional forms, that is, the relationship between the exercise of power and social awareness. The idea of freedom vanishes in the context of the self-regulating market or system of prices and in the absence of the regulatory mechanisms of the state. Polanyi maintains that the unregulated capitalism of the nineteenth century led to the erosion of the concept of liberty.[82] This assumption embodies the limits of overlap between the two models of democracy, libertarian and egalitarian, which alternated in Europe between 800 and 1800.[83] Although the two models overlap when it comes to the forms of constitutional democracy, they also contain profound differences that make them mutually exclusive: "In fact equality is never achieved by law but at the cost of liberty, nor was liberty secured in an unequal society but at the price of maintaining inequality."[84]

Polanyi's reflections on the limits of freedom intersect with his criticism of economic determinism.[85] Polanyi claims that the development of freedom is independent from technology or any type of economic organization, since "[i]nstitutional guarantees of personal freedom are in principle compatible with any economic system."[86] The phenomenon of the self-regulating market is therefore contingent, and an extension of political democracy throughout society is possible through the democratization of industry.[87]

Polanyi's call for realism, however, is even stronger and more radical when it is about the possible model for a social state. He asserts:

> The actual forms of material existence of man are those of worldwide interdependence. The political forms of human existence must also be worldwide. Either within the boundaries of a world empire or in those of a world federation – either through conquest and subjection or by international cooperation – the nations of the globe must be brought within the folds of one embracing body if our civilization is to survive.[88]

This point seems to be at the center of Polanyi's thought. War and cooperation are in fact tools, used without distinction in interactions between social classes, between the victors and the vanquished, and between the haves and the have-nots. They are the forms through which an individual and a society are compatible or incompatible.

The connection between capitalism and democracy is linked to the compatibility between economics and politics. Abandonment of democratic forms necessarily impacts the multiplicity of human relations, and more generally the manifestations of social existence. By necessity, the sphere of democracy has to be inclusive; democracy cannot benefit some individuals but not others. Politics must, then, conform to the realities of material existence[89] and not vice versa, as was the case with the rise of fascist regimes.[90] The role of politics cannot be solely to allow risk to produce uncontrollable effects. In fact, were this to happen, modern rationality would inevitably be neutralized by the incalculability of the market, instead of performing its primary task of managing risk.[91]

In such a process, the idea of conflict[92] represents the central nucleus of constitutional forms, in both national and international law.[93] Joerges has argued, with reference to Polanyi, for a tripartite perspective on what he calls "conflicts law" – the conflict deriving from the multiplicity of institutional decisions made in a multilevel system – which confronts the present postnational constellation: the search for meta-norms that become operational in cases of substantially different regulatory systems; the implementation of international accords; and the inclusion of nongovernmental actors.[94]

Polanyi did not live long enough to witness the commodification of rights,[95] which was one of the very forms he hypothesized as a tool for economic reintegration. Nor did he see the decline of the social democracies in the 1970s, and thus the era when the state began delegating risk management to informal powers.[96] He did, however, witness the growth of a type of international cooperation that followed the 1944 Bretton Woods Conference. Its goal was to avoid devastation of the sort experienced in the world wars while leaving plenty of room for operation of the invisible hand of capitalism[97] – a program shortly afterward enacted in 1947 through the General Agreement on Tariffs and Trade (GATT). During that same period he saw the creation of a similar system in Europe following on the Marshall Plan, which led to the formation of the European Coal and Steel Community (ECSC) in 1949. As Polanyi writes in the essay "For a New West," after which this book is named, the challenge that faced the West was to initiate a true cultural revolution – one that challenged a perverse system in which science, technology, and economic organization had assumed uncontrollable dimensions. The roots of this phenomenon date back to the nineteenth century, when liberal capitalism began separating itself from representative democracy.[98] Curbing an unchecked progress would have meant sacrificing efficiency for the sake of humanity, namely democratic social integration.[99] Polanyi never lost faith in the possibility for social reintegration; and yet he was equally aware of the intrinsic limitations of an intervention that was merely legislative. That awareness emerges clearly in his critical analysis of the advent and crisis of the market economy. In comparing his thoughts with current events, we might infer that laws, important though they may be, cannot, in and of themselves, guarantee "a sufficiently stable outlook on the future, such as would allow laying the foundations of human character and raising a new generation."[100] That guarantee must come from something more powerful than laws, which Polanyi identifies as the values inherent in our shared culture – that is, in our act of establishing a community, as a project of collective and inclusive existence.[101] Laws without culture may prove to be weak, but most of all they run the risk of not serving an integrative function in society.

Polanyi's thoughts open unusual avenues of inquiry, which may either prove attractive to legal scholars or inspire their distrust. In the midst of a cultural and financial crisis that implicates human life rather than "structures," these works invite us not to lose sight of the "forgotten man"[102] and his unfolding throughout the world.

Translated by Carl Ipsen and Michael Ipsen

Notes to Postface

1. Michele Cangiani and Jérôme Maucourant, "Introduction," in Michele Cangiani and Jérôme Maucourant, eds., *Essais de Karl Polanyi* (Paris: Éditions du Seuil, 2008), 9–46, at pp. 9–11.
2. For a reconstruction of the major aspects of the author's biography, see Kari Polanyi-Levitt and Marguerite Mendell, "Introduzione," in Karl Polanyi, *La libertà in una società complessa*, edited by Alfredo Salsano (Turin: Bollati Boringhieri, 1987), xix–xlix
3. Kari Polanyi, "Karl Polanyi as Socialist," in Kenneth McRobbie, ed., *Humanity, Society and Commitment: On Karl Polanyi* (Montreal, Canada: Black Rose Books, 1994), 115–34.
4. On the concept of embeddedness, see Michele Cangiani, *Economia e democrazia: Saggio su Karl Polanyi* (Padua: Il Poligrafo, 1998), p. 58.
5. Polanyi's idea differs from Durkheim's concept of the social fact as "external coercion"; see Émile Durkheim, *The Rules of Sociological Method* (New York: Free Press, 1966), p. 11. For Polanyi, a social fact is, so to speak, verified by the ambit of its effect: see Karl Polanyi, "Nuove considerazioni sulla nostra teoria e pratica," in Polanyi, *La libertà in una società complessa*, 52–61, at p. 59.
6. Bronisław Malinowski, *Argonauts of the Western Pacific: An Account of Native Enterprise and Adventure in the Archipelagoes of Melanesia New Guinea* (London: Routledge, 1932), pp. 350, 392–4.
7. Marcel Mauss, *The Gift: The Form and Reason for Exchange in Archaic Societies* (London: Routledge, 2002) (though Marcel Mauss is rarely cited in the works of Polanyi).
8. See Chapter 18 in this book, "The Eclipse of Panic and the Outlook of Socialism," p. 206.
9. On this point, see Amanda Perry-Kessaris, "Reading the Story of Law and Embededness through a Community Lens: A Polanyi-Meets-Cotterrell Economic Sociology of Law?" *Northern Ireland Legal Quarterly*, 62.4 (2011), 401–13, at p. 410.
10. See Chapter 19 in this book, "Five Lectures on the Present Age of Transformation: The Passing of the Nineteenth-Century Civilization," p. 212.

11. Karl Polanyi, "Über die Freiheit," in his *Chronik der großen Transformation: Artikel und Aufsätze (1920–1945)*, edited by Michele Cangiani, Kari Polanyi-Levitt, and Claus Thomasberger, vol. 3 (Marburg: Metropolis, 2005), 137–64, at p. 145.

12. Karl Polanyi, *The Great Transformation* (Boston, MA: Beacon Press, 1957), pp. 77–85.

13. See Gareth Dale, *Karl Polanyi: The Limits of the Market* (Cambridge: Polity, 2010), p. 85.

14. As is well known, it consisted of a system of subsidies for the poor designed to supplement their salaries and was based on a sliding scale dependent on the price of bread, the goal being to insure a minimum wage; see Polanyi, *The Great Transformation.* p. 78.

15. On this point, see Alexander Ebner, "Transnational Markets and the Polanyi Problem," in Christian Joerges and Josef Falke, eds., *Karl Polanyi: Globalisation and the Potential of Law in Transnational Markets* (Oxford: Hart, 2011), 19–41, at p. 24.

16. In this regard it is useful to consider the position put forward in Sabine Frerichs, "Re-Embedding Neo-Liberal Constitutionalism: A Polanyian Case for the Economic Sociology of Law," in Joerges and Falke, eds., *Karl Polanyi*, 65–84, at p. 81: "A critical Polanyian perspective has thus, first, to de-construct the Hayekian way of embedding even the law (and its inherent normativity) in economic rationalities and, secondly, to reconstruct law as a social institution which also reflects the rationalities and values of the other social spheres."

17. Polanyi, *The Great Transformation*, pp. 33–42. On this subject, see the careful analysis by Alexander Ebner, *Polanyi's Theory of Public Policies Embeddedness, Commodification and the Institutional Dynamism of the Welfare State* (Habilitation thesis, Staatswissenschaftliche Fakultät, University of Erfurt, 2008), p. 44.

18. Polanyi, *The Great Transformation*, p. 92: "Both enclosures of the common and consolidations into compact holdings, which accompanied the new great advance in agricultural methods, had a powerfully unsettling effect. The war on cottages, the absorption of cottage gardens and grounds, the confiscation of rights in the common deprived cottage industry of its two mainstays: family earnings and agricultural background."

19. Chapter 9 in this book.

20. Polanyi, *The Great Transformation*, p. 139.

21. On this point, see Ebner, *Transnational Markets and the Polanyi Problem*, p. 23.

22. Polanyi, *The Great Transformation*, p. 69.

23. Ibid., pp. 69–71.

24. Ibid., p. 141.

25. See Chapter 18 in this book, "The Eclipse of Panic and the Outlook of Socialism," pp. 207–8.

26. Polanyi, *The Great Transformation*, p. 250.

27. Ibid.

28. See Chapter 20 in this book, "Five Lectures on the Present Age of Transformation: The Trend toward an Integrated Society," p. 218.
29. See Chapter 14 in this book, "General Economic History," p. 136.
30. Karl Polanyi, "The Economy as Instituted Process," in Karl Polanyi, Conrad M. Arsenberg, and Harry W. Pearson, eds., *Trade and Markets in the Early Empires* (Glencoe, IL: Free Press, 1957), pp. 243–69.
31. In these writings Polanyi confronts the problem of the sustainability of a transitional socialist economy as an alternative to liberal capitalism. Starting from the impact of the law on the costs of production through what he terms "intervention effect" and "framing effect," Polanyi seeks to demonstrate that in a functional model of a socialist economy the distribution of societal production has the advantage of neutralizing the intervention effect. Conversely, in a capitalist economy it would have the effect of nullifying the cost principle, since in that case the costs would be those produced by the society itself, and those would appear only to affect the production process. Thus a socialist economy would not negate the cost principle and would ensure separate calculations for both production and social costs. An economy of this type is a functionally organized socialist economy, in which the costs of production and the social costs are agreed upon between the community and the association in charge of production, which can take the form of either a union or a production cooperative. See Karl Polanyi, "La contabilità socialista," pp. 26, 28, and "La teoria funzionale della società e la contabilità socialista," p. 44, both in Polanyi, *La libertà in una società complessa*, 10–41 and 42–51. See also Polanyi, "Über die Freiheit," p. 141, where he discusses positions expressed by Karl Marx in *Grundrisse*, vol. 1 and in *Capital*, vol. 2, Book i. For a more in-depth study of the complex relationship between Polanyi and Marx, see Cangiani, *Economia e democrazia*, pp. 71–8.
32. Polanyi, "La contabilità socialista," p. 22.
33. Giandomenica Becchio, "Polanyi e la visione austriaca del mercato," Working Paper 03/2002, Economics Department, University of Turin, p. 6, at http://www.cesmep.unito.it/WP/3_WP_Cesmep.pdf (accessed April 1, 2014).
34. On this subject, see Polanyi, "La contabilità socialista," "La teoria funzionale della società e la contabilità socialista," "Nuove considerazioni sulla nostra teoria e pratica," all in Polanyi, *La libertà in una società complessa*. Deserving of deeper study is the fact, related to his 1919 thesis, that the ideal socialist model of redistribution of the products of labor would take place through the market and on the basis of need. Yet the 1922 piece on socialist accountability includes an alternative to communism that predicts distribution of goods on the basis of worker productivity, corrected by "social law" and linked to minimum needs.
35. See Chapter 16 in this book, "The Crucial Issue Today: A Response," p. 169. On the so-called "interior vision" of the economy, see

Polanyi, "Nuove considerazioni sulla nostra teoria e pratica," p. 56.

36. On the complex problems arising from the relationship between capitalism and agriculture, of which Polanyi was well aware, see Paul Mantoux, *The Industrial Revolution in the Eighteenth Century: An Outline of the Beginnings of the Modern Factory System in England* (London: J. Cape, 1955), pp. 156, 168; Henri Pirenne, *Histoire économique de l'occident médiéval* (Bruges: Desclée de Brouwer, 1951), p. 217.

37. See Chapter 16 in this book, "The Crucial Issue Today: A Response," p. 170.

38. See Chapter 11 in this book, "How to Make Use of the Social Sciences," p. 109.

39. On this point Polanyi refers expressly to Robert S. Lynd, *Knowledge for What? The Place of Social Science in American Culture* (Princeton, NJ: Princeton University Press, 1939), p. 21.

40. On the notion of "innate interest," see Chapter 11 in this book.

41. This thesis is largely taken from Émile Durkheim, "The Realm of Sociology as a Science," *Social Forces*, 59.4 (1981), 1054–70, at p. 1062: "When elements are combined there emerges from their combination a new reality presenting entirely new qualities, sometimes quite contrary to those observed in their constituent elements."

42. See Chapter 12 in this book, "On Political Theory," pp. 119–24.

43. What emerges here is the possible cultural influence of Georg Simmel, who in 1890 elaborated on the thesis of social differentiation (Georg Simmel, *Über soziale Differenzierung: Soziologische und psychologische Untersuchungen* (Leipzig: Duncker & Humblot, 1890). In fact there is a fair chance that Polanyi came to elaborate on the concept of differentiation after his encounter with György Lukács, a former pupil of Simmel and a member of the Hungarian Galileo Circle; see Gareth Dale, "Karl Polanyi in Budapest: On his Political and Intellectual Formation," *Archives of European Sociology*, 50.1 (2009), 97–130, at p. 97. The concept of differentiation played an important role in Polanyi's thought, so much so that it has been picked up today even in legal writing: see Moritz Renner, "Transnational Economic Constitutionalism," in Joerges and Falke, eds., *Karl Polanyi*, 419–33, at p. 421.

44. See Chapter 12 in this book, "On Political Theory," p. 123. With regard to the relationship between science and knowledge, it would be interesting to study closely the relationship with Veblen, whom Polanyi cites frequently; see Thorstein Veblen, *The Place of Science in Modern Civilisation and Other Essays* (New York: B. W. Hübsch, 1919), p. 10: "The habits of thought that rule in the working-out of a system of knowledge are such as are fostered by the more impressive affairs of life, by the institutional structure under which the community lives."

45. Carl Schmitt, *The Concept of the Political* (Chicago: University of Chicago Press, 2007) pp. 27–9, or p. 33, where he claims: "[War] is

the most extreme consequence of enmity." In the same vein, see Michele Cangiani, "Cittadinanza e politica estera: Prefazione," in Karl Polanyi, *Europa '37*, edited by Michele Cangiani (Rome: Donzelli, 1995), ix–xxii, at pp. xvii–xix.

46. See Chapter 6 in this book, "The Nature of International Understanding."
47. Ibid.
48. Benjamin Constant, *The Liberty of Ancients Compared with That of Moderns* [1819], at http://firstsearch.oclc.org.ezproxy.lib.indiana.edu/WebZ/FSPage?pagetype=return_frameset:sessionid=fsapp7-48372-hp6zr25u-nzafqe:entitypagenum=5:0:entityframedurl=http%3A%2F%2Foll.libertyfund.org%2Ftitle%2F2251:entityframedtitle=WorldCat:entityframedtimeout=20:entityopenTitle=:entityopenAuthor=:entityopenNumber=: (accessed December 14, 2013).
49. See Chapter 13 in this book, "Public Opinion and Statesmanship," p. 131.
50. Polanyi's notion of civilization echoes some of the ideas of Émile Durkheim, *The Division of Labor in Society* (New York/London: Free Press/Collier Macmillan, 1933).
51. See Chapter 9 in this book, "Culture in a Democratic England of the Future," pp. 94–5.
52. For an introspective look at public opinion, see Karl Polanyi, "Sein und Denken," in Idem, *Chronik der großen Transformation: Artikel und Aufsätze (1920–1945)*, edited by Michele Cangiani and Claus Thomasberger, vol. 1 (Marburg: Metropolis, 2002), p. 203.
53. See Chapters 14 and 17 in this book, "General Economic History" and "Conflicting Philosophies in Modern Society.
54. In an essay of June 20, 1935, Polanyi openly claims that the essence of the American constitution is not the simple separation of powers but rather the real constitutional separation of the president and congress, their placement by the constitution in positions of mutual suspicion:

The president will always be suspected of aspiring to absolute power, while congress will instead be suspected of favoring special interests or groups of electors (if not the members of congress themselves) to the detriment of the collectivity. The constitution guarantees that the two will remain firmly in a position of mutual suspicion. Every line of the constitution expresses the profound aversion for the state, for any sort of constituted power, that characterized the founding fathers who were fundamentally anarchists. The prohibition against agreements between the head of state and the legislature was intended to protect the freedom of the individual. It is that purpose that explains a drastic measure like the separation of the executive from the legislative branch. (Karl Polanyi, "Roosevelt im Verfassungskampf," in his *Chronik der großen Transformation*, vol. 1, 264–70)

55. See Karl Polanyi, "America im Schmelztiegel," in his *Chronik der großen Transformation*, vol. 1, 271–8, at p. 271.

56. See Hans Kelsen, "Wer soll der Hüter der Verfassung sein?" *Die Justiz*, 6 (1931), 576–628.

57. "A constitutional form is viable only when final decisions rest with one of the institutions that are constitutionally recognized" (Polanyi, "La teoria funzionale della società," p. 45); for a more in-depth look at the debate between Polanyi and Mises, along with a reference to the question of constitutional form, see Becchio, "Polanyi e la visione austriaca del mercato," p. 8.

58. Karl Polanyi, "Jean-Jacques Rousseau, o è possibile una società libera?" in his *La libertà in una società complessa*, p. 68; Polanyi, "Über die Freiheit," p. 146.

59. For a global perspective, see Malcolm Rutherford, "Institutionalism between the Wars," *Journal of Economic Issues*, 34.2 (2000), 291–303, at pp. 298–301; Glenn Morgan and Sigrid Quack, "Law as a Governing Institution," in Glenn Morgan, John L. Campbell, Coulin Crouch, Ove Kai Pedersen, and Richard Whitley, eds., *The Oxford Handbook of Institutional Comparative Analysis* (Oxford: Oxford University Press, 2011), 275–308, at p. 279; Alan G. Gruchy, "The Current State of Institutional Economics: The Movement's Limited Impact on the Conventional Science Is Ascribed to Disunity, Disinterest in General Theory," *American Journal of Economics and Sociology*, 41.3 (1982), 225–42, at p. 228.

60. See Chapter 7 in this book, "The Meaning of Peace," p. 79.

61. See Chapters 6–8 in this book, "The Nature of International Understanding," "The Meaning of Peace," and "The Roots of Pacifism."

62. Karl Polanyi, *Europa '37*, edited by Michele Cangiani (Rome: Donzelli, 1995).

63. Hans Kelsen, *Peace through Law* (Chapel Hill: University of North Carolina Press, 1944).

64. Carl Schmitt, *The nomos of the Earth in the International Law of the jus publicum Europaeum* (New York: Telos Press, 2003).

65. See Chapter 7 in this book, "The Meaning of Peace," p. 79.

66. See Philippe d'Iribarne, "A Check to Enlightened Capitalism," in Coulin Crouch and Wolfgang Streek, eds., *Political Economy of Modern Capitalism: Mapping Convergence and Diversity* (London: Sage, 1997), 161–73.

67. See Chapter 7 in this book, "The Meaning of Peace," p. 79.

68. Polanyi does not rule out the kind of voluntarism that should ideally derive from the motive of social cooperation; see his "Über die Freiheit," p. 146.

69. See Chapter 6 in this book, "The Nature of International Understanding," p. 52.

70. See note 45.

71. Schmitt, *The nomos of the Earth*.

72. Carlo Galli, *Genealogia della politica: Carl Schmitt e la crisi del pensiero politico moderno* (Bologna: Il Mulino, 1996), pp. 927–36.
73. Carl Schmitt, *Land and Sea* (Washington, DC: Plutarch Press, 1997).
74. See Chapter 10 in this volume, "Experiences in Vienna and America: America," pp. 101–6.
75. Ibid., p. 104.
76. See Chapter 17 in this book, "Conflicting Philosophies in Modern Society," pp. 177–83.
77. Ibid., p. 184.
78. See Chapter 10 in this book, "Experiences in Vienna and America: America," pp. 102–4.
79. See Chapter 3 in this book, "Economic History and the Problem of Freedom," p. 39.
80. See Chapter 6 in this book, "The Nature of International Understanding," p. 72.
81. Karl Polanyi, "Economia e democrazia" [1932], in his *La libertà in una società complessa*, 65–9, at p. 67.
82. See Chapter 2 in this book, "Economics and the Freedom to Shape Our Social Destiny," pp. 33–8.
83. See Chapter 17 in this book, "Conflicting Philosophies in Modern Society," pp. 177–83.
84. Ibid., p. 181.
85. Karl Polanyi, "Über den Glauben an den Oekonomischen Determinismus" [1947], in his *Chronik der großen Transformation*, vol. 3, 325–34, at p. 325.
86. See Chapter 14 in this book, "General Economic History," p. 145.
87. See Chapter 17 in this book, "Conflicting Philosophies in Modern Society," pp. 183–4.
88. See Chapter 8 in this book, "The Roots of Pacifism," p. 87.
89. Polanyi, "Über die Freiheit," p. 141: " 'Capital' and 'prices' only appear to dominate humankind; what is actually happening is that some groups of people are dominating other groups."
90. See Chapter 17 in this book, "Conflicting Philosophies in Modern Society," p. 198.
91. See Carlo Galli, *Spazi politici: L'età moderna e l'età globale* (Bologna: Il Mulino, 2001), p. 165.
92. For a comparison with the concept of conflict in Simmel, see Georg Simmel, "Der Streit," in his *Soziologie: Untersuchungen über die Formen der Vergesellschaftung* (Leipzig: Duncker & Humblot, 1908), 186–205.
93. The theme of diversity arises in both law and economy; on this point, see Colin Crouch and Wolfgang Streek, "Introduction: The Future of Capitalist Diversity," in their *Political Economy of Modern Capitalism*, 1–18, at p. 16.
94. Christian Joerges, "A New Type of Conflicts Law as the Legal Paradigm of the Postnational Constellation," in Joerges and Falke, eds., *Karl Polanyi*, 465–501, at p. 501.

95. For an astute analysis of the influence of laws "over the hegemony of the markets," see Stefano Rodotà, *Il diritto di avere diritti* (Rome-Bari: Laterza, 2012), pp. 3–5, 28; see also Salvatore Settis, *Azione popolare: Cittadini per il bene comune* (Turin: Einaudi, 2012), 3–228, at p. 4.

96. Jürgen Habermas, "The Postnational Constellation and the Future of Democracy," in his *The Postnational Constellation: Political Essays* (Cambridge, MA: MIT Press, 2001), 58–112, at pp. 61, 70.

97. Luciana Castellina, *Cinquant'anni di Europa: Una lettura antieroica* (Turin: Utet, 2007), p. 29.

98. See Chapter 19 in this book, "Five Lectures on the Present Age of Transformation: The Passing of the Nineteenth-Century Civilization."

99. For a perspective on the case of East Germany, see Claus Offe, "Capitalism by Democratic Design? Democratic Theory Facing the Triple Transition in East Central Europe," in his *Varieties in Transition: The East European and East German Experience* (Cambridge, MA: MIT Press, 1997), 29–49, at p. 35.

100. See Chapter 20 in this book, "Five Lectures on the Present Age of Transformation: The Trend toward an Integrated Society," p. 217; see also Durkheim, *The Division of Labor in Society*.

101. On the relationship between culture and constitutionalism, see Peter Häberle, *Verfgassungslehre als Wissenschaft* (Berlin: Duncker & Humblot, 1998), pp. 117, 584, 1066.

102. Franklin D. Roosevelt, "The Forgotten Man's Speech," radio discussion in Albany, NY, April 7, 1932, in *The Public Papers and Addresses of Franklin D. Roosevelt*, vol. 1: *The Genesis of the New Deal, 1928–32* (New York: Random House, 1938), 624–7, at p. 624.

Index